The Academic Librarian as Blended Professional

Chandos
Information Professional Series

Series Editor: Ruth Rikowski
(email: Rikowskigr@aol.com)

Chandos' new series of books is aimed at the busy information professional. They have been specially commissioned to provide the reader with an authoritative view of current thinking. They are designed to provide easy-to-read and (most importantly) practical coverage of topics that are of interest to librarians and other information professionals. If you would like a full listing of current and forthcoming titles, please visit www.chandospublishing.com.

New authors: we are always pleased to receive ideas for new titles; if you would like to write a book for Chandos, please contact Dr Glyn Jones on g.jones.2@elsevier.com or telephone +44 (0) 1865 843000.

The Academic Librarian as Blended Professional

Reassessing and Redefining the Role

Michael Perini

ELSEVIER

AMSTERDAM • BOSTON • CAMBRIDGE • HEIDELBERG
LONDON • NEW YORK • OXFORD • PARIS • SAN DIEGO
SAN FRANCISCO • SINGAPORE • SYDNEY • TOKYO
Chandos Publishing is an imprint of Elsevier

CP
CHANDOS
PUBLISHING

Chandos Publishing is an imprint of Elsevier
50 Hampshire Street, 5th Floor, Cambridge, MA 02139, USA
The Boulevard, Langford Lane, Kidlington, OX5 1GB, UK

British Library Cataloguing-in-Publication Data
A catalogue record for this book is available from the British Library

Library of Congress Cataloging-in-Publication Data
A catalog record for this book is available from the Library of Congress

ISBN: 978-0-08-100927-7 (print)
ISBN: 978-0-08-101015-0 (online)

For information on all Chandos Publishing publications visit our website at https://www.elsevier.com/

Publisher: Glyn Jones
Acquisition Editor: George Knott
Editorial Project Manager: Harriet Clayton
Production Project Manager: Omer Mukthar
Designer: Maria Inês Cruz

Typeset by TNQ Books and Journals

For Alexandra—know that you are loved, always

Contents

Biography

Dr. Michael Perini spent more than 10 years working in collegiate libraries, and he has had additional higher education professional experience in admissions, academic advising, student affairs, and of late, administration. He holds a Doctor of Arts in Higher Education, a Master of Arts in History, and a Bachelor of Arts in Classics and History. Michael has published on a variety of topics, including for-profit education, the public and civic good, distance education, library management and theory, student engagement, and martial arts theory.

An active martial artist, Michael served as the Head Instructor of his undergraduate university's intercollegiate Taekwondo team. Michael currently holds the Kukkiwon Certified master ranking of fourth-degree black belt (License 05204570). Also a Brazilian Jiu-Jitsu competitor, he acquired numerous titles and championships through active competition in a variety of regional, national, and international striking and grappling events.

Michael is a member of several charitable organizations associated with his colleges and the Catholic Church. He resides with his family in the United States.

Foreword

As a liaison librarian in a research university, this discussion of librarians as blended professionals makes a lot of sense to me. We are, in fact, blended professionals by definition and work in a unique space within academia that is both administrative and academic. I've been a librarian for 9 years. The positions I've held were all in the liaison model and at universities. The first university I worked for had no formal review process. The other two, including my current position, have formal review processes and fall under the Dean of Faculty, but the librarians do not have faculty status. These experiences allow me to relate to the findings of the study.

I've known the author for years, and we worked together in a university library prior to this study. I witnessed the diligence with which he approaches his studies, as he was working toward his doctorate in Higher Education during the time we were colleagues. We have also collaborated on research projects and presented together at conferences. When working on my own research, I often reach out to him for guidance and support. His education and experience provide him with a unique perspective and one that is well suited to a study such as this one. It is not often that librarians are studied through the lens of higher education research, and, I think, it is a welcome change.

Although this is a singular case study, with pitfalls well acknowledged by the author, I think most liaison librarians would recognize many of the discussions, challenges, and attitudes described. It would be interesting to see this method applied to librarians with different status, as I suspect those similar to the librarians studied here would see the most commonality. That is, those who do not have faculty status but are required to go through a tenure-like review process may relate most closely to the uncertainty that creates. One wonders if librarians with faculty status or administrative status without review, whose expectations are more clearly delineated, experience this as strongly. I'm curious to know how my own colleagues would respond to this line of questioning, as I feel as though there may be even greater disparity in individual liaisons relationships with their departments and faculty here. Would similar themes emerge?

What I find intriguing about this type of work are the other avenues for potential exploration and application that could follow this study. For instance, the author asked the interviewees "What are the barriers to your success?" Not all librarians aspire to the same things. An additional definition of success and a question assessing the interviewee's perception of their own success would add another layer to this interesting discussion on professional role identity.

Still, this adds a new layer of consideration for future research and provides immediate relevance and applicability for professionals in the field. This is the benefit of having a perspective provided by an author who has an understanding of the role that academic librarians can and do play within the academy, but an academic expertise outside of the discipline.

I look forward to seeing the application of this study and the benefits that it will have for academic librarians. As a group, we spend a great deal of time considering our identity and relevance but are perhaps too influenced by history and administrative pressure. Establishing a new identity, that of a blended professional, may be a way to end the conversations about being faculty versus service personnel, and begin new ones that more clearly explain our roles and how we fit into the academic community.

Andrea Baruzzi

Prologue

In the course of my investigations both for this project and elsewhere, I often have found that qualitative research requires the researcher to look within in order to find explanations for why he or she came to their particular conclusions. Therefore, I am beginning with a bit of a background that will explain in part why I chose to complete a dissertation—and now a book—involving academic librarians. This is especially so, given that my chosen career path likely will not find me working in a library ever again.

Let me start by saying this: I am not a librarian by education or profession. Some of you may discount my message after reading that clause. I implore you to read nonetheless because I share a similar perspective as many of my librarian colleagues.

When I conducted this study of the academic librarians at St. Jerome University—the pseudonym of an actual institution in the United States—I was a nonfaculty, classified researcher in an academic library's reference department. I performed many of the same tasks as librarians though. I would log hours on the reference desk, teach classes on library resources and information literacy, seek out and find materials for collection development, and so on. Through these professional duties, I came to understand the role of the academic librarian. Yet due to my staff role, I could never be considered a "librarian," either in practice or in social interactions.

At the same time, consider my academic career. I am a doctoral graduate of a higher education program. However, I was a part-time student, not privy to teaching assistantships, internships, or other prospects available to full-time students. This experience in the higher education program provided me with associations that transcended some of the established campus and disciplinary silos but still ensured that I would be considered an outsider. Like the librarians that I will speak about in this book, I had a blended role that bridged many third spaces, but I was confined by the culture(s) with whom I circulated.

In this way, I can empathize with some of the perceptions expressed by the academic librarians that I interacted with and interviewed as part of this study. Due to my professional work, I understood the challenges of the librarians' practice. My academic studies facilitated a more complete consideration of the culture that hindered the acceptance of academic librarians as anything greater than service providers.

There are hierarchies in higher education. People in this environment care a great deal about the letters after one's name. It is a reality of the workplace. The librarians in this study held a supposed position that was inferior to the tenure-track faculty. How they were considered, or rather, how they perceived that they were considered, affected their ability to grow and develop as professionals in their academic community.

This, of course, limited their success and efficacy in networking with the faculty, staff, and students of the university.

Due to my interactions with other higher education professionals in the field, I suspect some of these prejudices extend well past this case study into the larger academic community. In fact, I often have attempted to present library-oriented research at higher education or interdisciplinary conferences. The responses usually follow this pattern: "The proposed presentation does not address the themes of [this higher education and/or interdisciplinary conference]. However, the proposal as submitted may fit well on the program of [a semi-random library conference]."

I completed this study in 2014, and it is now the autumn of 2015. I am working at a new university in a dean/director-level position that is in charge of the General Education Department, Faculty Development, and Research. While I interact with the library frequently due to my research obligations, I am no longer directly in that professional realm. I really do not foresee returning to school to obtain a library science degree. I suspect my professional time in the libraries has come to a close. Yet my perspective remains the same. Academic libraries and their librarians offer many collaborative opportunities that supersede the "service" mentality that the library employees are often afforded.

About a month ago, I was sitting in an academic affairs meeting at my new job with the provost and other deans and school directors. One dean, in reference to the library, said: "I don't mean this in a derogatory way but you [the library] are just a service for the students. You're not at the same level as we [the academic schools] are at." Once again it struck me that the library and its librarians were held at a lower perceived level than the rest of the academic community. There is work to do, both from within and without.

The first step is to consider the blended role and identity of academic librarians. This book will guide you through the details of my study on academic librarians as blended professionals. The applied model originated in higher education theory and literature. The hope is that you will find applicability of the frame and employ it in your own libraries so that academic librarians will have an enhanced and accurate understanding of their true role and identity within the context of higher education.

Michael Perini
Fall 2015

Introduction

1

There is a compelling dynamic in academic libraries between the librarians and the support staff. Historically, there have been distinct divisions regarding the roles and duties of the librarians and the staff, with the latter tending to handle the simpler tasks (Oberg, 1995). Classified circulation staff will check books in and out for patrons, but the academic librarians will aid the patrons in identification of proper sources. The librarian duties are more complex and generally require more experience and training. The demarcation of duties has long been justified by the requirement that unlike the support staff, academic librarians must hold a masters degree in library science (Rubin, 2004). Therefore, an academic librarian's education validated and rationalized their position and rank in the library community.

However, the roles within the academic library, especially with the influx and escalation of the usage of technology, have hastily begun to blur actual roles and create tension among the tiers of employees. "The rapidly changing library workplace has created tension, even resentment, among support staff. Paraprofessionals see themselves performing the tasks they have watched librarians perform for years, as well as the challenging new tasks created by automation, but for less money and lower status" (Oberg, 1995). Classified staff personnel now often perform similar duties, yet they do not regularly enjoy the same level of compensation or esteem within the libraries (Simpson, 2013).

This certainly was true in my own experience. I began full-time library work as a Circulation Supervisor, and I eventually joined a reference department as a "Reference and Research Specialist." I specifically made sure that my title did not have the word "assistant" in it, as I was concerned about how the transition from "supervisor" to "assistant" would be interpreted on a resume. Nevertheless, I continuously was referred to as an "LA" or "Librarian Assistant" by reference librarians right up until the time that I left that position. While it never was meant maliciously, this would be a semiotic ding to my ego every time someone referred to me in that manner.

Through the course of this study though, it occurred to me that the librarians were attempting to define their own space and role. The changing activity role of all individuals in the libraries has resulted in librarians examining their own function within the academy (Simpson, 2013). This assessment has fueled debate as to whether academic librarians are in fact faculty, based upon their professional activities (Coker, van Duinkerken, & Bales, 2010).

Interestingly, outside of the libraries, academic librarians themselves experience similar difficulties gaining acknowledgment for their roles and activities, particularly among the faculty (Coker et al., 2010). Traditional faculty in the academy value the service offerings of librarians that aid in faculty research, such as collection development and document acquisition (Yousef, 2010); however, faculty do not view librarians as collaborative equals due to long-standing historical roles that place the librarian as auxiliary to in-class instruction (Hardesty, 1995; Rubin, 2004). Similar to the strain

The Academic Librarian as Blended Professional.

placed upon relationships and roles in the library proper, external tension between faculty and academic librarians has developed over the role and status of the latter, especially with the expanding demands of the position (Hardesty, 1995). More or less, the librarians have the same treatment from the faculty that the classified "LAs" receive from the librarians themselves. Therefore, reconciling and defining the role of academic librarians is a key component of this study.

Furthermore, there exists a dichotomy in the concept of role and identity for professionals. Role is the mechanics of a position. It is what an individual performs in their profession on a daily basis. The professional identity is a construction of the attitudes, understanding, and beliefs associated with that role (Clarke, Hyde, & Drennan, 2013); it is the mental configuration of the physical responsibilities. Herein the difference between professional role and professional identity is illustrated. Role is the function, whereas identity is the personal perception.

My experience will lend a prime example of this dichotomy. My last job within a library was as a "Reference, Research, and Instruction Specialist," a classified staff position a paygrade above the aforementioned "Reference and Research Specialist." My role entailed sitting at the reference desk or on Virtual Reference/IM for roughly 20h per week, teaching individual library skills classes and working on random research projects. Research and academic productivity was only a portion of my responsibilities in that role. If I were at a dinner party or some social function where the majority of people were not library employees though, then I would define myself as "an academic researcher who works in a library." To me, the research and publication that I conducted embodied the most fulfilling aspect of the job and by defining myself with that perceived identity, I was better able to explain my relative functions in the profession.

Academic librarians have a similar opportunity to define themselves by portions of their roles, especially considering the multifaceted components of the position. Librarians have a complex set of responsibilities, working within the library, interacting with other academic departments and units around campus, and in various communities in and around the campus (Crawford, 2012). These activities create a unique position among the academic community, as their roles create opportunities to interact and communicate on several different planes of influence with a variety of the population. The librarians interrelate with faculty, graduate students, undergraduate students, and members of the community in tasks as simple as locating a book within the library to collaborating on high-level research projects, and the intricacy of the responsibilities varies often without notice. The librarians' exchanges occur in a similarly complex set of locations such as the physical libraries, academic departments, and through virtual communication. Understanding the impact of the role and its subsequent status on the professional identity of academic librarians is an important topic that bares examination and will be a key component of this work.

1.1 Background of the study

Lovitts (2007, p. 19) produced a study whose chief aim was "for departments, disciplines, and universities to develop objective standards for the outcomes of doctoral training- the dissertation." However, what about activities and student preparation during the program? If the goal of an academic department is the adequate preparation of a future graduate and extends beyond the culmination of the dissertation to the entirety of the doctoral program, then the program offerings required assessment. I subsequently developed a project that looked at doctoral studies beyond the scope of just the dissertation.

A colleague and I examined the curriculum in history and computer science programs and the successive academic professionalism[1] of doctoral students at the five largest public institutions in the country (Perini & Calcagno, 2013). Many department websites and their marketing suggest that their particular program would prepare prospective students for professional careers of their choosing. However, not all programs offer curricular courses on publication, or alternatively, either student- or faculty-led workshops or groups that focus on that aspect of academic professionalism. The study suggested that there is indeed a sizable gap between the number of students in the programs and the number of students who produce scholarship in their fields.

These findings were troubling. First, it demonstrated that potentially a significant portion of doctoral students are not engaging in published scholarly productivity concurrent with their studies. This becomes problematic because many of these students will seek employment in academe and be at a disadvantage when compared to their peers who do publish. Second, it is difficult to evoke changes to a doctoral program without a doctoral-level terminal degree in hand. In addition to the difficulty associated with the introduction of courses through a university curriculum committee, it seems unlikely that program populated by doctorate-holding faculty with years or decades of instruction experience would be receptive to curricular critiques fielded by a doctoral student and a librarian.

Academic librarians though often engage in professional activities that might aid doctoral students in their development of academic professionalism. In fact, a subsequent study found that 74 percent of academic librarians had experience publishing formal research papers (Baruzzi & Calcagno, 2015), which is a skill easily passed along to receptive doctoral students. Thus, the librarians were found to have engaged in at least a portion of the activities that traditional faculty are noted for, specifically research.

This revelation led to a series questions involving the actual role of academic librarians throughout the university system. For instance, what type and quality of research do academic librarians perform? How often do they instruct? What type of service activities are they involved in? Essentially, in academe, who are librarians and what do they do?

In addition to the issues regarding librarian function, questions emerge when considering the individuals who occupy the position. This study will be gender specific

[1] Academic professionalism in the context of that paper referred to the professional role of the doctoral student once they had graduated and entered their place in the academy. Aspects of this process no doubt occurred within the doctoral program itself, such as what the new graduate might expect in the acculturation process of their future department. However, since that study concerned the librarian's role in the process, the focus was on the aspects of this training that the academic librarian realistically could alter, such as exposure to a publication process. As a result, professionalism related to the preparation for anticipated academic output: publications, presentations, and so on.

in studying the identity of female academic librarians. This is significant, as since its inception, in contrast to traditional faculty, the role of academic librarian historically has been a female profession. In fact, of the 20 original students in 1887 at the first library school at Columbia, 17 were female (Rubin, 2004). Of the 15 schools in existence in 1919, 10 were established by women (Maack, 1986). Yet there are consistent inequities by gender. In 1999, the American Library Association reported that 67.99% of academic librarians and 57% of academic library directors were female. Yet the average salary for a male director was $62,961, whereas the female directors averaged $58,202, a difference of nearly $5000 (American Library Association, 1999).

Similar inequalities persist between men and women in the traditional professoriate. Thus, the role of librarian has historically been occupied by women, and their experiences of bias in the academy merge with those of their full-time tenure-track female faculty counterparts (Schuster & Finkelstein, 2006). Even though their historical pathways evolved in different manners, the perception of roles of female academic librarians and female faculty occupy a similar experiential space within their respective fields. While the female faculty role inherently may be different from that of the female academic librarian, the biased treatment of the individuals in relation to their gender is comparable. By additionally introducing the consideration of gender, the discussion may deliberate on the effect that the role as a female academic librarian has on professional identity.

Make no mistake: the frame applied in this study is not gender specific. If you choose to replicate my work in order to analyze your own institutional environment, then this method will be valid. In fact, in later sections of the book, I address the legitimacy of the process by offering provisions for future research. However, as the following chapters will indicate, I believe that the librarian status among the university hierarchy is determined by the misuse and misunderstanding of the function of the role of the academic librarian. This perception closely mimics the overall experience of females within the academy. As a result, the sample not only reflects the prevailing historical image of librarians, but it illustrates a social dynamic as well, thereby providing a viable context for the discussion here.

When considering the individual's place in the academy, there emerges the split between role and identity. In the context of this work, the *role* of faculty is defined by the actual responsibilities of the individual as characterized by their job description. Some theorists add additional responsibilities to the faculty position, such as governance (Bowen & Schuster, 1986) and the actual level of faculty scholarship and goals differ by institution (Boyer, 1990). Contemporary academics most often distill the function of faculty in some fashion into three categories: research, instruction, and service (Lucas, 2006). For librarians, these activities often carry an ambiguous tone. As faculty, academic librarians are expected to publish. Since the librarians are not tenure-track faculty though, the projected complexity of this research and publication is vague. Which research role has supremacy, librarian as faculty or nontenure-track librarian? In this work, the functional role will be measured by job description and subsequent activity, and the attempt will be made to tease out some of the ambiguities in the academic librarian role.

In contrast, *identity* may be a more subjective and malleable term than role dependent upon the individual perception. "Identity encompasses how individuals understand themselves, how they interpret experiences, how they present themselves and wish to be perceived by others and how they are recognized by the broader community" (Lieff et al., 2012, p. 208). A faculty member may spend the majority of their time involved in classroom instruction, yet identify themselves as an academic researcher. Role and identity differ in this way. While there may be some overlap to the entities, the role and the identity of faculty remain distinct.

Levin and Shaker (2011, p. 1465) also state that "articulation of identity brings together personal experiences and expectations with the social-cultural environment, specifically, the university, including its structures, norms, and practices." Therefore, the environment in which the faculty operates shapes identity, and as intimated, the workplace atmosphere tends to be more difficult for female faculty and academic librarians, and this is a suggested premise in this work. How a faculty member—to include all classifications of faculty, such as academic librarians—perceives any professional experience, regardless of the interface, has a direct positive or negative effect on the individual's identity (Whitchurch, 2009).

1.2 Conclusion

Thus, what began as a study on doctoral student academic professionalism emerged into an examination of the roles and functionality of academic librarians to include considerations of their roles and professional identities. The full evolution of the process and the subsequent consideration of the literature led to more complex questioning. For instance, if librarians engage in activities akin to formal faculty (research, instruction, and service), what is their role and position in the professoriate? Should academic librarians be considered faculty? These are the questions that required investigation on a larger scale, and therefore led to this current study.

References

American Library Association (ALA). (1999). *Library directors: Gender and salary*. Retrieved from http://www.ala.org/research/librarystaffstats/diversity/libdirectors.

Baruzzi, A., & Calcagno, T. (2015). Academic librarians and graduate students: an exploratory study. *Portal: Libraries and the Academy*, *15*(3), 393–407.

Bowen, H., & Schuster, J. (1986). *American professors: A national resource imperiled*. New York: Oxford University Press.

Boyer, E. L. (1990). *Scholarship reconsidered: Priorities of the professoriate*. San Francisco: Jossey-Bass, Inc.

Clarke, M., Hyde, A., & Drennan, J. (2013). Professional identity in higher education. In *The academic profession in Europe: New tasks and new challenges* (pp. 7–21). Netherlands: Springer.

Coker, C., van Duinkerken, W., & Bales, S. (2010). Seeking full citizenship: a defense of tenure faculty status for librarians. *College & Research Libraries*, *71*(5), 406–420.

Crawford, A. (2012). *New directions for academic liaison librarians*. Cambridge: Woodhead Publishing Limited.

Hardesty, L. (1995). Faculty culture and bibliographic instruction: an exploratory analysis. *Library Trends*, *44*(2), 339–367.

Levin, J. S., & Shaker, G. G. (2011). The hybrid and dualistic identity of full-time non-tenure-track faculty. *American Behavioral Scientist*, *55*(11), 1461–1484.

Lieff, S., Baker, L., Mori, B., Egan-Lee, E., Chin, K., & Reeves, S. (2012). Who am I? Key influences on the formation of academic identity within a faculty development program. *Medical Teacher*, *34*(3), e208–e215.

Lovitts, B. E. (2007). *Making the implicit explicit: Creating performance expectation for the dissertation*. Sterling, VA: Stylus.

Lucas, C. (2006). *American higher education: A history* (2nd ed.). New York: Palgrave Macmillan.

Maack, M. N. (1986). Toward a new model of the information professions: embracing empowerment. *Journal of Education for Library and Information Science*, *38*, 283–302.

Oberg, L. R. (1995). *Library support staff in an age of change: Utilization, role, definition, and status*. Retrieved from http://www.ala.org/offices/hrdr/librarysupportstaff/library_support_staff_in_an_age_of_change.

Perini, M., & Calcagno, T. (2013). Research and preparation for academic professionalism: the role of the academic librarian. *World Universities Forum*, *6*(2), 13–25.

Rubin, R. E. (2004). *Foundations of library and information science* (2nd ed.). New York: Neal-Schuman Publishers, Inc.

Schuster, J. H., & Finkelstein, M. J. (2006). *The American faculty: Restructuring of academic work and careers*. Baltimore: The Johns Hopkins University Press.

Simpson, B. (2013). Hiring non-MLS librarians: trends and training implications. *Library Leadership & Management*, *28*(1), 1–15.

Whitchurch, C. (2009). The rise of the blended professional in higher education: a comparison between the United Kingdom, Australia and the United States. *Higher Education*, *58*(3), 407–418.

Yousef, A. (2010). Faculty attitudes toward collaboration with librarians. *Library Philosophy and Practice*, *12*(2), 1–15.

Purpose of the study and research questions

2

At this point, the conversation turns to the topic of the roles of librarians versus tenure-track faculty. As you will see in this chapter and throughout the rest of the work, I believe that the basis of the productivity of the tenure-track faculty and academic librarians are similar. However, the substance of the tenure-track faculty is on a different, more advanced level. Of course, this is not a universal absolute, but it certainly is the prevailing trend.

This assertion is not to denigrate librarians or their place in academe at all. I do not believe that the role and perception of the academic librarian should be relegated to "servitude," which it has in many cases throughout the academic community. Instead, it is an accurate affirmation that provides a more positive understanding of the librarian's roles in higher education. As such, this study aims to help define the role of the academic librarian and provide a more realistic and defined role and space for the academic librarians.

2.1 Purpose of the study

When speaking of "faculty," the general implication is of the tenure-track variety, that is, a professor who splits their time teaching classes and performing research for their next book or article, all the while attending conferences for their particular discipline. Even at that connotative and simplified level though, the actual role of faculty in the established tenure-track line is at times itself murky. For example, a 2007 COACHE study found that while the tenure expectations regarding scholarship and instruction remained clear, the role of faculty in community and service was vague. Still, the priorities of the role retained consistency: research, instruction, and service (COACHE, 2007).

Yet there are wrinkles in the actual roles of faculty themselves as "economic, political, and cultural forces have contributed to the ways in which the nature of faculty work has changed over time" (Robbins, 2013, p. 191). These pressures are pervasive, regardless of the institution, as revised role requirements created new positions and expectations of duty (Robbins, 2013). In addition, across the academy, assumptions about the activities and role of the faculty vary by level and classification, as there are other members of the university community who have faculty status but perform nontraditional and/or nontenured roles. Department chairs, for example, are full-time faculty but occupy a position that involves more administrative duties than average tenure-track faculty (Riley & Russell, 2013). Student affairs professionals are one example of personnel who often hold faculty titles but have different expected competencies and may not even teach or research at all (Ahren, 2008; Dickerson et al., 2011). There are many complex hybrids of faculty across campuses that do not fit the traditional tenure-track notion and as a result, struggle to gain recognition as either defined or accepted faculty.

The segment of that underrecognized population examined in this discussion of course is the academic librarian. The historical image of a librarian sitting at a desk dispensing information is prevalent, but it has evolved into a position that includes instruction (both in person and virtual), service and society memberships, academic scholarship, collection development, and other substantial tasks. Also, similar to student affairs professionals and other factions of the faculty, academic librarians exist in a malleable spot at the university due to these mixed roles as scholar, educator, and administrator (Coker, van Duinkerken, & Bales, 2010). They are a balance between the academic faculty and other departments on campus, such as student services. Their work enhances the in-class learning provided by the faculty by extending that formal learning with supplemental literature and resources.

However, the literature regarding academic librarians does not look favorably upon the premise that academic librarians are, in fact, faculty. Higher education literature and the discussion on faculty habitually overlook the role of the academic librarian, since the role is considered an intrinsically different form and level of academic faculty (Association of College & Research Libraries, 2013). At the same time, literature by librarians concerning their role rarely considers higher education theory in an attempt to bolster their argument that they are, in fact, equivalents to their professorial counterparts (Hardesty, 1991). In short, higher education theorists and proponents of the tradition faculty role view librarians as nonfaculty, whereas academic librarians argue the opposite.

This discussion asserts through a case study analysis of academic librarians at St. Jerome University (St. Jerome)[1] that academic librarians do not, in fact, deserve faculty status. The activities of the academic librarians do involve traditional faculty mores of research, instruction, and service. However, these activities occur on a different plane of involvement than do those of the tenure-track faculty.

The consideration of academic librarians as true tenure-track-style faculty, at least among higher education theorists, is peripheral at best; academic librarians argue that their roles are consistent with faculty. As I mentioned, due to my academic and professional background, I bridge the gap between the higher education theorists and the libraries. I understand both sides of the argument. Part of the bias from the higher education perspective emerges from the mentality that the library and its workers are in the service role. Faculty depict the librarians as persons who will help students or faculty find materials and habitually little more. The academic librarian is often in a subordinate role, one that I do not agree with, for the record. Partnerships may be unequal, but they do not have to be inferior or superior in perceived or actual rank. Librarians, on the other hand, still struggle to overcome this subservient image and validate the collaborative roles that they might play within the academy. Due to

[1] St. Jerome University (St. Jerome) is the pseudonym for the real university at which the case study occurred. Citations related to St. Jerome will not be listed with the references due to the potential for human subject identification.

realities in the identities of the librarians though, which will be discussed later, I suspect that this fight will continue for some time.

If academic librarians are not on the level of tenure-track faculty, then what is their classification? The aim of this study, therefore, is to determine what the actual role of female academic librarians by investigating their positions with higher education theory. By establishing through empirical evidence and qualitative research that their active roles significantly differ from the traditional model of tenure-track faculty, the research therefore seeks to determine the exact features of this position. Once the study concludes *what* they are, the discussion may turn to *who* they are. By solidifying the professional roles, the study then may consider the perceived identities of the librarians. How do they view themselves within the academic community? The higher education framework by which the question of identity of these individuals may be studied is called *blended professionalism*.

As institutions have evolved to meet the demands of their age, the exact specifications of the roles of the roles of various forms of academicians subsequently changed as well (Gordon & Whitchurch, 2007). The combination of these new, actual roles and perceived identity create what Whitchurch (2009) defines as the *blended professional*. Blended professionals are individuals who "are characterized by an ability to build common ground with a range of colleagues, internal and external to the university, and to develop new forms of professional space, knowledge, relationships and legitimacies associated with broadly based institutional projects such as student life, business development and community partnership" (Whitchurch, 2009, p. 417). Basically, blended professionals bridge gaps in both institutional and external silos in order to perform their professional and academic duties; the roles and the environment in which they are performed create professional identities.

Blended professionalism is influenced by and enhances prior identity models. Regarding individual self-identity, Giddens's (1992) model has a noteworthy impact. Giddens (1992, p. 5) regards identity as a "reflexively organized endeavor...which consists in the sustaining of coherent, yet continuously revised, biographical narratives [and] takes place in the context of multiple choice as filtered through abstract systems." External influences and spaces such as jobs and professional roles therefore impact individual identity (Whitchurch, 2009). Whitchurch also cites Rhoades's (2005) development of professional identities of management in academe. Rhoades (2005, p. 39) asserted that shifting roles for nonfaculty administrative managers influenced their faculty identity as *managed professionals* and affected shared governance. The modification of management ultimately was found to have impacted faculty socialization and roles (Deem, Hillyard, & Reed, 2007; Rhoades, 2007). Faculty identity has also been tied to the activities of research and instruction (Deem, 2006), yet like Giddens's (1992) general model is fluid and in constant flux because it is internally perceived (Beijaard, Meijer, & Verloop, 2004). The key addition of Whitchurch's model is that though the prior models acknowledged shifts in roles, they did not overly develop considerations of the blurring of specific professional responsibilities and the resultant outcome on identity. As such, the relative activities of these blended individuals merge and develop a new professional identity not readily codified in previously existing identity theories.

Whitchurch considers and surveys several members of what she considers blended professionals, such as those individuals whose "areas of work variously described as learning or business partnership, student life, diversity, outreach, institutional research, program management and community development" (Whitchurch, 2009, p. 408). A major area of thought left out of Whitchurch's analysis, though, is the role of the academic librarian in the institution. It is clear from a study of Whitchurch's (2013) subsequent work that academic librarians do not even come under consideration with respect to the blended professional concept.

So what is the value of this higher education-based model called blended professional for the analysis of academic librarians? Consider the description of the blended professional again. Blended professionals "are characterized by an ability to build common ground with a range of colleagues, internal and external to the university, and to develop new forms of professional space, knowledge, relationships and legitimacies associated with broadly based institutional projects such as student life, business development and community partnership" (Whitchurch, 2009, p. 417). When I initially read this description, I immediately thought of my librarian colleagues because their work spanned across several spheres of influence within the academy. That portrayal above essentially applies to every facet of the academic librarian's role.

In fact, academic librarians perform a variety of functions in the academy that comprise aspects of research, instruction, and service, and require networking and influence in a variety of physical and virtual spaces (Crawford, 2012). Academic librarians, with their numerous and sometimes ambiguous roles, also may be considered blended professionals. The exact specifics depends upon the academic librarians' personal interpretation of their roles and the associated perceptional identity of their positions. By applying this frame to librarians, administrators and researchers might be better able to understand the professional role and identity of the academic librarians.

Therefore the first guiding question of this study is:

What is the blended professional identity of female faculty librarians?

I argue that the traditional mold of tenure-track faculty does not fit the roles of academic librarians. However, by utilizing Whitchurch's blended professional model, the study better establishes the specifics of the position in the context of their professional duties. Whitchurch's four-tiered frame considering space, knowledge, relationships, and legitimacies is an apt model for analysis, as librarians operate in a blended professional manner on a daily basis. The explicit use of female academic librarians also provides additional insight into the blended professional, specifically due to the additional concept known as *third space*.

Whitchurch (2009, p. 408) asserts that blended professionals are individuals "who not only cross internal and external institutional boundaries, but also contribute to the development of new forms of third space between professional and academic domains." Third space is a theoretical sphere built through an individual's ability to interact and intertwine with many different communities, thereby developing commonalities between diverse populations (Whitchurch, 2013, 2008). With this in mind, the second guiding question of the study becomes:

What is the third space that female academic librarians occupy?

In addition to the library, interactions for and by academic librarians occur in a variety of physical and virtual settings across institutions and with a diverse assortment of the populace to include other library staff, faculty, and students. The role and identity of academic librarians is often an afterthought for higher education theorists. In contrast, literature from the standpoint of the library expounds on the positive additions that academic librarians provide at the academy. The specifics of the position beyond the relative boundaries of the library and its personnel are mitigated due to prevailing perceptions, creating a confusing and complicated professional and academic environment for the librarian.

Part of the difficulty arises from the theoretical conception of the environment. Third space encompasses both the actual role and space of the librarians as well as their perception of that situational setting. This may be a positive opinion if the individual feels supported. However, internal and external forces can create real or artificial boundaries for mobility, thereby potentially limiting growth and development. This environment, in turn, develops the professional identity. The supposition here is that due to their status as female faculty and their professional positions, the academic librarians operate on a difficult plane of third space due to preexisting biases. This space of operation has a significant chance of influencing the academic librarians' professional development.

This reality provides the third guiding question of this work:

How does the blended professional identity shape the female academic librarians' professional growth?

Numerous studies document the historical discrimination and gender inequality that almost always favors men (Blau, Gielen, & Zimmermann, 2012; Lorber, 2010; Vianello & Siemienska, 1990). The prior section of this work mentioned the biased gender trends in academic libraries, where despite the greater number of female librarians, women earn less compensation in directorships. This is perpetuated throughout higher education. For example, in the academic year 2005–06, only 31% of tenure-track positions were filled by women (West & Curtis, 2006), despite the fact that the majority of master's (62.3%) and doctorates (53.3%) in the United States were conferred to women (National Center for Education Statistics, 2012). Another example in higher education is leadership positions, as in 2006, only 23% of university president positions were filled by women (American Council on Education, 2007). The historical model of the tenure-track faculty is based upon an image of a profession that developed from a male-only role. Women gradually gained positions in the professesoriate, but there always have been consistent gender-based inequities concerning course loads, student and faculty expectations, and domestic responsibilities (Trower, 2012). Compound this with the prevailing perception that librarians on not on equal footing with tenure-track faculty counterparts (Coker et al., 2010).

The combination of all of these factors creates a presumably difficult third space in which female academic librarians might thrive. The purpose of this investigation is to determine how the confluence of these dynamics affects the academic librarians' ability to thrive as blended professionals in the collegiate environment. This is a significant conceptual addition, as Whitchurch (2009) primarily considered the fractured divisions in the workers' professional positions. The linking and codification of these academic librarians in a distinctive third space creates a unique prism through which members of the faculty might be examined.

2.2 Significance of the study

At the base level, this study extends multiple conversations regarding academic librarians and their place in the professoriate. Misunderstanding of the role has led to an underappreciation of the contributions of the librarians on campus, and this study in part attempts to clarify the involvement of these individuals within the collective whole. This study gains significance by analyzing this issue; the work recasts academic librarians as blended professionals, and as such, provides the opportunity to reevaluate their worth and significance to the goals of the university system.

Additionally, through the employment of this higher education-based frame and theory, the work provides a wholly new prism through which librarians might investigate their roles in the context of higher education theory. Librarians have complex and sometimes ambiguous roles and duties within the university, the understanding of which might facilitate a more complete understanding of the perception of the position. This study offers insight into the roles and development of female academic librarians and provides a model that might be replicated in other geographic and demographic settings to the benefit of staff and management alike. Simply put, this study ascertains a new, reimagined understanding of the professional identity of academic librarian. The blended professional identity approach enhances the appreciation of what librarians do at the academy and who they are (or more accurately, who they think they are).

On an individual perspective, this study and its replication offer professional individuals an opportunity for self-reflection and analysis, which may have a positive individual outcome (Cooper, 1999). The primary argument put forward here is that the role of the librarian remains so inherently different from a tenure-track route that classifying them as faculty becomes problematic and incorrect. However, librarians gain alternative analytical perspective on their roles and consequently may better understand and articulate their identity when evaluated through the higher education scope.

From a managerial perspective, the study potentially provides the opportunity to discover obstacles preventing staff members' successes in regard to performance and professional development. While this study focuses on one segment of the faculty in the form of academic librarians at one specific university, it is applicable in other units and departments. This is to include positions interior to the library, such as a cataloging librarian, and exterior departments in student affairs that also nominally qualify as faculty but share blended roles, such as career services. The process also may be replicated in other positional demographics, geographies, and manners of collegiate institutions. This study's significance derives from the contextualization and codification of the attendant contributing factors to librarian role and identity construction while employing higher education framework of blended professionalism.

2.3 Conclusion

In this chapter, the framework of the questions of the study was defined in hopes of explaining the purpose and impact that the work might have on the definition of academic librarian role and identity. The following chapter will discuss literature regarding the evolution of the faculty role and the development of the position of the academic librarian in the context of historical narrative. In addition, through preliminary role comparisons, the chapter will establish that the academic librarians in this study do not share the same functionality as tenured-track faculty. A further historical discussion on the inequities regarding the experience of women in higher education will follow. The chapter will conclude with a critique of the literature and underscore the means by which the application of the theory of blended professionalism will address gaps in the arguments.

References

Ahren, C. (2008). Closing the gap with student affairs staff: from margin to mainstream. *New Directions for Higher Education, 143*, 83–91.

American Council on Higher Education. (2007). *The American college president: 2007 edition*. Washington, DC: American Council on Education.

Association of College and Research Libraries (ACRL). (2012). Guidelines for academic librarians without faculty status. *College & Research Libraries News, 73*(3), 161–162.

Beijaard, D., Meijer, P. C., & Verloop, N. (2004). Reconsidering research on teachers', professional identity. *Teaching and Teacher Education, 20*, 107–128.

Blau, F. D., Gielen, A. C., & Zimmermann, K. F. (2012). *Gender, inequality, and wages*. Oxford: Oxford University Press.

Coker, C., van Duinkerken, W., & Bales, S. (2010). Seeking full citizenship: a defense, of tenure faculty status for librarians. *College & Research Libraries, 71*(5), 406–420.

The Collaborative on Academic Careers in Higher Education (COACHE). (2007). *Tenure-track faculty job satisfaction survey highlights report*. Harvard School of Education. Retrieved from http://isites.harvard.edu/fs/docs/icb.topic1023643.files/COACHE_ReportHighlights_20070801.pdf.

Cooper, J. M. (1999). The teacher as a decision-maker. In J. M. Cooper (Ed.), *Classroom teaching skills* (6th ed.). Boston: Houghton-Mifflin.

Crawford, A. (2012). *New directions for academic liaison librarians*. Cambridge: Woodhead Publishing Limited.

Deem, R. (2006). Changing research perspectives on the management of higher, education: can research permeate the activities of manager-academics? *Higher Education Quarterly, 60*(3), 203–228.

Deem, R., Hillyard, S., & Reed, M. (2007). *Knowledge, higher education, and the new, managerialism: The changing management of UK universities*. Oxford: Oxford University Press.

Dickerson, A. M., Hoffman, J. L., Anan, B., Brown, K. F., Vong, L. K., Bresciani, M. J., & Oyler, J. (2011). A comparison of senior student affairs officer and student affairs preparatory program faculty expectations of entry-level professionals' competencies. *Journal of Student Affairs Research & Practice, 48*(4), 463–479.

Giddens, A. (1992). *Modernity and self-identity: Self and society in the late modern age*. Stanford: Stanford University Press.

Gordon, G., & Whitchurch, C. (2007). Managing human resources in higher education: the implications of a diversifying workforce. *Higher Education Management and Policy, 19*(2), 135–155.

Hardesty, L. (1991). The bottomless pit revisited. *College & Research Libraries, 52*, 219–230.

Lorber, J. (2010). *Gender inequality: Feminist theories and politics* (4th ed.). New York: Oxford University Press.

National Center for Education Statistics. (2012). *Degrees conferred by sex and race*. Retrieved from http://nces.ed.gov/fastfacts/display.asp?id=72.

Rhoades, G. (2005). Capitalism, academic style, and shared governance. *Academe*, *91*(3), 38–42.

Rhoades, G. (2007). The study of the academic profession. In P. J. Gumport (Ed.), *Sociology of higher education: Contributions and their contexts* (pp. 113–146). Baltimore: The Johns Hopkins University Press.

Riley, T. A., & Russell, C. (2013). Leadership in higher education examining, professional development needs for department chairs. *Review of Higher Education & Self-Learning*, *6*(21), 38–57.

Robbins, S. P. (2013). From the editor-balancing the personal and professional in an era, of transformed faculty roles. *Journal of Social Work Education*, *49*, 191–193.

Trower, C. A. (2012). *Success on the tenure track: Five keys to faculty job satisfaction*. Baltimore: Johns Hopkins University Press.

Vianello, M., & Siemienska, R. (1990). *Gender inequality: A comparative study of discrimination and participation*. London: SAGE.

West, M. S., & Curtis, J. W. (2006). *AAUP faculty gender equity indicators*. Retrieved from http://www.aaup.org/NR/rdonlyres/63396944-44BE-4ABA-9815-5792D93856F1/0/AAUPGenderEquityIndicators2006.pdf.

Whitchurch, C. (2008). Beyond administration and management: reconstructing the identities of professional staff in UK higher education. *Journal of Higher Education Policy and Management*, *30*(4), 375–386.

Whitchurch, C. (2009). The rise of the blended professional in higher education: a comparison between the United Kingdom, Australia and the United States. *Higher Education*, *58*(3), 407–418.

Whitchurch, C. (2013). *Reconstructing identities in higher education: The rise of third, space professionals*. New York: Routledge.

Historical roles

3

When reviewing literature regarding academic librarians as faculty, two distinct themes emerge. Scholars from a library background assert that academic librarian duties are similar enough to those of tenure-track faculty that the librarian position should be considered true faculty. Conversely, most literature written from the higher education perspective regards the academic librarian as a form of subfaculty, if the work even thinks to include a discussion on librarians at all. Here, the position will be that of the latter stance; academic librarians are not on the same level as tenure-track faculty.

First through a historical narrative and then through preliminary comparison, it becomes apparent in the American experience that although tenure-track faculty and academic librarians share the similar responsibilities and expectations regarding research, instruction, and service, the substance of the activities is inherently different. While the basis of this discussion is within the framework of American history, the experience, particularly involving biases, extends far past the borders of the United States. The following chapter will outline the literature regarding these professional roles, as well as discuss the difficulties facing women in higher education in the context of a chronological description.

3.1 Role of academic faculty

The contemporary role of academic faculty is something that has been scrutinized through a good deal of literature to include Finkelstein (1984), Boyer (1990), Lucas (2006), and Schuster and Finkelstein (2006). Still, the actual faculty roles have shifted over time, beginning as lecturer and evolving into the current research–instruction–service model (Thelin, 2004). Therefore, it seems apt to briefly describe the basic modifications that have taken place through the history of American higher education.

Historically, the faculty of early American colleges would probably be better classified as "instructors" or "tutors" as opposed to a practiced professoriate who lectured on all topics of instruction instead of specializing in one discipline or another. The early faculty came from an established social class, though their wages did not reflect upon their upbringing. "The faculty were similar to clerics in that they were expected to teach for the privilege of affiliating with the college" (Cohen & Kisker, 2010, p. 32). Stratification of the role, such as junior and senior positions, did not occur until the mid-19th century. Not until the late 1800s did the notion of a career as a professor become a viable and respected opportunity, leading to the growth of faculty size and disciplinary specializations (Finkelstein, 1984).

Colleges seemingly existed as more of a male finishing school (all early colleges were male-only) that prepped young gentlemen for civil positions such as ministers, doctors, and public servants (Lucas, 1994), although early faculty often dealt

The Academic Librarian as Blended Professional.

with mischief among the student body. "Drunkenness was rampant, as were violent assaults, uncontrolled gambling, and debauchery of one sort or another" (Lucas, 1994, p. 111). As a result, interactions between faculty and students occurred both within the classroom and on the grounds of the campus, as "college life was characterized by perpetual tensions between students and faculty" (Thelin, 2004, p. 21). As such, the early faculty also carried a "headmaster" disciplinary role in addition to their instructional roles.

The concept of the position's role began to change in the 1800s as bidding wars orchestrated by institutions, particularly the University of Chicago and its president William Rainey Harper, began to push faculty salaries upward (Cohen & Kisker, 2010). The commoditization of the job also afforded the ability of faculty to reduce their in-class teaching time as well as schools to attract scholars from fields to this point not traditionally academic, such as scientists who did research in addition to teaching duties (Lucas, 2006). Additionally, the Morrill Act passage in 1862 noticeably enhanced the number of positions available, which in turn provided for the subdivision of "professorial ranks into assistant, associate, and full, and [systematized] the procedures for advancement in rank and the probationary period prior to tenure" (Gappa, Austin, & Trice, 2007, p. 51). The key attribute of the faculty around the turn of the 20th century was that they were full-time employees.

Indeed, the stratification of the ranks provided the basis for institutions (and their administrators and boards of directors) to create expectations of the incoming faculty's function, such as education level, teaching requirements, and publication. The former role of exclusive instruction was essentially eliminated as "promotion, tenure, salary, and professional esteem were all associated with research and scholarship" (Lucas, 2006, p. 305). Colleges also codified their organizational structures, introducing administrative positions that supported the educational goals of the system, albeit in a business-like mode (Lucas, 2006). It also bears importance because it introduced the concept of academic freedom among the professoriate.

The American Association of University Professors (AAUP) was founded in 1915, with the intention of stemming a series of well-publicized academic firings around the turn of the 20th century (Fruman, 2009). Establishing a codified structure of tenure and its subsequent privileges became a primary goal of the AAUP. In addition, faculty desired the provision of "freedom of expression and economic security" (Gappa et al., 2007). "It took decades for many colleges and universities to accept that unless professors were secure in their jobs, after a probationary period of no more than seven years, genuine academic freedom would be constantly threatened" (Fruman, 2009, p. 342). The AAUP spent 25 years of negotiations with the colleges themselves to produce the "1940 Statement of Principles on Academic Freedom and Tenure" that ultimately defined academic freedom and tenure as the model of the professoriate.

In addition, the introduction of seminal college funding programs such as the GI Bill (Mettler, 2007; Pusser, 2006), the National Merit program (Turner, 2006), and the Higher Education Act (HEA) of 1965 and its succeeding editions (Pusser, 2006), as well as innovations to travel (Turner, 2006) during the middle decades of the 20th century created an influx of students with the ability to attend collegiate institutions. In response to these mainly federal- and state-backed initiatives, faculty enjoyed an "academic job market [that] became a seller's market, in which individual professors negotiated premium salaries and the average salary improved significantly" (Gappa et al., 2007, p. 52). The professoriate became a highly desirable and respected position.

This "golden age" of faculty was not to last, however, as social and economic concerns arose (Sorey & Gregory, 2010). As mentioned, though violence between parties on campus was not a new concept, those conflicts occurred either out of drunken buffoonery or dissatisfaction with college rules and regulations (Bledstein, 1976). Instead, these later demonstrations of the 1960s and 1970s carried a political shade that compromised the notion of the institution of the faculty. Tied to political remonstrations of the era, "student protests during the late 1960s and early 1970s attacked irrelevant courses and uninspiring teaching. Since the protests took place at universities with the greatest concentration of leading scholars, they exposed the myth that all that is required to be a good teacher is to know one's subject" (Gaff & Simpson, 1994, p. 168). In essence, students of this era, inspired by the questioning of political authority of the time, latched on their own dissatisfactions with the educational system and its faculty to the ongoing protests.

This development is not necessarily a detriment because it demonstrates a growth of cultural and communal awareness by the student base, thereby indicating that some of the educational development garnered in a college education took hold. However, it predicated a general downtrend in the esteem of the profession, especially when financial considerations also drove institutions to find means to alter personnel regulations. This resulted in the (still continuing) downturn in the number of the tenured faculty and the revision of instructional roles around academe (Bowen & Schuster, 1986; Marcus, 2000; Nelson, 2008).

Resulting from the decline of tenured numbers was the increased amount of part-time and contract faculty employed in the instructional role. "Outside academe, the tendency in the 1990s was to reduce the number of full-time staff who had rights to their jobs and to employ temporary staff...the universities...were among the last bastions of career security and norms of professionalism" (Cohen & Kisker, 2010, p. 361). Resistance to the adjunctification of the faculty did not last though, as by 1995, 41 percent of faculty was part-time, almost double of that in 1970 (Cohen & Kisker, 2010).

The reduction in full-time roles was caused "not by a shortage of qualified candidates but by the desire of administrators to save money at a time of rapidly increasing expenditures" (Cohen & Kisker, 2010, p. 223). Administrators were beginning to see a reduction in the amount of federal and state monies supporting the institution of higher education and as a corollary, sought to trim down faculty expenditures. Consequently, these changes "helped institutions balance the budget, but at the same time they diminished faculty professionalization because they did not adhere to the traditional core values that included not only teaching but also research, public service, service to the institution, and commitment to a career in which they were judged by their peers" (Cohen & Kisker, 2010, p. 364).

Full-time and tenure-track faculty still retained their previous responsibilities though (Lucas, 2006). For example, total workloads remained heavy and participation in service, both internal to the institution and in external associations were emphasized. By the 1990s, full-time instructors were working around 53 hours per week (Cohen & Kisker, 2010).

For tenure-track faculty, this included not only the expected responsibilities of teaching, but also research and service, both to the public and to the institution (O'Meara, LaPointe Terosky, & Neumann, 2008). Mentoring (Houser, Lemmons, & Cahill, 2013; Lechuga, 2011) and advising (Baker & Griffin, 2010) are commonplace responsibilities of contemporary faculty. Consequently, despite the adjunctification of the faculty, in many sectors, the professor's role has returned to its previous incarnations with the reemphasis on research and publication (Lucas, 2006).

Therefore, in summary, the role of the faculty in American higher education has evolved from primarily a lecturer to a researcher, instructor, and service-minded individual. As well, contemporary conditions of the higher education field have split the professoriate into increasingly distinct full-time or part-time positions, although the permanent positions and their responsibilities largely reflect the later historical model. The evolution of academic librarian roles follows a similar path to that of the faculty.

3.2 Role of academic librarians

Similarly to faculty roles, the role of academic librarians and its evolution has also been discussed extensively in historical analyses (DeVinney, 1986; Greer, Grover, & Fowler, 2007; Mullins, 2012; Rubin, 2004). In its current incarnation, academic libraries offer a substantial connectivity to the university academic collective, as they provide assistance and guidance to both students and faculty. Libraries and their librarians aid the acquisition of information for the student that supplements in-class learning. Historically, however, an academic librarian's role followed an evolutionary path similar to that of the faculty as the position progressed from a stationary data organizer into a dynamic and multifaceted university role.

The concept of the academic librarian is a relatively more modern development that coincided with the evolution of the faculty role during the 19th century. The position of academic librarian emerged in the 1800s as the model of the collegiate institution itself evolved. Rubin (2004, p. 278) cites three specific catalysts that led to the development of the academic librarian role: changes in the curriculum, the rise of the research model, and the Morrill Land Grant Act of 1862. As mentioned, the curriculum shifted from a liberal arts and classics-based core to more pragmatic disciplines (Lucas, 2006). This changed the faculty's instructional techniques from lecture-based learning to a model that required more research outside of the classroom, particularly at the library (Hanson, 1989).

The research model university developed from both the alteration to the instructional style and American's borrowing the German university form (Adrian, 2003). "The seminar model of teaching was emphasized and students were encouraged to consult a wide variety of published sources" (Rubin, 2004, p. 280). The university repositories required professionals to sort through and direct students and faculty to these materials, creating the need for a librarian.

The Morrill Land Grant Act produced federally backed universities across the country. The act provided land for the establishment of institutions that expanded educational curriculum beyond classical studies to include mechanical and agricultural arts (Duemer, 2007), again denoting the need for more research outside the classroom. As well, the goal was to expand access to academe to more than just the individuals who could afford to entertain the idea of attending a Harvard or Yale. As mentioned, the Morrill Act created a building boom. The legitimacy of the universities rested upon their ability to develop academic repositories, again generating a need for formal academic librarians (Rubin, 2004).

Thus, as the role expanded, the education required to practice as a librarian developed as well. Rubin cites the major influence of Mevil Dewey as the driving force behind the codification of library science as a discipline. "Dewey was not alone in promoting the field of librarianship and library education, but he was a central figure whose energy and devotion advanced the profession" (Rubin, 2004, p. 441). Dewey was instrumental in establishing the first library school at Columbia in 1887 and helped organize the American Library Association, not to mention the eponymous library classification system (O'Reilly, 2013). Though O'Reilly (2013) faults Dewey for helping establish an ideology that library work was less demanding and therefore deserved less compensation, his work nevertheless led to the organization and proliferation of library science programs.

By 1919, 15 library programs existed (Maack, 1986) and a variety of degree levels—bachelor's and master's—emerged (Robbins-Carter & Seavey, 1986). A review of the value of these 15 schools led to the Williamson Report of 1923, which above all recommended that library education take place at the university (Hansen, 2004). The report "affirmed that a substantial part of librarianship was, or should be, a form of education...and forced the profession to consider the importance of consistency and high quality in the curricula, administration, and teaching in library schools" (Rubin, 2004, p. 450). Essentially, library education was formulized, and it somewhat minimized the likelihood of an oversaturation of the degree. In fact, currently in 2014, there are only 63 American Library Association-accredited programs in the United States, Canada, and Puerto Rico (American Library Association, 2014a).

Subsequent to the addition of the Morrill Act, other government supported initiatives followed, increasing the number of financially capable students. Work-study, a federal program that subsidized student labor on campus, continued to be provided for students during the Great Depression (Lucas, 2006). The introduction of influential college funding programs such as the GI Bill (Mettler, 2007; Pusser, 2006), the National Merit program (Turner, 2006), and the Higher Education Act (HEA) of 1965 and its succeeding editions (Pusser, 2006) created an influx of students with the ability to attend collegiate institutions. All of these initiatives led to an ever-increasing need to expand and professionalize the librarian positions that would be needed to supplement the educational learning of the rapidly expanding student base.

As with the faculty, librarian's status increased throughout the 20th century, when the scope of the librarian role expanded as universities branched out and associated technology improved and increased in availability. As opposed to being confined to the physical space of the libraries, academic librarians were able to explore marketing and interaction avenues in different departments across physical and virtual academic campuses. Graham (2004) asserts that the evolved definition of "an academic librarian is an individual possessing a Master's in Library Science and working in a college or university library or library system" (p. 11). This is a generalization of the role, as academic librarians participated in instruction (Sproles, Johnson, & Farison, 2008), collection development (Bracke, Herubel, & Ward, 2010), peer mentoring and management (Fyn, 2013), and their own research and subsequent productivity (Schrimsher & Northrup, 2013).

Academic librarians also gained several modes of outreach and interaction with students on campuses, such as invited lectures, roving reference (where librarians carrying laptops aid research at different locations on campus), and in-class instruction, but the marketing of their abilities was usually done by the individual librarian by a variety of means (Aguilar, Keating, Schadl, & Van Reenen, 2011). As well, Shupe and Pung (2011) note that in the "traditional model, the librarian managed informational resources of the local holdings in the library" (p. 409). The physical library and collection were no longer the boundaries of expertise, as advancing technology has resulted in the availability of more research tools for the librarians to utilize (Cardina & Wicks, 2004). The changes in the ability to outreach increased the spaces and spheres of influence within which academic librarians could operate.

The role of the academic librarian certainly evolved with this influx of technology. Tucci (2011) supports integrating librarians into the academic community outside of the library, particularly with faculty/librarian relationships, as a means to enhance student-learning outcomes. The popular suggestion to accomplish this is through embedment of the librarian in the classroom or program office, either virtually (Bennett & Simning, 2010; Hawes, 2011) or physically (Freiburger & Kramer, 2009; Tumbleson & Burke, 2010). Another means to interact with the campus community is through the highlighting of librarian experience (Nunn & Ruane, 2011).

As a result of these opportunities, and similarly to the tenure and non-tenure track counterparts though, librarians have experienced an increase in the volume and complexity of their work, although the status of the position continuously changes. They operate in many professional spaces at varying degrees of involvement and acceptance and as a result, fit the description of a blended professional. With faculty, many of the instructional roles are being filled by part-time and adjunct faculty. Librarians find that their roles are being reclassified as nonfaculty staff (Dunn, 2013) or filled by differently qualified individuals, such as non-MLS-holding librarians (Simpson, 2013). These trends have reignited the debate as to the actual and perceived role of the librarian in the academy.

3.3 Perception versus actuality of the librarian role

Perceptions of the academic librarian's role among members of the academic community remain questionable due to misconceptions about librarian instructional efficacy and training, scholastic ability, and service related activities (Association of College & Research Libraries, 2012). Librarians themselves view their position as seminal to an institution's mission (Lynch et al., 2007). "As academic personnel, librarians are at the core of the University's teaching, learning, research and service mission" (St. Jerome University Librarians' Handbook, 2012).[1] Yet the rest of the academic faculty,

[1] St. Jerome University (St. Jerome) is the pseudonym for the real university at which the case study occurred. Citations related to St. Jerome will not be listed with the references due to the potential for human subject identification.

particularly the deans and provosts, view libraries and librarians as a merely pragmatic means of finding information and are supplemental, not primary to the university's mission (Lynch et al., 2007). This is due to ambiguity in the description of the roles of faculty and librarians, as on the surface, they appear similar. Delving into the specifics makes the differences in the levels of the individuals.

O'Meara, LaPointe Terosky, and Rice (2008, p. 5) provide a standard description of faculty role:

> *As professionals, faculty apply their developed knowledge, skills, and values to complex problems, challenges, and goals for the benefit of society. Professionals such as faculty have significant autonomy and privilege and are expected to commit themselves to the highest standards of excellence and ethical behavior in exchange for this autonomy...Faculty, as professionals, will continue throughout their careers to update their knowledge, skills, and ethical and practical competence in the service to their profession.*

This description, though thorough, is nonetheless nebulous because a variety of professions may fit into that definition. Few, if any, librarians will not assert the value of their skill-base when addressing any variety of problems, and ethical behavior is something of an expected understanding in higher education. Librarians also assert privilege in their roles when compared to their colleagues, and frequently publish and participate in scholarly practices associated with their profession. Compare the above depiction to the definition of academic librarians from St. Jerome University's (the site of this study) Librarians' Handbook:

> *Librarians at the University are responsible for acquiring, organizing, managing, and providing access to a multitude of scholarly resources. In addition, librarians may fulfill research consultation and instruction responsibilities in the University. The multiplicity of functions performed and the varied specialties possessed by librarians at the University reflect the diversity of the Libraries' programs, collections, and related service obligations. All librarians share a responsibility to perform at the highest level of professional competence, provide consistently high quality service to students and faculty, and to engage actively with and meaningfully contribute to the academic and research enterprise of the University (p. 19).*

Here, librarians categorize materials, teach on campus, retain professional competence, and participate in service and research activities. While the description leaves room for more of a service-based orientation, the librarian role may be interpreted as comparable to the faculty.

St. Jerome's Faculty Handbook echoes much of what has been said about the expectations of the faculty role, specifically concerning instruction, research, and service. "Candidates for renewal, promotion and tenure will be evaluated in light of the missions of the University which are teaching, research and scholarship, both theoretical and applied, and service" (p. 26). The St. Jerome University Librarians' Handbook also addresses these responsibilities. Beginning with instruction, the St. Jerome University Librarians' Handbook states that librarians are responsible for "instruction responsibilities in the University" (p. 19) and "teaching courses or giving lectures beyond the library's instruction program" (p. 24). Librarians do engage in a good deal of instruction in the university, both in person (Hall, 2013; Margino, 2013) and virtually (LaGuardia, 2011; Stiwinter, 2013). As well, they cater to varying levels of educational expertise, covering undergraduate (Clark & Chinburg, 2010; Lieberthal, 2009), graduate (O'Malley & Delwiche, 2012; Shaffer, 2011), and faculty (Watson et al., 2013). Extensive research demonstrated the efficacy of librarian instruction in a variety of settings, including community colleges (Arp, Woodard, & Warren, 2006; Johnson, 2004), 4-year institutions (Clark & Chinburg, 2010; Cooke & Rosenthal, 2011), graduate schools (O'Malley & Delwiche, 2012; Shaffer, 2011), and in distance settings (Charnigo, 2009; Hemmig & Montet, 2010; Hines, 2008; Shiao-Feng & Kuo, 2010). Research suggested that the actual institution, library, or funding had less influence on the quality of the instruction than the individual librarian themselves (Hines, 2008). Roles did not predicate effectiveness; motivation did.

Opponents of librarians as faculty suggest the role and responsibilities of librarians differs too drastically from traditional faculty. Of the conversation, Coker, van Duinkerken, and Bales (2010) note that "academic librarians do not often 'teach,' at least in the manner typically attributed to teaching faculty, nor are librarians required to obtain the PhD for employment (leading to the conclusion that they must play catch-up in research or their research is of lower quality)" (p. 408). Other institutions have librarians instructing formal for-credit classes similar to the faculty, usually dealing with information literacy (Rogers, 2013). At St. Jerome though, the instruction that the librarians perform is more workshop oriented (Hanz & Lange, 2013; Jacklin & Robinson, 2013) or through individual consultations (Meyer, Forbes, & Bowers, 2010). The comparison of the instruction between faculty and librarians at the institution of study, while still defined as instruction, is fundamentally different.

Next, consider research requirements. Faculty are expected to research and publish. "Genuine excellence must be exhibited in the areas of teaching or research and scholarship and high competence must be exhibited in both" (St. Jerome University Faculty Handbook, p. 27). Librarians also carry the expectation that they will contribute to the field through scholarship. "Librarians have privileges and responsibilities commensurate with their academic role as professional faculty at the University. As members of a profession, librarians are expected to keep current with and contribute to the advancement of the profession" (St. Jerome University Librarian Handbook, p. 24). Academic librarians publish. A recent study found that from a survey of 347 active collegiate librarians, 78 percent actively published researched material (Baruzzi & Calcagno, 2015). Lamothe (2012) advocated publishing due to its facilitation of discussion among individuals in the academic environment. "Writing and publishing is an opportunity for conversation among professionals where ideas are exchanged, agreed upon or argued, elaborated, and clarified" (Lamothe, 2012, p. 157). This can also include collaborative ventures, as librarian and faculty collaboration has been proven successful (Kennedy & Monty, 2011).

Due to mixed responsibilities of librarians at different institutions though, librarians do not always emphasize their professionalism through publication (Lamothe, 2012). This likely contributes to the misunderstanding of the role of the librarian around campuses. Tenure-track faculty have to publish. An easy way for librarians to gain their attention, if not respect, is to do the same. Hansson and Johannesson (2013) found that despite the knowledge of the processes, the daily duties of the librarians (ie, collection development, research consultations, etc.) took away from the librarians' time for research, and in fact, Schrimsher and Northrup (2013) suggest such duties make them wary of that researcher role. This is unfortunate because as Wolfe, Naylor, and Drueke (2010) assert, "reference librarians are perfectly positioned to collaborate with other stakeholders…[as] they operate in integrated virtual and physical worlds, where the human and the computer work together" (p. 110). Opportunities are therefore missed due to misconceptions about the actual role and abilities of the academic librarians.

Moreover, the nature of the institution shapes the productivity of the academic librarian. At some institutions, librarians are full, tenure-track members of the faculty; at other institutions, they may be professional or contract faculty, or even staff. These differences affect the productivity of the librarians, as for example, the tenured faculty librarian will have publishing expectations that the librarian staff will not have to address. However, tenured faculty librarians regularly do not have the same goals as their counterparts in academic departments. "Often, the publishing and service requirements for tenure are lower for librarians than for other tenured faculty. This is not because of a lack of academic rigor, but rather because of a lack of time and funding" (Coker, van Duinkerken, & Bales, 2010, p. 415). This partly is due to the fact that the responsibilities of librarians, tenured or otherwise, inherently differ from the traditional faculty.

The relative quality of library publications also bears reflection. Nixon (2013) revisited a 1985 article by Kohl and Davis that ranked the value of library journals by aspects such as acceptance rate and impact factors. Acceptance rates are the percentages of submitted manuscripts that are subsequently published. A lower acceptance rate traditionally has meant more scrutiny in the editorial process and therefore more quality in the finished product (Haensly, Hodges, & Davenport, 2009). Impact factors measure the number of citations taken from recent issues of a specific journal; the higher the number, the more influence that journal has on the field. Nixon (2013) cited the top library journals as *College and Research Libraries*, *Information Technology and Libraries*, and *Journal of Academic Librarianship*. Compare the acceptance rates and impact factors to top journals in a different field, such as Higher Education. Beach (2014) lists *The Journal of Higher Education*, *The Review of Higher Education*, and *Research in Higher Education* as leading journals in that field. For a list of acceptance rates and impact factors of the top three journals in the fields of Library Science and Higher Education, see Table 3.1.

All of these journals are peer-reviewed, meaning that article submissions are judged for worthiness by members of the (theoretically) same academic community. It is considered an extra level of quality assurance since it adds additional scrutiny to the arguments presented. The comparison of the acceptance rates shows that all of the higher education journals had a substantially lower acceptance rate when compared to the library journals. In addition, the impact factor tended to be higher for the higher education journals. These statistics are not flawless. For example, the way in which acceptance rates are calculated is not universal (Perry & Michalski, 2010), and the

Table 3.1 The acceptance rates and impact factors of the top three journals in the fields of Library Science and Higher Education

Journal title	Review process	Acceptance rate (%)	Impact factor
College and Research Libraries	Peer reviewed	30	0.683
Information Technology and Libraries	Peer reviewed	40	0.528
Journal of Academic Librarianship	Peer reviewed	40	0.87
The Journal of Higher Education	Peer reviewed	8	1.157
The Review of Higher Education	Peer reviewed	6–10	0.758
Research in Higher Education	Peer reviewed	11–20	1.221

Statistics are from: Nixon, J. M. (2013). Core journals and information science: Developing a methodology for ranking LIS journals. College & Research Libraries. Retrieved from http://crl.acrl.org/content/early/2012/07/23/crl12-387.short?rss=1 and Cabell's Directory (2011). Education journals impact factors and acceptance rates. Retrieved from http://classguides.lib.uconn.edu/content.php?pid=65298&sid=1310559.

impact factor can be manipulated by self-citation (Mannino, 2005). However, if these criteria are one of the considerations when judging the quality of faculty productivity during tenure review, they cannot be discounted (Campanario, 2010).

Finally the question of service is considered. Service is an inherent aspect of faculty work. "Departments are established to carry out programs of instruction, research and scholarship, and public service in particular fields of knowledge" (p. 12) and "some specific administrative or service functions may also be attached to the teaching, research, or clinical focus" (p. 17). While service can be a nebulous term, O'Meara et al. (2008) categorize service as institutional, disciplinary, community, and scholarly (p. 76). Institutional service refers to the work done at the employing university, such as interdepartmental committee work and disciplinary service follows a similar vein, only the service comes through work in professional organizations. Community service affects the process of providing information to the community at large. Scholarly service is the interesting frame, because it pertains to the professional expertise of the faculty member. Scholarly service, therefore, may concern dissertation and thesis committee advisement and participation, academic advising, and other forms of direct mentorship.

Similarly, librarians are charged with providing "service to the University and/or the University Libraries through participation in the work of committees, task forces and special projects at the University, Libraries, or departmental level" and "service to the community through participation in educational service activities external to the University community such as library boards, literacy programs, or other appropriate volunteer work" (St. Jerome University Librarians' Handbook, 2012, p. 24). Librarians are expected to serve on a variety of institutional committees (St. Jerome

University Librarians' Handbook, 2012). Just like the faculty, librarians are meant and expected to participate in all manner of disciplinary service activities and national associations, such as the American Library Association. In fact, the Association of College and Research Libraries—the university-oriented division of the American Library Association—had 11,944 members in 2013 (American Library Association, 2014b). In addition, many librarians have supplemental memberships in subject-specific associations, such as a chemistry librarian retaining an affiliation in the American Chemical Society (Bennett, 2011). Librarians also participate in community service outside of the university, providing information and resources to the larger population (de la Pena McCook, 2000; Press & Diggs-Hobson, 2005).

The scholarly frame is where the service models of faculty and librarians diverge. At some institutions, academic librarians serve as advisers to members of the student population (Kelleher & Laidlaw, 2009), but not at St. Jerome. In fact, part of the difficulty faced by librarians in the scholarly service sector deals with their terminal degree level. In order to serve on doctoral dissertation or master's thesis committees, faculty members must have an equivalent degree (St. Jerome University Academic Catalog, 2014). Given that the terminal degree for a librarian is often at the master's level, this limits their ability to serve in that capacity in a doctoral granting institution.

Another issue with librarians is that the role becomes blended between *service* and *services*. In contrast to the service provided by the faculty, librarians are viewed as auxiliary service personnel, present to assist students and faculty with the simple acquisition of resources. Service, not instruction or research, is viewed as their primary role. Steven J. Bell, president of the Association of College and Research Libraries, states: "We see ourselves as being closely connected to the educational mission, yet librarians are often perceived as academic-support personnel" (Dunn, 2013). In this manner, academic librarians frequently are viewed as service-oriented, noncollaborative subfaculty (Given & Julien, 2005; Julien & Given, 2002; Wyss, 2010). This position or marketing affects other issues, such as librarian participation in governance issues. Librarians are often left out of decision-making processes available to other faculty members around campus, to their detriment. "[Librarians] should be involved in library governance, and that involvement in university governance improves the perception among the teaching faculty of academic librarians" (Wyss, 2010, p. 381). Despite the discussed evolution of the role of the librarian, the perception of their work in service to the community is often mitigated and renders their influence ineffective.

Academic librarians fill a variety of roles on campus—researcher, collaborator, administrator, instructor—that blend some of the responsibilities of traditional faculty with the role of a librarian. Yet their comparative position on campus is tenuous, as the services provided by librarians often supersede their instruction and research endeavors. Whereas with faculty service appears to be a tertiary consideration, it is the primary focus of the academic librarian, potentially to the detriment of the perception of their role and identity. At the same time, the level, type, and quality of instruction and research performed by libraries appears to be of lesser substance than that offered by the academic faculty.

Because of the relative ambiguity of their professional and academic roles, the librarians fit the concept of a blended professional. The question then becomes whether or not their role influences their perceptions of their personal professional identities. This becomes all the more relevant when considering female role and identity throughout higher education, particularly as faculty and academic librarians.

3.4 Women in higher education

If academic librarians are to be considered second-tier in faculty due to their roles, they share similar perceptive experiences with women, particularly women faculty, in higher education. Based upon their roles, academic librarians have historically found it difficult to gain ascendancy of any kind within the professoriate. Female members of the academic community have long experienced the same difficulties and operate in a similar plane of third space, struggling to obtain even equality in academe.

Even so, women and other underrepresented minorities first obtained faculty positions in the 18th and 19th centuries. For example, in 1783, Washington College hired Elizabeth Callister Peele and Sarah Callister to instruct in painting and drawing (Washington College, 2013), and Sarah Jane Woodson Early was the first female African American college professor at Wilberforce College in 1858 (Lawson & Merrill, 1984). Opportunities were not plentiful, but one of the first successful incarnations of female higher education was the Southern Women's Colleges of the 1800s. Several contributions of women's education during this period include the creation of elective courses, standardization of instruction, growth of the public school system, and furthering employment opportunities (Farnham, 1994). Most importantly, in a fixed and male dominant society, these colleges demonstrated that women could learn and be successful outside the home.

Women in the Southern Women's Colleges were educated in curriculum on par with what was being taught at the men's colleges and the Seven Sisters. Math, English grammar, and sciences (botany, astronomy, mineralogy, anatomy) were commonplace courses. "The classics were considered the core of a liberal arts education and the fact that by custom they were not forbidden to Southern women as inappropriate to their gender is of special significance" (Farnham, 1994, p. 73). The women were also taught a variety of classical and foreign languages, such as Greek, Latin, French, and Spanish, and the education was on par with counterpart male institutions (Thelin, 2004). For instance, the Southern Carolina Female Collegiate Institute at Barhamville had an (native German) instructor that taught both German and instrumental and vocal music (Farnham, 1994). In contrast to prevailing society, in the collegiate environment, men and women were found to be intellectual equals, although parity of access was not ensured.

One might mention the contemporary existence of northern women's colleges such as the Seven Sisters, the first of which, Mount Holyoke College, was founded in 1837. These colleges were established as female "companion" schools to their male-only Ivy League counterparts (Rosenberg, 2004). Unfortunately, they also had similar restrictions to race and ethnicity well into the 20th century, paralleling faults of access similar to Ivy League schools at the time (Johnson, 2008; Rosenberg, 2004). For example, Barnard's Dean Virginia Gildersleeve developed a series of complicated application forms, tests, and subjective interviews similar to those utilized at Princeton at the time meant to limit the number of nonwhite, Christian women admitted (Karabel, 2005; Rosenberg, 2004). Indeed, Barnard did not admit an African American woman until the 1920s (Rosenberg, 2004).

Despite the shortcomings regarding race equality, the education received at women's-only institutions was stout. The students' acquisition of knowledge represented a level of curricular and civic education that might translate to a measureable production of public good in an assortment of social eras, including the present. These schools succeeded in spite of the societal restrictions in place during their time of operation. The same cannot be said for other incarnations of male-only educational institutions, due to varying combinations of restricted or flawed access, curricular shortcomings, or financial limitations.

The integration of women and faculty into male-only institutions was a slow and progressive journal. Echoing Oberlin's original model, coeducational institutions began to emerge after the Civil War at institutions like Cornell University, although single-sexed colleges continued to be the overwhelming standard (Thelin, 2004). Admissions opportunities emerged, as between 1890 and 1910, women accounted for 40 percent of undergraduate enrollment (Thelin, 2004, p. 226). It did not result in a plethora of higher-level graduates though. Columbia only conferred eight doctorates to women in 1900 (Rosenberg, 2004, p. 91). In addition, many of the leadership positions and clubs on campuses remained exclusive to men, either in practice or policy (Cohen & Brawer, 2008).

Later programs, like the GI Bill in the 1940s and Title IX in the 1970s, increased access for women and provided increased entry into traditionally male disciplines such as engineering and the sciences (Cohen & Brawer, 2010). Enrollment percentages continued to increase in favor of female students. In 1976, women represented 48% and 46% of the undergraduate and graduate population, respectively; by 1993, that percentage jumped to 56% and 54% (Cohen & Brawer, 2010, p. 334). Again though, the progress was sluggish and deliberate, with equitable treatment difficult to find. Yale did not even admit a female student until 1969 (Harvard Crimson, 1968). For the female faculty, improvements equally were trying.

3.5 Female faculty and administration

The historical female faculty role and experience might be best summed up with the statement that equal distribution of and compensation for the professorial roles were (and still are) not on level with male faculty (Bowen, 2005; Chisholm-Burns et al., 2012; Fowler et al., 2004; Guillory, 2001; Lanier, Tanner, & Guidry, 2009). The initial difficulty of equality emerged in the curricular offerings to which women had access.

Women were somewhat preemptively placed in detrimental spaces that limited their opportunities within academe. While the curriculum at the Southern Women's Colleges and Seven Sisters was on par with what was studied at male institutions, it often remained in the classical and liberal arts fields. Women were slow to receive admittance to scientific fields, and when they eventually did matriculate and graduate, employment opportunities were few. "Women students were often pigeonholed and thwarted in the curriculum and in campus life; and most, invidiously, those who completed advanced degrees encountered blatant discrimination in the academic job market" (Thelin, 2004, p. 143). Slow acquisition of degrees and positions continued until World War II (Cohen & Brawer, 2010).

Professional opportunities for women following World War II were more obtainable on a larger scale than in any previous era, and a move toward more diversified and inclusive curriculum ensued (Lucas, 2006). Women in the profession increased by 13% from 1945 to 1975 (Cohen & Kisker, 2010). That does not speak to the true struggle. Even today, despite the fact that women now receive the majority of conferred doctorates. Women account for only 23% of full professors (Mason, 2011). "Academic women…continue to be 20% less likely than men to perceive equitable treatment. Moreover, the percentage of women strongly agreeing that gender equity has been achieved is only half that of men" (Schuster & Finkelstein, 2006, p. 139). In spite of studies showing a higher level of intrinsic motivation in female faculty, thereby indicating a propensity for academic productivity that exceeds that of male counterparts (Chen & Zhao, 2013), financial recognition for female faculty remains lower.

Salary differential is far from equal, especially at the higher ranks of the professoriate (Fowler et al., 2004). Only one in four college presidents are women (Ward & Eddy, 2013). No one single factor can be pinpointed as the culprit for these present inequities, though several explanations have been offered. For instance, gender biases have been cited as reasons for the dearth of women in leadership positions (Bagilhole & White, 2008; Fulmer, 2010; Garn & Brown, 2008). By far, the most cited factor is time on the job, which predicates the possibility of time of service, amount of publications, and tenure prospects (Guillory, 2001). That discussion then leads to the implications of maternity leave.

Child rearing also impeded professional growth and development of the female faculty role, particularly in tenure where expectations of productivity are established. "It is noteworthy that women on the tenure-track are more likely than men to avoid marriage, delay parenting, or limit the number of children they raise" (Jackson, 2008, p. 227). Mason (2013) suggested that having children as a young professional negatively affected professional development because professors "get little or no childbirth support from the university and often receive a great deal of discouragement from their mentors." Gibbard Cook (2004) reiterated that children also hampered job possibilities due to a lesser amount of relative mobility when compared to nonparents. Available childcare for working moms in higher education is problematic as well (Jackson, 2008). Consider the simple biological window. If female faculty wish to have children, then it likely will occur during when it is physically feasible to conceive, either during their doctoral studies or during the first few years of postdoctoral work (Gibbard Cook, 2004). It then becomes a matter of choice: work and potentially struggle as a professional mother, or lose time and productivity in the workforce.

Additionally, any increase in women faculty members and doctoral recipients has not promoted an equally friendly work environment. Politics and sexist work environments have also impeded women gaining stronger footholds in leadership roles (Ward & Eddy, 2013). "Despite earning doctorates in ever-increasing numbers, many women…are eschewing academic careers altogether or exiting the academy prior to the tenure decision because both groups experience social isolation, a chilly environment, bias, and hostility" (Trower & Chait, 2002). Such working environments amplify job-related stress and workplace dissatisfaction (Lease, 1999).

Thus, research suggests that while opportunities are available, the environments in which women faculty's identity may be shaped are historically and contemporaneously inequitable, and this creates complicated and challenging spaces of influence. "[Female faculty] in the coeducational university faced marginalization at every turn. They were expected to be simultaneously a part and apart from the faculty culture" (Thelin, 2004, p. 144). Female faculty, in essence, was tiered into a caste system of rank in higher education setup for inequity, and interestingly, this leveled perception is similarly felt by faculty academic librarians in the third space of the professoriate.

3.6 Faculty identity and historical narrative critique

Similar to the analyses on roles, the professional identity of collegiate faculty has been explored in a variety of settings. For example, scholars have analyzed full-time faculty, both tenure-track (Abu-Alruz & Khasawneh, 2013; Lieff et al., 2012) and non-tenure-track (Levin & Shaker, 2011). Tenure-track faculty defines its identity through a combination of the department environment, communication with colleagues and mentors, and personal motivations and initiatives (Lieff et al., 2012). Nontenure-track faculty are something of a hybrid (Levin & Shaker, 2011). They require the same form of training and education as tenure-track (Schuster & Finkelstein, 2006), but occupy a position that is often lacking the benefits (actual and perceived) of tenure-track faculty, such as autonomy and job security (Kezar & Sam, 2013). Depending upon the institution, academic librarians may obtain either position, although the suggested perceptions around academic campuses tend to force librarians into a placement similar to nontenure track faculty.

Part-time or adjuncts' identity, both at community colleges and 4-year institutions, has also been considered in literature (Daffron, 2010; Dolan, 2011; Levin, Walker, Haberler, & Jackson-Boothby, 2013; Outcalt, 2002; Thirolf, 2013, 2012), though the research suggests that the experience is mixed. The mission of community colleges is inherently different, as they serve continuing, community, and teacher education in addition to traditional college-aged students, and therefore the roles of the faculty accordingly adjust (Vaughn, 2006). They also have a high ratio of adjunct instructors limiting the cohesiveness of departments and organizations within the actual college (Cohen & Brawer, 2008). However, the core role of the profession, instruction, does not change. "It is readily apparent that the distinctiveness of the clientele served by community college faculty exists in nominal form only" (Outcalt, 2002). In essence, the professors are still teaching college students, regardless of their own professional title and instructional platform. As was mentioned though, these conversations considered full-semester instruction as the standard, which librarians at St. Jerome do not perform.

Academic librarians carry similar traits to nontenure-track faculty and adjuncts, at least in their perception around campus. They fulfill many roles, but balance between the faculty role and function of academic librarians has been greatly discussed

(Bhuiya, 1981; Jablonski, 2006; Wyss, 2010, 2008). For example, Hosburgh (2011) noted that librarian roles affect tenure opportunities, salary, and research or presentation funding. Indeed, even the term "blended librarian" has found traction in literature (Bell & Shank, 2004; Shank & Bell, 2011); however, in that context, "blended" referred to the actual role and the relative skills connected with librarianship, not the perception, or professional identity, associated with the position in academe.

The identity of academic librarians only has been examined in passing. Bennett (1987) suggested that institutional structures promoted a secondary identity for librarians, but does not delve into the professional identity. Downing (2009) utilized social identity theory to examine the roles of librarians, finding that the roles were influenced by variables such as race, gender, and age. The key component of Downing's study was to assert that a diverse workplace benefits that collective library whole. What about the individual though? How does that personal identity influence concepts of professionalism? This question concerning the professional role and identity of the academic librarian is a major gap in both higher education and library science literature.

A major frame by which librarians have yet to be formally analyzed is blended professionalism, put forth by Whitchurch (2009). As noted earlier, blended professionals are individuals who operate internally and externally through a variety of academic and professional realms (Whitchurch, 2009), which is precisely what academic librarians do in the course of their daily work. To this point, the discussion has noted "binary perceptions" among the faculty and the librarians (Whitchurch, 2013). Each side marginalizes the role of the other, thereby creating strain. However, the expansion of the historical roles of both faculty and librarians calls into question this inherent bias, as "a diversifying workforce raises questions about what it means to be a professional in contemporary higher education" (Whitchurch, 2013, p. 8). All parties in higher education appear to be moving to a "third space" of interaction, one that transcends purely academic and professional roles (Whitchurch, 2009). The concept of third space is employed here "as a way of exploring groups of staff in higher education who do not fit conventional binary descriptors" (Whitchurch, 2013, p. 21). As is customary in higher education literature though, Whitchurch did not consider academic librarians in the blended professional role.

Based in part on Giddens (1992) self-identity theory and Rhoades (2007, 2005) managed professional identity theories, Whitchurch's system provides a model to develop professional identity through the criteria of *spaces, knowledges, relationships, and legitimacies*. *Spaces* are the physical, virtual and theoretical (through third space) spheres in which an individual operates, though the blended professional readily adapts to change and operates outside of formal organizational boundaries. *Knowledges* are assimilated professional and academic knowledge, which may be utilized to investigate organizational activity and link together multiple settings on campus. *Relationships* allow the blended professional to network, function in academic conversation, develop cross-unit alliances, and establish autonomy of one's own organization. Finally, *legitimacies* are the letters after an individual's name on their business card and the relative productivity of the academic and professional person; they allow and establish access into academic environments. The malleable nature of these active roles develops the perceived professional identity of the individual. By examining academic librarian usage of Whitchurch's criteria of spaces, knowledges, relationships, and legitimacies (outlined in Appendix A), the function of the librarian and the subsequent professional identity may be mapped.

The goal of this work will be a qualitative case study analysis of how the blended professional role and identity of faculty academic librarians shapes their development as professionals. How do these librarians see themselves as faculty? Does their experience hinder or promote their academic achievements, communication, or collaborative opportunities? Do they believe their abilities to develop are similar to other faculty? Do the librarians feel loyal to certain departments or individuals in their field? These universal questions speak to the function of identity in the professional and will address a gap in both the academic library and higher education literature both in the United States and abroad. It is significant in this way because it will provide a new structure through which academic librarians may analyze their role, standing, and potentially development in the academy. It can identify barriers for librarians (internal and external) for finding promotional opportunities and establishment of full faculty status.

3.7 Conclusion

This chapter established that the role of tenure-track faculty varied over time, but the present incarnation is one that emphasizes research, instruction, and service as the primary tenants of faculty output and behavior. Further, it detailed the evolution of the academic librarian from an isolated repository position to one that becomes increasingly complicated due to escalation in technology and professional expectations. Still, the comparison of the research, instruction, and service conducted by librarians does not equally balance with that of tenure-track faculty. If it may be accepted that activities of librarians in this manifestation are not equivalent, the study might be able to better establish the true academic and professional role and identities of this particular group.

The corollary to that notion is gender, as this chapter also inferred that women have experienced a history of inequality as both students and faculty in higher education. Since this study solely will consider the identity of female academic librarians, it suggests that any environment in which the librarians work will provide obstacles to professional development. Until now, professional role and identity of academic librarians has been largely ignored by higher education literature, providing a significant gap in the literature and provides the basis for this study. The following chapter will detail the methodology through which this work was conducted.

References

Abu-Alruz, J., & Khasawneh, S. (2013). Professional identity of faculty members at higher education institutions: a criterion for workplace success. *Research in Post-Compulsory Education, 18*(4), 431–442.

Adrian, W. (2003). Perils of the life of the mind: lessons from the German university. *Christian Higher Education, 2*(2), 155.

Aguilar, P., Keating, K., Schadl, S., & Van Reenen, J. (2011). Reference as outreach: meeting users where they are. *Journal of Library Administration, 51*(4), 343–358.

American Library Association (ALA). (2014a). *Directory of ALA-accredited master's programs in library and information studies.* Retrieved from http://www.ala.org/accreditedprograms/directory.

American Library Association (ALA). (2014b). *ALA's membership statistics by division, 2000-present.* Retrieved from http://www.ala.org/membership/membershipstats_files/divisionstats#acrl.

Arp, L., Woodard, B. S., & Warren, L. A. (2006). Information literacy in community colleges. *Reference & User Services Quarterly, 45*(4), 297–303.

Association of College and Research Libraries (ACRL). (2012). Guidelines for academic librarians without faculty status. *College & Research Libraries News, 73*(3), 161–162.

Bagilhole, B., & White, K. (2008). Towards a gendered skills analysis of senior management positions in UK and Australian universities. *Tertiary Education & Management, 14*(1), 1–12.

Baker, V. L., & Griffin, K. A. (2010). Beyond mentoring and advising: toward understanding the role of faculty "developers" in student success. *About Campus, 14*(6), 2–8.

Baruzzi, A., & Calcagno, T. (2015). Academic librarians and graduate students: An exploratory study. *Portal.*

Beach, A. (2014). *Higher education journals and publications.* Retrieved from http://homepages.wmich.edu/~abeach/HEjournals.htm.

Bell, S. J., & Shank, J. (2004). The blended librarian: a blueprint for redefining the teaching and learning role of academic librarians. *College & Research Libraries News, 65,* 372–375.

Bennett, G. E. (1987). *Conventions of subordination: An interpretive analysis of the professional identity of academic librarians* (doctoral dissertation). Retrieved from proquest dissertations and theses.

Bennett, M. (2011). The benefits of non-library professional organization membership for liaison librarians. *Journal of Academic Librarianship, 37*(1), 46–53.

Bennett, E., & Simning, J. (2010). Embedded librarians and reference traffic: a quantitative analysis. *Journal of Library Administration, 50*(5/6), 443–457.

Bhuiya, M. A. (1981). *The faculty image of academic librarians in colleges and universities of Pennsylvania: A measure of attitude* (doctoral dissertation). Retrieved from proquest dissertations and theses.

Bledstein, B. J. (1976). *The culture of professionalism: The middle class and the development of higher education in America.* New York: Norton & Co., Inc.

Bowen, R. W. (2005). Gender inequity. *Academe, 91*(2), 128.

Bowen, H., & Schuster, J. (1986). *American professors: A national resource imperiled.* New York: Oxford University Press.

Boyer, E. L. (1990). *Scholarship reconsidered: Priorities of the professoriate.* San Francisco: Jossey-Bass, Inc.

Bracke, M., Herubel, J. M., & Ward, S. M. (2010). Some thoughts on opportunities for collection development librarians. *Collection Management, 35*(3/4), 255–259.

Campanario, J. M. (2010). Empirical study of journal impact factors obtained using the classical two-year citation window versus a five-year citation window. *Scientometrics, 87,* 189–204.

Cardina, C., & Wicks, D. (2004). The changing roles of academic reference librarians over a ten-year period. *Reference & User Services Quarterly, 44*(2), 133–142.

Charnigo, L. (2009). Lights! Camera! Action! Producing library instruction video tutorials using Camtasia Studio. *Journal of Library & Information Services in Distance Learning*, *3*(1), 23–30.

Chen, Y., & Zhao, Q. (2013). Gender differences in business faculty's research motivation. *Journal of Education for Business*, *88*(6), 314–324.

Chisholm-Burns, M. A., Spivey, C. A., Billheimer, D., Schlesselman, L. S., Flowers, S. K., Hammer, D., & Vaillancourt, A. M. (2012). Multi-institutional study of women and underrepresented minority faculty members in academic pharmacy. *American Journal of Pharmaceutical Education*, *76*(1), 1–13.

Clark, S., & Chinburg, S. (2010). Research performance in undergraduates receiving face to face versus online library instruction: a citation analysis. *Journal of Library Administration*, *50*(5/6), 530–542.

Cohen, A. M., & Brawer, F. B. (2008). *The American community college* (5th ed.). San Francisco: Jossey-Bass.

Cohen, A. M., & Kisker, C. B. (2010). *The shaping of American higher education: Emergence and growth of the contemporary system* (2nd ed.). San Francisco: Jossey-Bass, Inc.

Coker, C., van Duinkerken, W., & Bales, S. (2010). Seeking full citizenship: A defense of tenure faculty status for librarians. *College & Research Libraries*, *71*(5), 406–420.

Cooke, R., & Rosenthal, D. (2011). Students use more books after library instruction: an analysis of undergraduate paper citations. *College & Research Libraries*, *72*(4), 332–343.

Daffron, E. (2010). The university chameleon: identity and time issues faced by faculty in dual positions. *Academic Leadership (15337812)*, *8*(4), 14.

de la Pena McCook, K. (2000). Reconnecting library education and the mission of community. *Library Journal*, *125*(14), 164.

DeVinney, G. S. (1986). Academic librarians and academic freedom in the United States: a history and analysis. *Libri*, *36*, 24–39.

Dolan, V. (2011). The isolation of online adjunct faculty and its impact on their performance. *International Review of Research in Open and Distance Learning*, *12*(2), 62–77.

Downing, K. E. (2009). *The relationship between social identity and role performance among academic librarians* (doctoral dissertation). Retrieved from proquest dissertations and theses.

Duemer, L. S. (2007). The agricultural education origins of the Morrill Land Grant Act of 1862. *American Educational History Journal*, *34*(1), 135–146.

Dunn, S. (2013). Do librarians need tenure? Depends on which ones you ask. *The Chronicle of Higher Education*. Retrieved from https://chroniclevitae.com/news/139-do-librarians-need-tenure-depends-on-which-ones-you-ask.

Farnham, C. A. (1994). *Education of the southern belle: Higher education and student socialization in the antebellum south*. New York: NYU Press.

Finkelstein, M. J. (1984). *The American academic profession: A synthesis of social scientific inquiry since world war II*. Columbus, OH: Ohio State University Press.

Fowler, N., Arens, K., Gilbert, L. A., Payne, S. M., Reichl, L. E., & Staiger, J. (2004). Graphic stories: representing the status of female faculty. *Feminist Studies*, *30*(3), 689–701.

Freiburger, G., & Kramer, S. (2009). Embedded librarians: one library's model for decentralized service. *Journal of the Medical Library Association*, *97*(2), 139–142.

Fruman, N. (2009). The AAUP: a moral autopsy. *Academic Questions*, *22*(3), 340–350.

Fulmer, C. L. (2010). Unpacking evidence of gender bias. *Journal of Women in Educational Leadership*, *8*(2), 81–97.

Fyn, A. F. (2013). Peer group mentoring relationships and the role of narrative. *Journal of Academic Librarianship*, *39*(4), 330–334.

Gaff, J. G., & Simpson, R. D. (1994). Faculty development in the United States. *Innovative Higher Education, 18*(3), 167.
Gappa, J. M., Austin, A. E., & Trice, A. G. (2007). *Rethinking faculty work: Higher education's strategic imperative*. San Francisco: Jossey Bass, Inc.
Garn, G., & Brown, C. (2008). Women and the superintendency: perceptions of gender bias. *Journal of Women in Educational Leadership, 6*(1), 49–71.
Gibbard Cook, S. (2004). Mothers in the faculty pipeline. *Women in Higher Education, 13*(8).
Giddens, A. (1992). *Modernity and self-identity: Self and society in the late modern age*. Stanford: Stanford University Press.
Given, L. M., & Julien, H. (2005). Finding common ground: an analysis of librarians' expressed attitudes towards faculty. *Reference Librarian, 43*(89/90), 25–38.
Graham, J.-B. (2004). What's in a name? *Alabama Librarian, 54*(1), 10–14.
Greer, R. C., Grover, R. J., & Fowler, S. G. (2007). *Introduction to the library and information professions*. London: Libraries Unlimited.
Guillory, E. A. (2001). The black professoriate: explaining the salary gap for African-American female professors. *Race, Ethnicity & Education, 4*(3), 225–244.
Haensly, P. J., Hodges, P. E., & Davenport, S. A. (2009). Acceptance rates and journal quality: an analysis of journals in economics and finance. *Journal of Business & Finance Librarianship, 14*(1), 2–31.
Hall, R. A. (2013). Beyond the job ad: Employers and library instruction. *College & Research Libraries, 74*(1), 24–38.
Hansen, D. (2004). Professionalizing library education, the California connection: James Gillis, Everett Perry, and Joseph Daniels. *Library Trends, 52*(4), 963–987.
Hanson, E. R. (1989). College libraries: the colonial period to the twentieth century. *Advances in Library Administration and Organization, 8*, 171–199.
Hansson, J., & Johannesson, K. (2013). Librarians' views of academic library support for scholarly publishing: an every-day perspective. *Journal of Academic Librarianship, 39*(3), 232–240.
Hanz, K., & Lange, J. (2013). Using student questions to direct information literacy workshops. *Reference Services Review, 41*(3), 532–546.
Harvard Crimson. (1968). *Man and woman at Yale*. Retrieved from http://www.thecrimson.com/article/1968/11/18/man-and-woman-at-yale-pa/.
Hawes, S. (2011). Playing to win: embedded librarians in online classrooms. *Journal of Library & Information Services in Distance Learning, 5*(1/2), 56–66.
Hemmig, W., & Montet, M. (2010). The "just for me" virtual library: enhancing an embedded eBrarian Program. *Journal of Library Administration, 50*(5/6), 657–669.
Hines, S. (2008). How it's done: examining distance education library instruction and assessment. *Journal of Library Administration, 48*(3/4), 467–478.
Hosburgh, N. (2011). Librarian faculty status: what does it mean in academia? *Library Philosophy & Practice*, 31–37.
Houser, C., Lemmons, K., & Cahill, A. (2013). Role of the faculty mentor in an undergraduate research experience. *Journal of Geoscience Education, 61*(3), 297–305.
Jablonski, J. A. (2006). *Conceptualizing the field of library and information studies: The perspective of LIS faculty and LIS practitioners in the United States* (doctoral dissertation). Retrieved from proquest dissertations and theses.
Jacklin, M., & Robinson, K. (2013). Evolution of various library instruction strategies: using student feedback to create and enhance online active learning assignments. *Partnership: The Canadian Journal of Library & Information Practice & Research, 8*(1), 1–21.
Jackson, L. D. (2008). Reflections on obstacles and opportunities: suggestions for improving the retention of female faculty. *Women's Studies in Communication, 31*(2), 226–232.

Johnson, W. G. (2004). Information literacy standards and library instruction. *Community & Junior College Libraries, 13*(1), 25–32.
Johnson, J. M. (2008). *Southern women at the Seven Sister colleges: Feminist values and social activism, 1875–1915*. Athens: University of Georgia Press.
Julien, H., & Given, L. M. (2002). Faculty-librarian relationships in the information literacy context: a content analysis of librarians' expressed attitudes and experiences. *Canadian Journal of Information & Library Sciences, 27*(3), 65–87.
Karabel, J. (2005). *The chosen: The hidden history of admission and exclusion at Harvard, Yale and Princeton*. Boston: Houghton Mifflin.
Kelleher, M., & Laidlaw, S. (2009). A natural fit: the academic librarian advising in the first year experience. *College & Undergraduate Libraries, 16*(2/3), 153–163.
Kennedy, R., & Monty, V. (2011). Faculty-librarian collaboration and the development of critical skills through dynamic purposeful learning. *Libri, 61*(2), 116–124.
Kezar, A., & Sam, C. (2013). Institutionalizing equitable policies and practices for contingent faculty. *Journal of Higher Education, 84*(1), 56–87.
LaGuardia, C. (2011). Library instruction in the digital age. *Journal of Library Administration, 51*(3), 301–308.
Lamothe, A. R. (2012). The importance of encouraging librarians to publish in peer-reviewed publications. *Journal of Scholarly Publishing, 43*(2), 156–167.
Lanier, P. A., Tanner, J. R., & Guidry, B. N. (2009). A comparison of gender and gender-related issues in the business disciplines. *Public Personnel Management, 38*(3), 51–70.
Lawson, E., & Merrill, M. (1984). *The three Sarahs: Documents of antebellum black college women*. Lewiston, NY: Edwin Mellen Press.
Lease, S. H. (1999). Occupational role stressors, coping, support, and hardiness as predictors of strain in academic faculty: an emphasis on the new and female faculty. *Research in Higher Education, 40*(3), 285–307.
Lechuga, V. (2011). Faculty-graduate student mentoring relationships: mentors' perceived roles and responsibilities. *Higher Education, 62*(6), 757–771.
Levin, J. S., & Shaker, G. G. (2011). The hybrid and dualistic identity of full-time non-tenure-track faculty. *American Behavioral Scientist, 55*(11), 1461–1484.
Levin, J. S., Walker, L., Haberler, Z., & Jackson-Boothby, A. (2013). The divided self: the double consciousness of faculty of color in community colleges. *Community College Review, 41*(4), 311–329.
Lieberthal, S. P. (2009). Teaching undergraduate business students to access public company information: assessing students' use of library resources. *Journal of Business & Finance Librarianship, 14*(3), 230–247.
Lieff, S., Baker, L., Mori, B., Egan-Lee, E., Chin, K., & Reeves, S. (2012). Who am I? Key influences on the formation of academic identity within a faculty development program. *Medical Teacher, 34*(3), e208–e215.
Lucas, C. (2006). *American higher education: A history* (2nd ed.). New York: Palgrave, Macmillan.
Lucas, C. (1994). *American higher educaiton: A history* (1st ed.). New York: Palgrave, Macmillan.
Lynch, B. P., Murray-Rust, C., Parker, S. E., Turner, D., Walker, D. P., Wilkinson, F. C., & Zimmerman, J. (2007). Attitudes of presidents and provosts on the university library. *College & Research Libraries, 68*(3), 213–227.
Maack, M. N. (1986). Toward a new model of the information professions: embracing empowerment. *Journal of Education for Library and Information Science, 38*, 283–302.

Mannino, D. M. (2005). Impact factor, impact, and smoke and mirrors. *American Journal of Respiratory and Critical Care Medicine*, *171*(4), 117–118.

Marcus, J. (2000). American academic tenures in decline. *Times Higher Education* (Suppl. 1429), 64.

Margino, M. (2013). Revitalizing traditional information literacy instruction: exploring games in academic libraries. *Public Services Quarterly*, *9*(4), 333–341.

Mason, M. A. (2013). The baby penalty. *The Chronicle of Higher Education*. Retrieved from http://chronicle.com/article/The-Baby-Penalty/140813/.

Mason, M. A. (2011). The pyramid problem. *The Chronicle of Higher Education*. Retrieved from http://chronicle.com/article/The-Pyramid-Problem/126614/.

Mettler, S. (2007). *Soldiers to citizens: The GI Bill and the making of the greatest generation*. Oxford: Oxford University Press.

Meyer, E., Forbes, C., & Bowers, J. (2010). The research center: creating an environment for interactive research consultations. *Reference Services Review*, *38*(1), 57–70.

Mullins, J. L. (2012). Are MLS graduates being prepared for the changing and emerging roles that librarians must now assume within research libraries? *Journal of Library Administration*, *52*(1), 124–132.

Nelson, C. (September 2008). Across the great divide. *Academe*, 11–15.

Nixon, J. M. (2013). Core journals and information science: developing a methodology for ranking LIS journals. *College & Research Libraries*. Retrieved from http://crl.acrl.org/content/early/2012/07/23/crl12-387.short?rss=1.

Nunn, B., & Ruane, E. (2011). Marketing gets personal: promoting reference staff to reach users. *Journal of Library Administration*, *51*(3), 291–300.

O'Malley, D., & Delwiche, F. (2012). Aligning library instruction with the needs of basic sciences graduate students: a case study. *Journal of the Medical Library Association*, *100*(4), 284–290.

O'Meara, K., Terosky, A. L., & Neumann, A. (2008). *Faculty careers and work lives: A professional growth perspective*. San Francisco: Jossey Bass, Inc.

O'Reilly, M. (2013). Melvil's girls: still struggling to survive. *Feliciter*, *59*(2), 35–38.

Outcalt, C. L. (2002). Toward a professionalized community college professoriate. *New Directions for Community Colleges*, *2002*(118), 109.

O'Meara, K., Terosky, A. L., & Neumann, A. (2008). *Faculty careers and work lives: A professional growth perspective*. San Francisco: Jossey Bass, Inc.

Perry, S. D., & Michalski, L. (2010). Common acceptance rate calculation methods in communication journals: developing best practices. *Journalism & Mass Communication Educator*, *65*(2), 168–186.

Press, N., & Diggs-Hobson, M. (2005). Providing health information to community, members where they are: characteristics of the culturally competent librarian. *Library Trends*, *53*(3), 397–410.

Pusser, B. (2006). Higher education, markets, and the preservation of the public good. In D. W. Breneman, B. Pusser, & S. E. Turner (Eds.), *Earnings from learning: The rise of for-profit universities*. Albany, NY: State University of New York Press.

Rhoades, G. (2005). Capitalism, academic style, and shared governance. *Academe*, *91*(3), 38–42.

Rhoades, G. (2007). The study of the academic profession. In P. J. Gumport (Ed.), *Sociology of higher education: Contributions and their contexts* (pp. 113–146). Baltimore: The Johns Hopkins University Press.

Robbins-Carter, J., & Seavey, C. A. (1986). The master's degree: basic preparation for professional practice. *Library Trends*, *34*, 561–580.

Rogers, E. (2013). Teaching government information in information literacy credit classes. *Georgia Library Quarterly*, *50*(1), 13–22.

Rosenberg, R. (2004). *Changing the subject: How the women of Columbia shaped the way we think about sex and politics*. New York: Columbia University Press.

Rubin, R. E. (2004). *Foundations of library and information science* (2nd ed.). New York: Neal-Schuman Publishers, Inc.

Schrimsher, R. H., & Northrup, L. A. (2013). Helpful hints for every librarian's nightmare: publishing an article. *College & Undergraduate Libraries*, *20*(1), 87–94.

Schuster, J. H., & Finkelstein, M. J. (2006). *The American faculty: Restructuring of academic work and careers*. Baltimore: The Johns Hopkins University Press.

Shaffer, B. A. (2011). Graduate student library research skills: Is online instruction effective? *Journal of Library & Information Services in Distance Learning*, *5*(1/2), 35–55.

Shank, J. D., & Bell, S. (2011). Blended librarianship: [re]envisioning the role of librarian as, educator in the digital information age. *Reference & User Services Quarterly*, *51*(2), 105–110.

Shiao-Feng, S., & Kuo, J. (2010). Design and development of web-based information literacy tutorials. *Journal of Academic Librarianship*, *36*(4), 320–328.

Shupe, E. I., & Pung, S. K. (2011). Understanding the changing role of academic, librarians from a psychological perspective: a literature review. *Journal of Academic Librarianship*, *37*(5), 409–415.

Simpson, B. (2013). Hiring non-MLS librarians: trends and training implications. *Library Leadership & Management*, *28*(1), 1–15.

Sorey, K., & Gregory, D. (2010). Protests in the sixties. *College Student Affairs Journal*, *28*(2), 184–206.

Sproles, C., Johnson, A., & Farison, L. (2008). What the teachers are teaching: How MLIS programs are preparing academic librarians for instructional roles. *Journal of Education for Library & Information Science*, *49*(3), 195–209.

Stiwinter, K. (2013). Using an interactive online tutorial to expand library instruction. *Internet Reference Services Quarterly*, *18*(1), 15–41.

Thelin, J. R. (2004). *A history of American higher education* (2nd ed.). Baltimore: The Johns Hopkins University Press.

Thirolf, K. Q. (2012). The faculty identities of community college adjuncts teaching in the humanities: a discourse analysis study. *Community College Journal of Research & Practice*, *36*(4), 269–278.

Thirolf, K. Q. (2013). How faculty identity discourses of community college part-time faculty change over time. *Community College Journal of Research & Practice*, *37*(3), 177–184.

Trower, C. A., & Chait, R. P. (2002). Faculty diversity: too little for too long. *Harvard Magazine*, *104*(4), 33–37.

Tucci, V. K. (2011). Faculty/Librarian collaboration: catalyst for student learning and librarian growth. *Science & Technology Libraries*, *30*(3), 292–305.

Tumbleson, B. E., & Burke, J. J. (2010). When life hands you lemons: overcoming obstacles to expand services in an embedded librarian program. *Journal of Library Administration*, *50*(7/8), 972–988.

Turner, S. (2006). For-profit colleges in the context of the market for higher education. In D. W. Breneman, B. Pusser, & S. E. Turner (Eds.), *Earnings from learning: The rise of for-profit universities*. Albany, NY: State University of New York Press.

Vaughn, G. B. (2006). *The community college story* (3rd ed.). Washington, DC: American Association of Community Colleges.

Ward, K., & Eddy, P. L. (2013). Women and academic leadership: leaning out. *The Chronicle of Higher Education*. Retrieved from https://chronicle.com/article/WomenAcademic-Leadership-/143503/.

Washington College. (2013). *Art and art history*. Retrieved from http://www.washcoll.edu/catalog/art-and-art-history.php.

Watson, S. E., Rex, C., Markgraf, J., Kishel, H., Jennings, E., & Hinnant, K. (2013). Revising the "one-shot" through lesson study: collaborating with writing faculty to rebuild a library instruction session. *College & Research Libraries*, *74*(4), 381–398.

Whitchurch, C. (2009). The rise of the blended professional in higher education: a comparison between the United Kingdom, Australia and the United States. *Higher Education*, *58*(3), 407–418.

Whitchurch, C. (2013). *Reconstructing identities in higher education: The rise of third space professionals*. New York: Routledge.

Wolfe, J. A., Naylor, T., & Drueke, J. (2010). The role of the academic reference librarian in the learning commons. *Reference & User Services Quarterly*, *50*(2), 108–113.

Wyss, P. (2008). Library faculty member perceptions regarding faculty status for academic libraries (doctoral dissertation). Retrieved from proquest dissertations and theses.

Wyss, P. (2010). Library school faculty member perceptions regarding faculty status for academic librarians. *College & Research Libraries*, *71*(4), 375–388.

Methodology

4

During the conceptual phase of this project, several replicable methodological avenues were considered. The central construction of the research—the blended professional identity of female academic librarians—is perceived by the individual experiencing the role. Since these identities are individualized, it was believed that qualitative interviews would produce the most profound, direct feedback on the blended professional identities of the academic librarians and illuminate the working third spaces as well as the obstacles to professional development. Therefore, a qualitative case study was chosen.

Since this project is the study of a single case at an institution in the United States, some readers will question the study's universality. Given the complexity of higher education institutions (private, public, not-for-profit, for-profit, etc.) and the libraries therein, it would be difficult to provide an applicable study that would cover all institutions even within the United States, much less on the international level. For instance, if this book covered a review of librarians at the surveyed university's institutionally defined "peer" schools (that are all schools in the United States) in order to provide a larger sample, then there still would be an opportunity for a librarian from, say, Australia to mention that it is not a collective survey. Therefore, providing access to the method and the appropriate recommendations for the implementation of the study seems like the most suitable route.

As well, the hope is to offer a higher education-oriented model that would gain purchase with nonlibrarian faculty better than a simple comparison of duties. Most library-based analyses, including those mentioned in the previous chapter, create an argument from the standpoint of the libraries. In the higher education sector, this is less effective due to the relative role and placement of libraries and librarians in the hierarchy of the institution. While application of this study might not reveal a pleasant standing for the librarian's role and identity, it will provide the opportunity to address inhibitors to professional success in the respective institutions.

In practice, methodology sections tend to be somewhat sterile and drab. It is a necessity here though. The base goal of this book is to provide a replicable model that librarians and library administrators might reproduce in their own libraries and institutions. This could be done on the department level or the institution level. It is up to the reader to determine that greatest value. The following chapter will outline the methodology utilized in this study along with the procedures implemented.

4.1 Into the weeds

For these research questions, qualitative research presents a viable methodology. Mauch and Park (2003, p. 125) define "qualitative research as describing a situation as it exists, without involving formal hypothesis, but focusing on explaining social processes in great detail." The research concerning the identity of the librarians is subjective and based upon experiences of individual librarians within an academic community. A qualitatively collected sample would offer direct connection with the experiences of the academic librarians, as responses would be tied to experience and emotion.

This is of consequence, since "securing accurate information about feelings, sensitive behaviors, and other personal experiences is critical in many areas of research" (Mauch & Park, 2003, p. 18). The interviewee's personal experiences will educe relevant information that may be applied to the theoretical and actual role and identity of the academic librarian. It is possible to write a generic report regarding the roles of academic librarians without formal interviews; however, the direct experiences—to include the successes, the challenges, the frustrations, the emotions, and so on—produce personal recollections and anecdotes that create a fuller understanding of the person and the environment of study.

By interviewing the librarians, the hope is to gain a better understanding of the effect that the role has on the blended professional identity and development of the academic librarian. In addition, one of the prime benefits for faculty members to participate in a study such as this is that it allows the practitioner to self-reflect on their roles, challenges, and opportunities that exist in the navigation of their instructional responsibilities. This type of analysis has been demonstrated to have positive pedagogical effects on the participating members because of its ability to positively identify obstacles (Dausien, Hanses, Inowlocki, & Riemann, 2008; Zha, Adams, & Mathews-Ailsworth, 2013).

4.1.1 Method

The context of this study is developed with a historical role in mind, but the results are based upon contemporary experiences. Therefore, a case study method of analysis becomes the best option. "The case study relies on many of the same techniques as a history, but it adds two sources of evidence not usually included in the historian's repertoire: direct observation of the events being studied and interviews of the persons involved in the events" (Yin, 2009, p. 11). Historical works often analyze people, events, and environments where the seminal contributors to any theory are no longer available, rendering the evidence finite to a degree. This contrasts case studies examining contemporary situations where opinions are documented and witnessed by the researcher. As well, the case study "method is heuristic- a term for self-guided learning that employs analysis to help draw conclusions about a situation" (Ellet, 2007, p. 19). Unlike purely historical studies, where the availability of the studied individuals may not be accessible due to the distance of historical time, a case study offers the ability to study and interact with the individuals in a contemporary context.

Case studies become viable methods when the researcher has no influence on the individuals studied. "The case study is preferred in examining contemporary events, but when the relevant behaviors cannot be manipulated" (Yin, 2009, p. 11). The experiences of the academic librarians are developed through their relative experiences. This is relevant in this instance, as I, as the researcher, had no control over the events that lead to their beliefs, as I had no influence on the librarians' role requirements involving research, instruction, and service. I also was not in the position of librarian supervision and had no ability to develop policy or procedure that might sway the librarians' behavior.

4.1.2 Identification and recruitment of participants

Yin (2009, p. 93) affirms that "convenience, access, and geographic proximity can be the main criteria for selecting a pilot case or cases." In this particular case, the participants were identified due to my proximity to the sample organization, and geographically, it allowed for minimal travel for the qualitative process. As well, since I was not a librarian, I was not a member of any regional, national, or international professional library organizations. My professional affiliations were and are in the higher education sector, and there is not a great deal of organizational overlap with library associations. As a result, the vast majority of library contacts and associates for me were located at the sample institution, St. Jerome University (St. Jerome).

St. Jerome, the pseudonym of a real institution, is a mid-Atlantic state university with approximately 34,000 students spread across 200 degree programs located on three main campuses: St. Gabriel, St. Michael, and St. Raphael. St. Gabriel Campus is in an urban setting, St. Michael Campus is in the suburbs, and St. Raphael Campus is rural. About 6100 students live on campus, primarily at the St. Michael Campus. There are about 6400 faculty and staff working at St. Jerome. Of a total of about 130 full-time employees that include classified staff, between 40 and 45 jobs in the libraries at St. Jerome are academic librarian positions, though duties vary.

Just as with the faculty itself, librarians are stratified by their role and responsibilities. St. Jerome has several types of librarians on staff in departments such as technical services, cataloging, and circulation services. However, these librarians perform more administrative tasks and rarely engage in instruction of students and faculty. Also, there are classified staff that perform many of the same duties as librarians such as instruction, but do not have master's degrees in library science. As a result, the librarians surveyed in this sample were *liaison librarians* employed at St. Jerome.

As opposed to the traditional model of librarians that field either random or subject-specific inquiries at a physical desk in the library, liaison librarians are attached to a specific academic department or sector of the community, such as undergraduates in entry-level required English courses (Crawford, 2012). Crawford (2012, p. 3) defines liaison librarians as the "old subject librarian PLUS" who operates "beyond the traditional realms...to explore new possibilities." Therefore, the role of the liaison librarian fits the concept of blended professional in definition and function; as individuals who operate internally and externally through a variety of academic and professional realms, they work within the library and liaise with their academic department and its constituents in various communities around the campus. In addition, at St. Jerome, these librarians have renewable contracts and perform versions of the faculty role through instruction, research, and service.

At St. Jerome, the status of the librarians is based upon "professional competence, scholarship, service, and experience [as academic librarians]" (St. Jerome University Librarians' Handbook, 2012, p. 20). Four levels of librarian exist: I, II, III, and IV.

Table 4.1 The libraries and their corresponding campus

Library	Campus
Alexander VI Library	St. Michael Campus
Stephen VI Library	St. Michael Campus
Urban II Library	St. Gabriel Campus
Clement V Library	St. Raphael Campus

The length of appointment is determined by the rank; Librarian I is for 2 years, Librarian II is for 3 years, Librarian III is for 4 years, and Librarian IV is for 4 years. Similar to an academic department, there are a higher number of the lower-ranked positions available.

The librarians surveyed came from two sectors of the library: Research Services and Gateway Services. The main difference between these two departments is that the latter specifically markets to the undergraduate population, whereas the former interacts with all levels of patronage. Both departments report to the same Associate University Librarian. St. Jerome also has four distinct libraries spread across three different campuses. Table 4.1 indicates the library name and the campus location.

Each of these libraries has the position of "head" or "director." Gateway Services is located in the main undergraduate library at St. Jerome, Stephen VI Library, although the head of that department reports directly to the Associate University Librarian as opposed to the head of the Stephen VI Library.

This sample made a practical case study due to the demographics of the potential interviewees. Comparing the relative professional identities between male and female librarians in this case study makes little sense, as all but three of the librarians and the department heads were female. Therefore, the survey specifically examined the professional identity of the female librarians. In addition, the consideration of race did not appear a feasible topic of inquiry, as only one of the female librarians was of minority status.

At the time of research, there were 21 female academic librarians in these libraries; 17 of these librarians agreed to participate in this study. The librarians were recruited via an email, which was sent out July 7, 2014. A copy of this email is attached as Appendix B. Accordingly for the 17 librarians who responded to the mail, interview times and dates were arranged according to the librarians' schedules. I interviewed each librarian alone. The 17 interviews took place between July 7, 2014 and August 12, 2014.

The questions were designed around the juxtaposition of role and identity. As well, they used the framework of the concept of the blended professional put forth by Whitchurch, as such a model provides a researcher "ways of identifying and understanding important aspects of a situation and what they mean in relation to the overall situation" (Ellet, 2007, p. 19). The questions fielded by the librarians are found in Appendix C.

The interviews with librarians based on the St. Michael Campus, as well as one librarian working on the St. Raphael Campus, occurred in the Alexander VI Library conference rooms. The interviews with the librarians at the St. Gabriel Campus occurred in the Urban II Library conference room. The interview with the librarians at the St. Raphael Campus occurred in that librarian's office. All interviews were recorded with an Olympus VN-702PC Digital Voice Recorder. The 17 interviews totaled 788 min.

Following the interviews, I transferred the digital recordings to a 4 GB thumb drive. I then transcribed the interviews and double-checked them for veracity between July 8, 2014 and August 19, 2014. Following the completion of the transcriptions, the interviews were printed out and stored in a legal document folder in a locked desk in my office.

The Institutional Review Board approved consent forms were signed by the librarians prior to the start of each interview. These consent forms were stored in a separate folder within the same legal document binder. In order to mask the identity of the individuals who participated, the interviewed librarians were given pseudonyms during the transcription process. The names that appear in the text of this book are not the real names of the interviewed academic librarians.

In order to enhance the validity of the results, the responses from the qualitative interviews were triangulated. "Triangulation may be defined as the use of two or more methods of data collection in the study of some aspect of human behavior. Triangular techniques in the social sciences attempt to map out, or explain more fully, the richness and complexity of human behavior by studying it from more than one standpoint" (Cohen, Manion, & Morrison, 2007, p. 141). Similar to the construction of the questions, the triangulation techniques were designed with role and identity in mind.

To inspect blended professional roles concerning spaces and relationships, schedules were examined. These documents and observations gave me information on where the primary working spaces of the librarians were and with whom and how the total working time of librarians was being spent. I chose to examine the schedules of the interviewed librarians from Sunday, September 21, 2014 through Saturday, September 27, 2014. Depending on the discipline, librarians have varying responsibilities at different points in the semester. As a result, this week in September was chosen at random without catering to one discipline or another. In order to obtain the schedules, I contacted the respective librarians and mapped out their schedules on a standard calendar ledger. I then added the total time spent in various activities and tabulated the results.

Similarly, I studied librarian-developed Infoguides and Research Portals in order to establish activities regarding knowledges. The 17 interviewed librarians collectively created and continuously update 193 Infoguides and 21 Research Portals. While Infoguides and Research Portals are effectively the same thing—information on the resources available to library patrons—Infoguides are geared toward more generic undergraduate learning, whereas Research Portals are oriented toward graduate students with discipline- or program-specific problems and provide more in-depth tools for the viewing researcher. These documents are publically available via the internet on the St. Jerome University library website and required no contact with the librarians. The online materials detailed the librarians' subject knowledge expertise. Additionally, I arranged to observe instruction of eight librarians between July 9, 2014 and September 19, 2014. These classes took between 60 and 150 min in length.

For legitimacies, I examined physical artifacts such as business cards and office spaces to note presence of established credentials and experience. Items of interest included diplomas, award certificates, training certificates, mementos from academic conferences, and other miscellaneous objects that denoted professional experience and achievement. The inspection of the 17 librarians' offices and working spaces took place immediately following the interviews and generally lasted 15 minutes or less.

Field notes were compiled in a 5″×9″ spiral bound notepad. Upon return to my office, the notes were transferred to a confidential master spreadsheet stored on the same USB thumb drive as the transcriptions. A chart outlining the methods of inquiry is found in Appendix A.

4.1.3 Data analysis

One of the difficulties in constructing a qualitative research project is that there is "no precise or agreed-on terms describe varieties and processes of qualitative analysis" (Patton, 2002, p. 452). Many recommendations in literature vary in steps and terminology. As well, the process is subjective. "Qualitative research is 'interpretive' research in which you make a personal assessment as to a description that fits the situation or themes…the interpretation that you make of a transcript differs from the interpretation that someone else makes" (Creswell, 2005, p. 232). My understanding of the collected data may differ from the next researcher who either reads this report or conducts their own field work using a similar model.

In general though, this study followed Creswell's (2005, p. 231) "bottom-up" approach:

1. Collect data
2. Prepare data (transcription, etc.)
3. Read through data
4. Code data
5. Code text for themes
6. Interpret data

The interviews, transcriptions, and verification of the accuracy of the transcriptions, steps 1 and 2, were completed by August 19, 2014. The actual qualitative data analysis was developed with inductive analysis. "Inductive analysis involves discovering patterns, themes, and categories in one's data. Findings emerge out of the data, through the analyst's interactions with the data" (Patton, 2002, p. 453). Specifically, this study employed inductive content analysis to code the data and develop categories and themes. The intent of this method was to cultivate core concepts that emanated through the existing data (Glaser, 1992).

So that I might accomplish this task, I read the entirety of the interviews upon completion of the transcription process (step 3). I then did not look at the transcripts for 7 days and occupied myself with exercise, hobbies, and vacation in order to garner a fresh look during subsequent readings. Following the week respite, I began step 4 and numbered the survey questions and then noted in each text where that particular question was asked, which was the beginning of the open coding scheme (step 4).

"Open coding is the commencement of...working the raw data, through constant comparison, initial conceptual identification, and categorization" (Price, 2010, p. 157). Open coding, while a rigorous and exhaustive process, allowed me to identify relevant patterns and themes related to the framework of blended professionalism. I then underlined key sentences and phrases under each numbered question in the transcript text, thereby segmenting information (Creswell, 2005).

This process follows Patton's (2002, p. 454) recommendation suggesting that "a good place to begin inductive analysis is to inventory and define key phrases, terms, and practices that are special to the people in the setting studied." Following the completion of the underlining and note-taking process, I copied all underlined and noted phrases into a file with their corresponding numbered survey question. This process was replicated for all 14 of the formal survey questions asked of the interviewees. The reason for utilizing this method was to create a means of comparing the results with the existing literature on blended professionalism and the academic librarians' role in a more structured manner. By configuring the analysis in this way, I was better able to analyze and conceptualize simultaneously both individual segments and the totality of the emerging information within the data.

From there, the underlined sentences and phrases were distilled in order to create short, collective bullets. Finally, I bolded the significant words into "a manageable...coding scheme" within the bullets (Patton, 2002, p. 454). After developing the codes, I considered themes that emerged from this process. Themes were created (step 5) with the use of handwritten mind maps comprised of the codes (Creswell, 2005). A mind map is a model illustration used to visually consolidate and shape substantial information (Munim & Mahmud, 2011). Mind maps have been shown to enhance understanding of data by allowing a researcher to view problems on a multidimensional plane, which allows for more complete understanding of the information (Munim & Mahmud, 2011). The emergent themes from the mind maps became the core and structure of the interpretation of the findings (step 6) found in this chapter.

4.1.4 The researcher's role and limitations

Ideally, a researcher will approach the process from a purely objective position in order to develop rational and valid results (Greenbank, 2003). Rarely, though, is this perfect model obtainable, and in some ways it was not achieved in this model. Biases and suppositions, resulting in potential limitations in this study, exist due to my familiarity with the survey sample. Reflection and disclosure of these established perspectives, though, support the development of the validity regarding the total study (Greenbank, 2003). As such, in this case study, my role is that of an insider given that I had worked at the same institution as the interviewed librarians; yet due to my nonlibrarian job, I was an outsider, as I shared a different social and professional standing.

As a result of my employment at St. Jerome, I had also experienced similar challenges and opportunities that academic librarians might face as blended professionals, albeit at a nonfaculty level of classification. I had worked with the majority of the librarians in an assortment of professional capacities. In addition, I had developed assumptions about the roles and activities of the academic librarians through years of interaction in a variety of campus settings.

Consequently, it was difficult for me to divorce myself from some of the data, especially concerning productivity and academic professionalism. The administration celebrates the achievements of the academic librarians much more vociferously than the accomplishments of the classified staff. This is an annoyance and slight to the ego and difficult to overcome with an objective analytical perspective.

Upon reflection, though, it became apparent to me that the obstacles that limited the productivity and professional development of the librarians inherently were different due to the individuality of those who perceive them. My professional and personal roles varied significantly from the interviewees and projecting my own expectations on that community acted as a severe disservice and would mitigate the librarians' respective voices in the data.

In qualitative models, the researcher has the ability to become a member of the collective. Conversely, the researcher might find that the aim of objectivity creates a greater divide between the individual and the interviewed group (Punch, 1998). In my experience, I did improve communication with several interviewed librarians. In some cases the interview was the first formal in-person contact that I had with that particular librarian. Following the research, though, there was little impetus for the librarians to remain in contact with me, and these relationships and my capacity to engage in that particular academic realm became stagnant.

In truth, I did not have the realistic ability to become a member of the librarian community. It is true that I belonged to the same university, and in some cases, the same department as some of the interviewed librarians. However, within the academic hierarchy, I remained classified staff. No amount of personal or professional connections developed through research would ever have elevated me to the respective level and standing of the interviewed librarians. This research in some ways further defined the boundaries that prevent the mixing of the roles by codifying the role of the academic librarian at St. Jerome. Simply put, I was not a librarian and therefore could not join that exclusive community.

Further, my professional activities were usually as a separated function to the undertakings of the librarians. My instruction has been detached from that of the librarians; whereas librarians often teach library instruction, I focused on more discipline-oriented, lecture-based topics given in graduate student settings. At the time of research, I was not a member of any of the professional library service organizations, such as the American Library Association. I also had performed only one nonwork related collaborative research project with one of the liaison librarians. The rest of my projects were individual or conducted with nonlibrary staff. The professional roles of me and the academic librarians essentially diverged when considering research, instruction, and service.

Also, the premise of this study is to establish how academic librarians develop within the blended professional role. This may be done regardless of established professional relationships because the factors influencing the librarians' opinions were not controlled by me. No aspect of my professional or academic position then swayed any of the policies and procedures that governed the work environment of those librarians. Furthermore, as classified staff, I habitually occupied a lower hierarchical and theoretical organizational position than the librarians. Due to position rank, I did not participate at all in the librarian administrating committees that had the potential to modify the roles of the librarians. In short, though I worked in the same organizational unit, the spaces and spheres of influence were inherently separate.

The study also considers one segment of the population of the nontenure-track faculty at one mid-Atlantic university in the United States. Professional role experiences and opinions on identity will differ by department even at the studied institution, so the results cannot be considered comprehensive for the entirety of nontenure-track faculty and academic librarianship. The hope though is that through the demonstration of the viability of this model, other researchers might explore the concept of blended professionalism in varying departments and demographics.

4.2 Conclusion

This chapter established the framework of the qualitative research methodology that I utilized in this case study. Blended professional identities are perceptual, and therefore, these identities are personalized. These identities will fluctuate by institution and even by department within larger organizations. The model frame, though, provides the means to assess these perceptions at your respective institutions.

It was believed that qualitative interviews would generate the most reflective, direct opinions on the blended professional identities of the female academic librarians and provide insight into the third spaces as well as the obstacles to professional development. Following the completion of the interviews, coding, and analysis, this qualitative process seemed successful as it produced animated responses and viewpoints in spite of the aforementioned limitations. The next chapter will begin to discuss the findings of this case study.

4.2.1 Questions for researchers to consider

Since this was a case study analysis, your sample invariably will be different than mine. Prior to undertaking your work, reflect upon how your group might influence the results. As well, I have attached the questions that I asked of the librarians in my study in the appendices. The structure of the questions that I provide is sound because they are designed to deliver understanding of librarian role and identity with the blended professional frame in mind. You are free to replicate them for your work.

However, you may choose to modify slightly or add some additional questions based upon what you would like to learn from the research. Still, keep the focus on blended professionalism. The following are some straightforward considerations that will help you mold the specifics of your blended professional questionnaire.

How does your organization classify librarians? Institutions vary on how they categorize librarians within the hierarchy of the university. Some librarians are categorized as faculty, and some are viewed as staff. The professional expectations accordingly would correspond. In order to define the role of the academic librarian at your institution, catalog their responsibilities and develop conforming questions.

What is the nature of your institution? St. Jerome University is a large, public institution in the United States. Just as with the classification of the librarians, the type of institution might predicate professional expectations for the librarians in your study. Again, determine how the institution itself would have an effect on the academic librarians and create appropriate modifications to the questions.

What is the size of the sample that you want to study? The model is applicable for all sizes of study. However, the size will have an effect on the perception of components of the model, such as spaces and relationships.

Do you have a homogenous or mixed demographic? My research featured all females. Your study might have a more even mix of genders or even the inverse. Additionally, I did not examine race. This would be an option for the additional framing of questions when considering professional identity.

References

Cohen, L., Manion, L., & Morrison, K. (2007). *Research methods in education* (6th ed.). New York: Routledge.

Crawford, A. (2012). *New directions for academic liaison librarians.* Cambridge: Woodhead Publishing Limited.

Creswell, J. W. (2005). *Education research: Planning, conducting, and evaluating, quantitative and qualitative research.* Upper Saddle River, NJ: Pearson Education, Inc.

Dausien, B., Hanses, A., Inowlocki, L., & Riemann, G. (2008). The analysis of professional practice, the self-reflection of practitioners, and their way of doing things. Resources of biography analysis and other interpretative approaches. *Forum: Qualitative Social Research, 9*(1), 1–9.

Ellet, W. (2007). *The case study handbook: How to read, discuss, and write persuasively, about cases.* Boston: Harvard Business Press.

Glaser, B. (1992). *Basics of grounded theory analysis.* Mill Valley, CA: Sociology Press.

Greenbank, P. (2003). The role of values in educational research: the case for reflexivity. *British Educational Research Journal, 29*(6), 791–801.

Mauch, J. E., & Park, N. (2003). *Guide to the successful thesis and dissertation: A handbook for students and faculty* (5th ed.). New York: Marcel Dekker, Inc.

Munim, M., & Mahmud, I. (2011). Mindmap: a powerful tool to improve academic, reading, presentation and research performance. *Review of Higher Education & Self-Learning, 3*(11), 21–26.

Patton, M. Q. (2002). *Qualitative research and evaluation methods* (3rd ed.). Thousand, Oaks, CA: Sage Publications.

Price, J. (2010). Coding: open coding. In A. Mills, G. Durepos, & E. Wiebe (Eds.), *Encyclopedia of case study research* (pp. 156–158). Thousand Oaks, CA: Sage Publications, Inc.

Punch, K. F. (1998). *Introduction to social research: Qualitative and quantitative, approaches.* Beverly Hills, CA: Sage.

Yin, R. K. (2009). *Case study research: Design and methods.* Los Angeles: Sage Publications.

Zha, S., Adams, A., & Mathews-Ailsworth, J. (2013). Examining the blog use in a faculty, development programme: a multiple case study. *International Journal of Learning Technology, 8*(1), 5–19.

5 Academic librarians versus tenure-track faculty at St. Jerome

During the data analysis, several themes emerged from the findings, such as the distinctive differences between librarian and tenure-track faculty roles, the composition of the librarians' third space, the librarians' perceived role with respect to the blended professional model, and the obstacles to professional development and librarian success at St. Jerome. These themes are all tied together by the core theory produced from this study. Specifically, the functional aspects of the librarians' role places structural limitations on their influence; the perceptual and socially constructed limitations further enhance these issues by restricting the blended professional effectiveness and operational third space, which creates both artificial and actual obstacles to professional development. Simply put, the academic librarians at St. Jerome are in fact blended professionals that operate in a unique third space within higher education. However, real or manufactured limitations confine that blended role and third space.

To start, the comparison of the actual role of the academic librarians versus that of the tenure-track faculty at St. Jerome is required. This chapter will reaffirm the differences that emerged during the interviews between the tenure-track faculty and academic librarian role at St. Jerome. The discussion will turn to the consideration of the academic librarian as blended professional. Finally, the causes and validities of professional obstacles will be examined.

5.1 Role comparison: academic librarians versus tenure-track faculty

As asserted earlier, the roles between tenure-track faculty and academic librarians historically have been distinct. Gradually, the responsibilities of the librarians increased and began to resemble the activities of the tenure-track faculty in terms of research requirements, instructional duties, and provision of services. However, at St. Jerome, these core tasks of research, instruction, and service remain distinct between the two factions.

It was postulated earlier in this work that the roles of academic librarians and tenure-track faculty at St. Jerome are inherently different in the substance of their activities. Nothing in the findings refuted this assumption. In fact, this assertion was more firmly verified.

While academic librarians engaged in activities that mimicked tenure-track duties, the librarian workload might be best labeled as "tenure-track lite." Understanding of this realization might best be related through the words of Sofia.

I know a lot of tenure-track faculty very closely and that makes me want to say that it's nothing at all like it. I deliberately chose not to take that path so I tend to emphasize the distinctions. In terms of responsibilities, duties, burdens, workload… this is much less high stakes, right? There is no point in my job where I feel like it's "x" or perish.

In short, the pressures and the burdens of the librarians at St. Jerome at present are less severe than an individual faculty member pursuing tenure. In order to establish librarians as blended professionals and gain a better understanding of the third space that they occupy, a brief comparison to the tenure-track faculty role is required.

5.1.1 Research

The librarians feel that their administration is strongly encouraging that they create high-level research projects that replicate those produced by the tenure-track faculty. The librarians were skeptical of their ability to accomplish this aim.

> Irene: The research expectations that [the administration] might have…we're never going to have anything like that. I mean, we may have research expectations and it seems like the administration is pushing us that way but it's going to take a lot of years before the research that we do is anything like the same caliber of research that the tenure-track faculty have to do.

This is in part due to the disciplinary area that the librarians are focusing on, specifically library literature. When asked the question "What kinds of research do you do?" only two of the librarians responded saying that they did disciplinary research. The rest of the librarians' research related in some form to the libraries, such as technology used in instruction, library sustainability, and other pragmatic projects that furthered discussion on processes within the library.

However, library-oriented research did not garner respect even from the librarians themselves. As Valeria somewhat lightheartedly commented: "Don't get me going. Library literature being its own joke. I didn't say that on tape. But oh my gosh." Valeria later described the literature as "abysmal." I interpreted this perspective to relate to the lack of a difficulty gaining acceptance into library publications mentioned earlier in chapter "Historical Roles." An added problem stems from the supposed emphasis on quantity as opposed to quality. As Julia notes:

It doesn't seem to me that the type of literature that you're publishing matters very much. From what I've seen, it seems that I think we all think that library lit is garbage…but crank it out, but people do all sorts of things like book reviews and things like that, I wouldn't necessarily…and I don't think that other tenure-track faculty would get promoted for doing book reviews.

This type of commentary illustrates the difficulty that the librarians have in defining what is valuable research and what is merely symbolic productivity. As well, these types of mentalities feed into the systemic devaluing of the librarians' own contributions to the literature.

Both legitimate qualitative and quantitative projects produced by librarians are cycled through St. Jerome's Institutional Review Board. However, the librarians denigrated the output time and again as "not real research."

> Laura: It's not a real research thing. And [the Data Services Research Consultant] is helping us and maybe she can turn some switches on statistics and make it more…really what you're going to come out with is some sort of impression from this particular snapshot.
> Researcher: The librarians tend to use the terminology "we done good."
> Laura: Yes, yes. And that the kind of thing that I have [quote hands] published; more or less reports of projects that I did that turned out well. Yeah, things like that.

A "we done good" paper or presentation in the parlance of academic librarians is the equivalent of a report in other disciplines. The project generally did not require qualitative or quantitative analyses. It is often an experiment that involved applying conditions to a particular unit and reporting on the results. It generally will just feature a literature review, a summation of the steps in the process, and then end with considerations for future applications of a similar project.

The project Laura is listing above actually was more sophisticated than a "we done good" report. Laura and her coauthor analyzed the receptiveness of library users to instruction at the reference desk through a sophisticated survey approved by St. Jerome's Instructional Review Board. Even so, Laura and other librarians pursuing similar projects often lowered the perceptive quality of the project through their own interpretations. The librarians just did not appreciate the level of erudition required to complete some of their work.

It is possible—and likely, given the interview responses—for this perspective to stem from a lack of formal understanding of the substantive research process. As Valeria stated: "I can wing it. I can partner with people who know how to do it, but [I don't]." Another librarian noted that her article that featured 2 years of data collection might have been accepted in a "better journal," but it would have required more qualitative methods that she did not know how to complete, in large part due to the scholastic preparation that the librarians receive in library school.

The quality of research fundamentals covered in library school was seen as a pitfall for many of the librarians. In the librarians' eyes, this contributed to poorer literature output.

> Lucy: But I know a lot of librarians and I know to a degree that some of the library scholarship is or can be pretty sad and that people do it just because they have to and it's not always good quality. Because we don't get really exposure in our programs to that. Our programs, at least in my day because it's been awhile since I graduated, were way more vocational.
> Researcher: Yeah, there's not the quantitative or qualitative research courses.
> Lucy: Right. We took a research methods class but for goodness sakes it didn't teach us anything. I mean, I think that all I really had to do in that class was fake apply for a grant…like write a grant proposal and fake apply for a grant. We did not learn methods. Like we learned that there was difference between qualitative and quantitative but we didn't learn how to do it, you know?

The library science degree is a practical program designed to prepare librarians to work in the field (American Library Association, 2008). Theory, especially research methodology, is not emphasized in library school curriculum (American Library Association, 2008). This spoke to the level of methodological understanding that the librarians gained during their library school programs.

> Valeria: Even if I had all the time in the world to publish…[if] I had one of those jobs where I picked-and-choose where to go [publish], the MLS didn't give me the means to analyze the data in ways I need to in order to conduct a really methodologically sound study. I don't feel like I have that background.

For librarians, the term "research" predominantly refers to the acquisition and exploration of materials needed to complete a formal project. The American Library Association Standards for Accreditation of Master's Programs in Library and Information Studies states:

> *The curriculum of library and information studies encompasses information and knowledge creation, communication, identification, selection, acquisition, organization and description, storage and retrieval, preservation, analysis, interpretation, evaluation, synthesis, dissemination, and management.*
>
> *American Library Association (2008)*

Note that the word "production" or an equivalent is missing from that description. For accreditation purposes, the American Library Association emphasizes the "knowledge of" research as opposed to the ability to produce. Melania affirms: "We aren't trained in research methodology in library school. Maybe we will in the future but right now the curriculum is very resource oriented, which is not good for academics librarians." Research for tenure-track individuals includes both the knowledge and resource acquisition portion of the endeavor, as well as the composition of the completed project. At St. Jerome, research for tenure-track faculty is defined as:

> *Scholarly achievement is demonstrated by original publications and peer-reviewed contributions to the advancement of the discipline/field of study or the integration of the discipline with other fields; by original research, artistic work, software and media, exhibitions, and performance; and by the application of discipline- or field-based knowledge to the practice of a profession.*

Here is a fundamental difference in philosophy for the two roles. Academic librarians find; tenure-track faculty produce.

The librarians at St. Jerome are working within an environment where the constituents often have as much or greater education in terms of the complete definition of "research." The mission and substance of their education makes it highly challenging for the librarians to succeed in the equivalent production of research or gaining a collaborative foothold. They are the buttresses to the research process, not the foundation, walls, or the towering pillars that form the cathedral of academe at St. Jerome. This restricted role in the research process creates a constructed limitation on the extent of their influence and third space within the academy.

5.1.2 Instruction

As a whole, the instruction that librarians perform also falls short of that completed by their tenure-track counterparts. It is important to note that librarians view instruction on multiple planes of individual and group teaching. To the former, "in-person or online reference assistance often incorporates teaching" (Detmering & Sproles, 2012, p. 546). This may include individual interactions, either at the reference desk or in scheduled appointments. Librarians "teach" whenever they attempt to help an individual find information. When a patron visits a reference desk, or a group of students are receiving classroom instruction, and even remotely via email or instant messenger, librarians are performing some form of instruction.

The main difference between a transaction that occurs at a reference desk and the reference consultation is that the latter is scheduled and the former occurs randomly during a scheduled desk shift. The premise of both is the same though. "In the reference interview, the librarian's goals are to determine the most efficient and productive way, the nature, quantity, and level of information the user requires, and what information format is most appropriate for or preferred by the user" (Bopp & Smith, 1995, p. 36). The process therefore is similar to what occurs during the preparation for classroom instruction. The librarian must identify the appropriate resources for the patron. The interaction between the librarian and the individual will illuminate the level of sophistication required to complete the task.

Sometimes the librarians trip themselves up at this stage. Many times, I have observed librarians sometimes overeagerly provide information to the patron. For instance, if a patron is looking for printed books on a topic, the librarian will also show the individual databases, journals, research guides, and other superfluous information. This is referred to as data smog (Shenk, 1997) and often overcomplicates the transaction. As an observer, I could see the eyes of the patron glaze over while the librarian continued on in their presentation.

Regardless, the purpose of the individual instruction is to prepare the patron to perform research on their own. Catherine uses the fishing analogy: "The primary role [of an academic librarian that] I see is teaching people how to fish. I don't want to give them the fish. You [the learner] have to take this over. And you have to be comfortable with doing it your way." In theory, it is easy to find information for a student. If a student comes to the reference desk asking for information on Chaucer, the librarian could print out copies of relevant articles and send the student on their way. However, it is more effective and mutually beneficial to give details about the steps involved in the process and empower the student to succeed on their own. This is not a dissimilar mission from group instruction. The preparation is just different.

With group instruction, in general, the educational preparation that the librarians received in library school was somewhat incomplete in the provision of pedagogical skills. Some of the librarians did not have much faith in their instructional abilities and pinpointed teaching as a weakness in their professional roles.

> M: What type of instruction do you do?
>
> T: It's funny you should ask because I've been thinking that I really need...I really need somebody to assess me because I really don't think it's particularly good. I don't have a lot of confidence in my teaching ability.

Lucy claims: "Librarians historically...I don't know about now...but I know, historically we're not taught to teach like faculty. We're not taught to teach." Research, or at least the librarian-oriented view of research, was at least addressed in library school. Nowhere in the curriculum requirements of an ALA-accredited school will a reader notice the requirement that schools are to offer instructional assistance or practice. Most of the librarians began teaching with little or no formal background in instruction.

> Valeria: I do very little instruction now. I try to make it really active giving them exercises encouraging them to participate. Encouraging them to even look at an online tutorial so that we're at least beginning from the same place (or at least theoretically we are). I don't know what you call my approach. I don't have any educational background.

While she does not teach many of the formal classes, Valeria's position requires significant presentations to faculty and staff. The researcher observed her presentations, and they are very professional and successful in achieving the dissemination of information. Yet Valeria and many of her colleagues developed their skills through practical on-the-job learning. Librarians predominantly entered into the profession without a formal base in instructional methods, and learned pragmatically in the field. As Irene states: "It's all been the way I think it should be done based upon my own experiences."

The reliance upon instructional techniques developed through experiential means is systemic within the libraries at St. Jerome. Abilities may be gained at the initiative of the individual seeking them. Lucy asserts: "Everything we've learned is through external means of...you know, workshops, professional development opportunities." Training and assessment at St. Jerome seemingly is not provided by managers or administration. Laura related: "I don't like the lack of feedback...the lack of critical constructive evaluation. Constructive criticism would be helpful." This atmosphere does not appear likely to change in the near future. Irene mentioned that a proposal for instructional training, feedback, and assessment was suggested by one of the librarians. It was vetoed by the library administrator, with time restrictions being viewed as the main contributing factor.

In my own experience, I also did not receive much training or feedback with respect to instruction. As part of my professional responsibilities, I frequently taught library classes in a variety of settings. While as a student, I had formal classes in college teaching and previously had instructed semester-long for-credit college courses, I too learned to teach library classes through experience and without formal feedback. In fact, in all of the courses that I ever taught in the libraries, a supervisor only sat in on one instruction session, and that was nearly 4 years after I began instructing library courses. Given the feedback from the librarians, I understood that this was similar to their experiences as well. There was no training or assessment.

All of this is not to say that members of the tenure-track faculty necessarily ever have had formal pedagogical training. Many of them also are thrown into the fire, so to speak. One librarian had such an experience in her nonlibrary school graduate program.

Irene: I can remember when I started my [second master's] degree ...I had a teaching assistantship. And I was floored. I was 22 years old and they said "Okay, you're going to do two lab sections of such and such. Here's your syllabus and book." And there were a bunch of us doing the same lab sections but there was no guidance whatsoever on what we were supposed to do.

In some respects, this "trial by fire" is better than no experience at all. One of my degrees is a master's in history. In that program, all of the lower-level undergraduate courses and recitations were taught by full-time PhD students with assistantships. Master's students and doctoral students without full-time status or an assistantship gained no pedagogical experience at all. If I took a postgraduation job teaching history or social studies in a state that did not require additional educational training or certification, I would have had a difficult time learning the craft on the job. This is essentially what librarians experience once they enter the field.

Therefore, realistically, unless a faculty member, academic librarian, or any other professional in the instruction field had a student teaching internship or some variant form of teaching apprenticeship, their instruction is learned through observation and personal trial and error. However, where the instructional roles between tenure-track faculty and libraries additionally diverge is in the nature of the actual classes taught.

Consider the method of instructional style and delivery. In terms of delivery methodology, the librarians unanimously favored interactive instruction as opposed to lecture. Sofia stated: "The idea of lecturing horrifies me." She was not speaking in terms of fear, but rather thought that standing and speaking for 3 h without discussion was abhorrently boring. As a result, Sofia and the rest of the librarians incorporated interactive instruction. One of the driving factors in utilizing this manner of instruction was that interactive instruction breeds collaboration.

Researcher: Do you feel the students learn the library material better from the interactive?
Melania: Yeah.
Researcher: Why is that?
Melania: Because people learn by doing. I just did a [instruction-based project]...and the theory that I related it to was Vygotsky's zone of proximal development. So students...people are social in nature, so you learn in a social context and you learn when you have a problem to solve. They get something out of [it] because the problems are directly based on something that they're working on so scaffolding from one another as they're working...as they're partnered in groups. So one person might have better research skills than another so they learn collectively that way.

Interactive instruction provides the librarians with a means through which to encourage the students to pay attention and care. If the instruction is relevant to their homework or an ongoing or future project, they are more apt to pay attention to the entirety of the lesson (Brophy, 2008).

Unfortunately, interactive instruction often requires a commitment of time and the librarians frequently were not afforded a great deal of instruction time due to their manner of instruction. The overwhelming style in which the academic librarians teach at St. Jerome is in the form of the *one-shot*. "The one-shot library instruction session has long been a mainstay for many information literacy programs. Identifying realistic learning goals, integrating active learning techniques, and conducting meaningful assessment for a single lesson" (Watson et al., 2013, p. 381). One-shot instruction is formulaic. If the class is longer (and the students have access to computers, such as in one of the library instruction rooms), it consists of a four-step process. Specifically:

1. Introduction
2. Overview of resources
3. Interactive searching
4. Questions and conclusion

If the librarian has an abbreviated time or computers are not readily available, then step 3 from the above process is skipped. Step 2 may also vary in terms of complexity when librarians deliver a one-shot. Some of the classes in which the librarians speak, specifically those taught to incoming freshmen or students new to St. Jerome, require very basic resources. These often include more generic databases such as Academic Search Complete or Proquest Research Library.

Unfortunately, the one-shot hampers the librarians in a couple ways. In his 4-stage learning cycles model, Kolb (1984, p. 38) stated that "learning is the process whereby knowledge is created through the transformation of experience." Kolb (1984) asserted that the four stages consisted of concrete experience, reflective observation, abstract conceptualization, and active experimentation. The one-shots benefit the concrete experience aspect of learning because that stage emphasizes "doing." However, in the short amount of time, there is not necessarily enough opportunity for the students to progress through deep and thoughtful considerations. The major problem with this reality is that not all students learn in the same manner. Therefore, the active learner might gain a great deal from the interactive lessons designed by the librarian, but the reflective learner might find little or no value in that methodology.

I observed eight individual one-shot instructions performed by eight librarians. There were many positive aspects of the instruction sessions that validated the academic librarians' expertise on library resources. The librarians observed are adept at "gaining the buy in" from the students. They present the relevant resources that students in the respective classes might utilize. Mere mention of the cost of some of the database resources, especially when emphasizing the place that the students' tuition might play in their purchase, often grabs and keeps the attention of the classroom. They also explain the role of the librarian and encourage questions, visits to the library, and follow-up consultations.

It is very impressive to see the librarians work specifically within their subject. They "speak the language," which gives them instant legitimacy. For example, a student asked one librarian a question about a very specific disciplinary database. I had never even heard of the resource and probably could not even spell it, yet the librarian promptly and accurately responded to the student's question.

Several aspects of the one-shot role, though, reiterated the librarians' guest speaker status. For instance, librarians teach across several departments and sometimes instruct a class that is not within their specialized field. One librarian stated during her presentation that "I don't know what you guys do in [your discipline]" and "I have no idea what that [disciplinary term] means." It seems fine to enter an instructional situation without a complete grasp of the entirety of the disciplinary field. However, projecting that fact hinders the likelihood that a specialized student would contact the librarian and again demonstrates the ancillary nature of the librarian within the classroom.

The librarians did not engage in any grading or assessment for these classes, so when matters concerning the application of resources to projects arose the librarians conceded control of the classroom back to the professor. For example, when questions pertaining to the assignment come up, such as "Is this a resource that I can use for my paper?" the librarian always deferred the question to the professor. She responded to one student with "Ask your professor. I am not grading your paper." After providing a similar response to two more students, comparable questions were then directed to the professor and not the library instructor.

In another instance, the librarian was not present when questions of substance were fielded. The second half of the class consisted of research done by the students with minimal supervision. The librarian, in fact, left the room for the majority of this time, and the professor alone answered questions from the students. Most of these questions appeared to be pertaining to the assignment, such as with the structure of the upcoming written project. Students' actions in the librarian's absence, unfortunately, defined her role in the class.

Finally, nerves apparently affected the delivery of one librarian. Several times during the presentation, the librarian apologizes, saying that she is running out of time, causing the talk to be stunted, rushed, and awkward on occasion. In total, the librarians demonstrated their acumen concerning useful resources applicable to student study. Slight flaws in their deliveries might be addressed through simple coaching. In doing so, the academic librarians might better bridge the gap between "guest lecturer" and collaborative individual.

At present though there is also no real connection between the librarian and the students during the one-shots. In an article, Chambliss (2014) advocated that professors take the time to learn their students' names for the following reason:

> *Any person's name is emotionally loaded to that person, and has the power to pull him or her into whatever is going on. But more than that, calling a student by name opens the door to a more personal connection, inviting the student to see the professor (and professors generally) as a human being, maybe a role model or even a kind of friend.*
>
> *Chambliss (2014)*

Chambliss is clearly speaking to his colleagues in the professoriate, but the value of knowing the names is clear. It provides a bridge-building connection that is unavailable to the guest speaker. The librarian's role in the one-shot classroom is of an auxiliary individual, present only to supplement the instruction provided by the main librarian.

In some cases, librarians do have a more substantial role, such as when librarians are *embedded*. An embedded librarian is a librarian that either co-teaches a course with a faculty member or has a role that extends for a series of classes, or in some cases, the entirety of the semester (Kvenild & Calkins, 2011). The activities of the embedded librarian are more substantive, such as grading or assessing assignments semester (Kvenild & Calkins, 2011). For example, when the librarian is embedded in the course, the librarian has a better understanding of the needs of the faculty member for whom they are instructing. As Valeria states: "I think…that in those more enhanced relationships you get a better feeling for what the professor wants and is trying to achieve in terms of objectives, learning outcomes, and so on." The situation also provides the opportunity to develop more in-depth student–librarian relationships.

> Valeria: You get to development a better relationship with students. And as a consequence you build trust so they feel like they can come talk to you in a way that they might not consult their instructor. They know that you don't give them a grade. And when they're struggling a lot of times I felt like they would be more open with me than they would a professor.

It does, however, require the cooperation of the faculty member, and this was an issue confronting many of the academic librarians at St. Jerome. Faculty did not provide many embedded opportunities at this point for the librarians. As Bridget stated: "I think the liaison role provides access but I don't think that it necessarily provides inclusion." Thus, during the course of this project, none of the interviewed librarians participated in embedded classroom instruction, so unfortunately I was unable to observe the nuances in this altered version of instruction and its potential effects on the librarians' blended professional identity.

5.1.3 Service

Service for the librarians entails many activities as well as the mindset of the librarian. Briefly to the latter, some of the librarians considered the foundation of the role as service-based due to the ambiguity of the description of service activities. Service for librarians could involve everything from helping a student at a reference desk to buying books for the collection to attending conferences. These activities comprise a significant portion of the daily activities of the librarians and therefore represent the foundation of the role of the academic librarians at St. Jerome.

To start, similar to tenure-track faculty, the librarians of St. Jerome serve on a variety of committees. By virtue of being academic librarians at St. Jerome, the librarians interviewed were members of Librarians' Council, which is a committee that meets monthly to discuss matters such as library governance, professional reviews, and research leave considerations. Participation in Librarians' Council is high and voluntary, mainly because it is one of the only avenues where librarians at St. Jerome can manage the governance of their position.

There is a faculty senate at St. Jerome; however, the academic librarians have no representation in it. The Vice-Chair of the Librarians' Council attends the Faculty Senate meetings but only for the sake of gaining information. Neither the Vice-Chair nor the librarians themselves have any feedback, and this immediately creates a distinction between them and the tenure-track faculty at St. Jerome.

> Maria: I think we're isolated from a whole lot of things because to one sense not having a faculty status excludes us from the faculty senate. And having colleagues at other universities where they are faculty...I've seen the difference that it makes for those librarians on their curriculum committees, on the budget committees...you know, fairly significant committees to the point where one colleague I know, he's chair of the faculty senate budget committee.
> Researcher: That helps.
> Maria: That helps. Another one was chair for 2 or 3 years...I forget...of the curriculum committee for the whole university through the faculty senate. I don't know. Having worked at two institutions where you did have senate status and faculty status I can see where that does help. Whereas here we're in that limbo between the teaching faculty who get all the glory and wonder and classified staff. We're in this limbo of afterthought or "Oh yeah, those guys. We should ask them." But it's already too late or down the road and they haven't included.

Due to their classification, the experience of the librarians at St. Jerome is not universal among librarians at other institutions, particularly those where the librarians have full faculty status, tenure-track positions, or both. However, this likely is a trend across several types of institutions due to the perceived rank of the librarians in comparison to the other faculty.

In addition to Librarians' Council, the librarians also serve on a variety of committees known as "taskforces" that supposedly help administrators make educated decisions regarding planning for development initiatives. These committees are not well-liked because the work contributed by the groups is often not implemented.

> Bridget: I am occasionally asked to serve on library committees. They are not the committees of my personal interest, so I find some of them frustrating because they're not something that I'm interested in and on occasion I'm concerned that we're doing a lot of busywork because on more than one committee we've done a lot of work, we've submitted the report, and the report was either rejected outright or completely ignored.

This type of empty activity undermines the librarians' contributions and enhances the discord between the librarians and the library administrators.

> Lucy: I'm not sure also that there's a lot of intent around what's being done and why. Like planning and why projects are happening and what projects are happening. And I hate when they start projects and they either don't finish them or finish a report and never implement anything. I mean, there's a lot of busywork it seems that doesn't accomplish a lot of things.

Part of the contributing factor to this issue is that major decisions at St. Jerome take a significant amount of time to develop and come to fruition in a public institution (Cotton, Bailey, Warren, & Bissell, 2009; Siegfried & Getz, 1995). Bureaucratic approval processes retard expedient progress and change in that type of environment.

For example, I served on a committee that researched types of learning commons. I was the only nonlibrarian on that particular committee. We spent a year researching existing commons, interviewing administrators, traveling to other libraries, and compiling a comprehensive report. Formal implementation of any of the recommendations from that group would not be initiated for approximately 3 years after the committee first organized. I coauthored a book chapter related to that group's work that was proposed, peer-reviewed, edited, formatted, and published in less time than it took to apply any of the suggestions in that initial report! Therefore, a lot of the committee service that the librarians participate in seems less that productive or rewarding.

The other issue involves top-down communication from library administration at St. Jerome. As Maria's feedback indicates, the librarians already feel disconnected from the decision-making processes at St. Jerome due to the exclusion from Faculty Senate. Poor communication from the library administration was cited by many of the librarians and contributes to the perception that committee work is "busywork." Improved communication might address some of these concerns and improve overall morale (Crick, 2014; Saxena, 2010).

Now there are many members of the academic community, including wage staff and classified staff, right up through full professors and administrators that must participate in organizational activities such as committees that often times seem repetitive or insignificant. There are different levels of expected governance though. As a classified staff member, realistically I did not expect to have much input or feedback, or find recognition outside of my immediate unit. On the other hand, faculty, which the librarians were categorized as at St. Jerome, should have a prospect of some governance. The issue for the librarians at St. Jerome is that they do not have individual membership (and the corresponding voice) in the Faculty Senate, whose decisions may considerably impact the activities of the libraries and its academic librarians. In addition, the librarians feel that the library administration does a poor job of communicating during the decision-making process. This creates obstacles to the success of the librarians, which will be discussed later in chapter "Obstacles to Professional Success."

In terms of a holistic understanding of the concept though, service provides the foundation of the librarian role. Juxtaposed with the traditional tenure-track model with research being the significant foundational base of activities of that category of the faculty, the altered perspective of the librarian identity modified the external and internal understanding of the role for the interviewed librarians. Adele states: "I would say [tenure-track model] is kind of flipped on its head, which in some ways is why we don't get the same kind of respect." For other librarians, the term "service" equated to "support."

> Laura: I am definitely a support role to the tenured faculty and helping them and their students. Now I do see that I have a role in helping the tenured faculty with research because I know things that they don't know and I can help them. I have in the past been on grants with…PhDs and stuff and I know that there's a role that we can serve but I really do see it as a support role and not on the same level.

Because service is a foundation of the librarian role, the ability to create a distinction between collaborator and service provider is difficult, which results in issues relating to respect and minimizes opportunities for librarian–faculty collective ventures. This "support" ideology had implications, particularly concerning gender, which will be discussed later in this chapter.

While transdisciplinary, multidisciplinary, and interdisciplinary work can appear in instructional literature and best practice materials may bridge disciplinary gaps, the main body of research focuses on department-specific articles, books, and other forms of academic productivity. This actuality promotes difference and siloing among the university departments. This is not to say that tenure-track does not perform service and outreach, but the goal of tenure-track research promotes an inner-facing perspective.

Service, on the other hand, is outreach-based. The goal of the librarian is to help whomever, whenever, and wherever. Ideally, the librarian is working with department-specific people in the liaison role purposely, since the librarians are trained to "speak the language." However, the nature of the role promotes the instruction of all manner of patronage, from freshmen 101 students all the way up to tenured faculty and department chairs.

The librarian will help a patron regardless of the topic. Questions come to the reference desk from all manners of patronage. The problem is either solved therein, or the patron is referred to the appropriate party. This ideology predicates an interdisciplinary approach and role. The mindset emphasizes the blended professional model and validates the inclusion of librarians in conversations regarding the model's application.

5.2 Conclusion

Demonstrated in Table 5.1, the academic librarians' role at St. Jerome does not compare equally with the tenure-track faculty due to the differences in research, instruction, and service obligations.

These are legitimate, functional separations that define who and what the librarians are at this particular institution. Reading this, you might suggest that the comparison of tenure-track and nontenured librarians is not a fair comparison because the expectations inherently would be dissimilar. Why not compare the librarians to contract instructional faculty or adjunct faculty? Remember though, the comparison is based upon the components of both roles requiring research, instruction, and service. Those other forms of faculty generally only retain one of those responsibilities. One would expect that the teaching duties of an instructional faculty would exceed those of

Table 5.1 A brief summation of the roles of the academic librarians when compared to tenure-track faculty at St. Jerome

Activity	Tenure-track faculty	Academic librarians
Research	Discipline-focused; required; core to function; substantive research projects	Library research; not "publish or perish"; "we done good" reports
Instruction	Semester-long courses; integral role	"One-shots"; auxiliary presence
Service	Tertiary; may not contribute to tenure	Seminal for role

librarians because that is all that they are contracted to perform. Instructional faculty normally are not contracted to perform research or service to the extent that librarians are though.

Also, the comparison here is to formulate the specifications for the type of activity conducted by the librarians for the sake of understanding perceptions of role. While the findings place the librarians on a lower vertical standing than the tenure-track faculty in terms of role function, I believe that in the relative, professional identity would be outranked by most of the faculty at this particular institution regardless of specified function. In the total context of the hierarchy of academe, the contract and adjunct faculty often retain a higher social standing than the librarians—at least at a large, doctoral granting institution such as St. Jerome—because those faculty positions require terminal degrees. As I will discuss during the legitimacies section of the following chapter, the letters after one's name retain significant weight in this type of community.

All of this creates layers in the consideration of the librarians at St. Jerome. These strata will vary at different institutions, depending upon librarian rank, performance expectations, and so on. However, I believe that challenges to a librarian's role as a blended professional will exist regardless of the examined location, and the perceptions of these defined limitations of the librarians' role create socially constructed obstacles that further limit the effectiveness of their role as blended professionals. Findings related to the blended professional model are where the conversation now turns.

References

American Library Association (ALA). (2008). *Standards for accreditation of master's, programs in library & information studies*. Retrieved from http://www.ala.org/accreditedprograms/sites/ala.org.accreditedprograms/files/content/standards/standards_2008.pdf.

Bopp, R. E., & Smith, L. C. (1995). *Reference and information services: An introduction*. Englewood, CO: Libraries Unlimited.

Brophy, J. (2008). Developing students' appreciation for what is taught in school. *Educational, Psychologist*, *43*(3), 132–141.

Chambliss, D. F. (2014). Learn your students' names. *Inside Higher Education*. Retrieved from https://www.insidehighered.com/views/2014/08/26/essay-calling-faculty-members-learn-their-students-names.

Cotton, D., Bailey, I., Warren, M., & Bissell, S. (2009). Revolutions and second-best solutions: education for sustainable development in higher education. *Studies in Higher Education*, *34*(7), 719–733.

Crick, J. (2014). Effective team communication. *In Practice (0263841X)*, *36*(2), 96–98.

Detmering, R., & Sproles, C. (2012). Forget the desk job: current roles and responsibilities in, entry–level reference job advertisements. *College & Research Libraries*, *73*(6), 543–555.

Kolb, D. A. (1984). *Experiential learning experience as a source of learning and, development*. New Jersey: Prentice Hall.

Kvenild, C., & Calkins, K. (2011). *Embedded librarians: Moving beyond one-shot, instruction*. Chicago: Association of College and Research Libraries.

Saxena, R. (2010). Role of communication in employee development. *International, Transactions in Humanities & Social Sciences*, *2*(2), 115–121.
Shenk, D. (1997). *Data smog. Surviving the information glut*. San Francisco: Harper Edge.
Siegfried, J. J., & Getz, M. (1995). The snail's pace of innovation in higher education. *Chronicle of Higher Education*, *41*(36), A56.
Watson, S. E., Rex, C., Markgraf, J., Kishel, H., Jennings, E., & Hinnant, K. (2013). Revising the "one-shot" through lesson study: collaborating with writing faculty to rebuild a library instruction session. *College & Research Libraries*, *74*(4), 381–398.

The academic librarian as blended professional

6

As I repeatedly have asserted, academic librarians, with their numerous and sometimes ambiguous roles, also may be considered blended professionals. The academic librarians at St. Jerome perform an assortment of functions in the academy that comprise aspects of research, instruction, and service, and necessitate interaction and influence in a variety of physical and virtual spaces (Crawford, 2012). In this chapter, I present the findings that validate this assentation.

Since the findings are based upon the interpretation of qualitative data from an individual case, the results will be study-specific. However, the frame applied is transitional to other libraries and librarians. Additionally, some of the responses will be indicative of environments and the perceptions of professional identity elsewhere, so the results presented have universal relevance.

Once again though, blended professionals are individuals who "are characterized by an ability to build common ground with a range of colleagues, internal and external to the university, and to develop new forms of professional space, knowledge, relationships and legitimacies associated with broadly based institutional projects such as student life, business development and community partnership" (Whitchurch, 2009, p. 417). Principally, blended professionals engage with a variety of individuals and departments in order to perform their professional and academic duties; the actual roles and the surroundings in which they are executed generate perceived professional identities.

More so, the hierarchical and perceived placement in the process of curricular student learning between faculty and students places academic librarians in an exceptional space within the context of higher education. Whitchurch's four-tiered frame considering spaces, knowledges, relationships, and legitimacies is a suitable model for analysis, as librarians operate in a blended professional mode on an everyday basis. The librarians interact with nearly every facet of the university community in one way or another. Yet the librarians' role affects their perception of their abilities and limits the completeness of their capacity to blend into all real or perceived contexts around the university.

Each category in Table 6.1 has the ability to influence the librarians, as blended professionals' approach and style depending upon the perception of the activity. The resulting opinion then defines the workable ability of the librarians at St. Jerome to blend into different communities around the institution. In essence, the categories help explain the boundaries of the academic librarians at St. Jerome and form the basis for the following section.

Table 6.1 The table above lists the traits of the blended professional along with the categories that emerged from the qualitative interviews and field research and serves as a roadmap for Section II

	Spaces	Knowledges	Relationships	Legitimacies
Influences on blended professional role of academic librarians at St. Jerome	Geography Stigma & misunder-standing of role Technologies	Resource evaluation Disciplinary language Social language	Managerial perspectives Colleagues Faculty Students & staff	Workspace Legitimizing knowledge Status quo

The model is adapted from the model of Whitchurch, C. (2009). The rise of the blended professional in higher education: a comparison between the United Kingdom, Australia and the United States. *Higher Education, 58*(3), 407–418.

6.1 Spaces

The previous section affirmed that the academic librarians at St. Jerome have fundamentally similar roles as the tenure-track faculty, yet the output is less and the emphases are inverted. The following will discuss how the academic librarian fits into the blended professional model and how their particular position in the campus community creates a unique third space. The third space that the librarians occupy might best be explained with a quote from Veronica. After much petitioning, she finally was added to her department's email Listserv.

> *The email thread for that one was interesting for how many people it had to be punted to saying "Oh yeah, she can be on it" or…but I guess whoever was the gatekeeper was like "Yeah, you're not a student. You're not faculty. So you're not going to be a part of it."*

The librarians are not students or faculty, but they have the potential ability to balance between both entities and contribute to the complete campus collective. It is a unique space in that the librarians' purpose is to extend in-class learning. Other blended entities on campus, such as student affairs department, supplement purely academic student learning with extracurricular activities and functions.

Therefore, librarians have access to physical and perceptual communities on campus due to what they can provide. In Whitchurch's (2009, p. 410) words, the academic librarians of St. Jerome "accommodate the ambiguities of third space between professional and academic domains." Their role extends beyond administrative and professional responsibilities due to their contributions to the academic endeavors of the community, yet the limitations of their position and expertise thwart a wholly academic identity. Indeed, who they are prevents their complete acceptance into the communities with whom they interact. The contributing factors around their positions will now be examined.

6.1.1 Geography

One of the basic challenges concerning place that the librarians face at St. Jerome pertains to geography. As mentioned, St. Jerome's librarians are spread across three campuses: St. Michael, St. Raphael, and St. Gabriel. The Alexander VI and Stephen VI libraries are both on the St. Michael Campus, which is a sprawling residential campus in a suburban area. Clement V Library is located on the newly residential St. Raphael Campus, which is in a rural setting approximately 15 miles to the west of the St. Michael Campus. Urban II Library on the St. Gabriel Campus is in an urban setting and caters primarily to professional, nonresidential students.

St. Jerome is in a metro area where traffic congestion makes travel between campuses problematic. This reality in itself creates artificial siloing between the libraries at the campuses that has implications beyond mere isolation.

> Susanna: St. Michael…I feel totally isolated from. St. Raphael I tend to forget about. Unless one of them contacts me I tend to forget that they even exist. Being out here [St. Michael's librarians] completely forget what we can do out here and sometimes they forget that we're out here in general. Then they also don't realize that sometimes, because they don't interact with us, what our specialties are.

Again, remember that the librarians at St. Jerome are liaison librarians. The liaison librarian fits the concept of blended professional in definition and function; they work within the library and liaise with their academic department and its constituents, and in various communities around the campus. One of the benefits of this model is that specialists exist and when complicated disciplinary questions emerge, the patron may be referred to a particular librarian with a background in that field. In Susanna's case, she has a very unique social science specialty that may be considered a subset of other disciplines. As Susanna is implying, the librarians at St. Michael, due to a lack of sustained interaction, tend to disregard her abilities and refer patrons to more generic disciplines. This may create problems for the patron because they are potentially referred to an individual without the expertise to solve the problem. It also complicates the role of the librarian who is being asked to resolve an issue that they might not have the ability to grasp in its entirety.

The geographic situation also exacerbates other manners of isolation. One librarian described her boss as a micromanager who required all staff to have approval to travel to different campuses. The librarian had made some collaborative connections with librarians located on different campuses, but in her opinion, her supervisor prevented travel because there was a personality dispute. Melania states: "I feel isolated now in my own library and also isolated from what's going on at other campuses."

At one point in my career, I worked at one of the distributed campus' libraries and found the experience to be exactly the same as what the librarians described. For instance, every year there was a massive holiday party intended for all the St. Jerome libraries held at the St. Michael Campus. The refreshments are catered and plentiful. It is toward the end of the exam period during the fall semester, usually during the third week of December. Most students have left campus and the patronage in the libraries dramatically drops.

Still, all of the libraries need to remain open just in case, and as a result, many of the librarians and staff at the distributed campuses' libraries do not or cannot attend the large party. In order to provide an equal opportunity for these library employees to enjoy in festivities, money normally is provided so that the distributed libraries might host smaller, separate parties. In contrast to the larger party at St. Michael, these gatherings are rather Spartan. One year, I recall our library being given enough money to order three pizzas, which amounted to just less than two slices of pizza per employee at the time. I remember my colleagues being quite perturbed at the gesture.

In other instances, siloing emerged between libraries on the same campus. In the past 2 years, the librarians at Stephen VI have begun to focus heavily on instruction and outreach to the undergraduate community. Alexander VI in contrast has shifted its charge by attempting to provide services focused on the graduate and faculty populations at the St. Michael Campus. The ideology of "facilitating information to students and faculty" of St. Jerome remains the same. However, graduate and faculty work is seen as "real research" and more pedantic in substance. It intensifies division. As Lucy stated:

> *I felt like the Alexander VI librarians were very…like, "We are the subject liaisons, and we are…" I don't know where they get that attitude. I'm not saying that translates to everyone but they sometimes come off as elite…or better than the other librarians. And I've heard them say bad things about other librarians on the other campuses if that…as if the other campuses are inferior. Which I think goes back to the whole "We are one library" thing, but we're not really becoming one library.*

Part of the problem with Lucy's statement is that regardless of whether or not the Alexander VI librarians have or display elitist attitudes, the sensitivity exists. Perceived belief may have just as much likelihood to create negative professional opinions as an actual attitude or obstacle.

Perhaps a contributing factor to this concern is the location of the library administration for St. Jerome. The librarians at Alexander VI have offices located in a "cubicle farm." Within that room is the supervisor of all the librarians at St. Jerome. Across the hall is the office of the Dean of the Libraries. The decision-making process consistently was described as Alexander VI-centric. Important meetings, trainings, and even the aforesaid holiday parties are planned with this library in mind. The implication was that the location of the administration itself influenced this process, again providing the perception of favoritism and further isolating the other libraries.

Communication, or lack thereof, does not help the siloing. Yes, decisions are made frequently with the St. Michael Campus libraries at the forefront of the process. However, the policy decisions are universal, often without definitive explanation:

> Gwen: I definitely feel like some decisions are made within the library system centrally that…like unless I'm very aggressive and or nosy, don't always necessarily trickle down or then maybe they just trickle down later than other things that are happening.

A formal example of this occurred in the summer of 2014 when the research for this project was ongoing. Circulation staff was to receive uniform training on answering reference questions. All circulation staff at St. Michael attended four weekly 1.5 hour trainings during the month of July. One librarian, located at the St. Gabriel Campus, stated that their staff training would be a single session and occur just prior to the start of classes at the end of August. It also would be taught by a different librarian than the one instructing the four sessions at the St. Michael Campus. The quality of training at the St. Gabriel Campus invariably was different than that received at the St. Michael Campus due to the amount of time spent. In addition, the librarian who taught the classes at the St. Michael Campus developed the training. St. Gabriel essentially received a distilled training from a supplemental trainer.

Throughout the community of librarians, geography encouraged siloing, creating situations where librarians move primarily within their own spheres of influence, be that a specific library or campus. These findings are significant because this compounds the academic librarians' isolation among the greater academic community because it restricts the limits of blended professional's spatial mobility.

6.1.2 Stigma and misunderstanding

The academic librarians at St. Jerome have difficulty gaining acceptance in the greater academic community, in part due to some of the differences in the roles of the librarians and the tenure-track faculty outlined in the previous chapter. The level of research is different between the two entities, which frequently puts the librarians into a service-oriented role. The lack of a foothold in the academic community was often credited to a misunderstanding of the role of the librarian.

> Laura: Generally I don't think that faculty recognize what we...because we haven't educated them, or they just don't know, or they're too busy, or whatever...they don't recognize what we can contribute. So we're isolated in that kind of context.

Again, this misunderstanding by the faculty may directly relate to the conflicted role that the librarians have of themselves. They view themselves as service providers, yet the administration emphasizes collaboration. Collaboration suggests equal or at least similar standing in role. Service retains the connotation of "servant." These are completely different ideologies that are difficult to reconcile, resulting in a lack of shared ventures and a prevalent and restricting stigma about the librarians' role. The mere perception of that identity creates a formidable challenge to overcome.

Unfortunately, college faculty primarily still utilize the library and its librarians principally for the acquisition of materials and occasionally as space for research labors (Marcus, Covert-Vail, & Mandel, 2007). For example, one study found that a vast majority of faculty value library services, but only a fraction utilized their liaisons for instruction, finding the greatest use of the library to be ordering books or serials for the faculty (Yang, 2000). As repeatedly asserted, collaboration is not viewed as the purpose of the space in which librarians at St. Jerome occupy.

> Bridget: [Faculty] don't do research the way we [librarians] think about research. They know people in their specialty so they're going directly to them. So in some ways they see the librarian as very much for the students but they're not going to use them necessarily for themselves unless it's something very, very tricky.

Essentially, research has shown that faculty like and seemingly appreciate the services provided by the libraries (Bausman, Ward, & Pell, 2014; Oakleaf, 2010; O'Clair, 2012), but the faculty does not wish to maintain or initiate said services, and therefore, they may not provide long-term opportunities for collaboration.

As a result, librarians have found it difficult to gain respect for collaboration or outreach in the academic departments. According to Elizabeth: "I've put out feelers about collaboration, collaborating on research, but nothing's ever come out of it." In fact, the survey of librarian schedules at St. Jerome found that only 3.9% of their time was scheduled to be in office hours located in an academic department. This is unfortunate because activities like office hours provide a means for the librarians to engage with the university community outside of the physical confines of the library.

> Julia: When I'm over there [in the department for office hours], I am not only meeting students, I am in a physical place where faculty members come through that particular office all the time too. So if someone needs to ask me a question, I'll tell them I'll be over there on Tuesday from 5 to 7, you can pop in and some people just come by and say hello because they know that I'm there or they need something or whatever. So it's really an advantage to have a known presence in a building like that.

Without a physical presence provided by office hours, outreach becomes more challenging and time-consuming for the academic librarians.

Even on a real social level, there appears to be a significant barrier between the occupied places of the librarians and the tenure-track faculty. Jessica related the following example.

> *The faculty, it's weird. This is so weird. I was going to someone's retirement party a couple months ago and I actually ended up running in to a couple of English faculty members, one of whom turned out to come from the same part of the country as I do. And it was weird because it was very collegial. I almost felt out of place. I felt odd and I wasn't quite sure what to make of it. But then when I saw one of them later at a conference, it felt much more distant. I don't know. It's a little uneven.*

McHenry and Sharkey (2014, p. 35) assert that "growing distinction between tenured and tenure-track faculty members on the one hand and tenure-ineligible lecturers or part-time adjuncts on the other has produced an academic caste system that is undermining the raison d'être of our institutions of higher learning." Similar to the geographic restrictions, these limitations are also perceived in that there is no written or physical barrier truly preventing interaction. Yet the perceptions of both the faculty and the librarians engage to create a socially constructed boundary that inhibits the interactions of the blended professional.

Therefore, librarians at St. Jerome do not achieve complete acceptance into communities around campus, perhaps because they have a lower rank in social capital (Burns, 2004). They have the ability to interact but cannot achieve a true foothold, and their space is defined by what they are not. These discoveries therefore suggest that the academic librarians exist on a third space that is subordinate to tenure-track faculty, and at the same time, the librarians find socially constructed restraints preventing the complete amalgamation of blended professional their role.

6.1.3 Technology and space

It was mentioned that the purpose of the librarian role is often misinterpreted by members of the academic community. Part of that stems from the historic model of the librarian working within a building crammed with volumes of books and journals.

> Valeria: I think there are a lot of truly academic organizations out there that really don't see the purpose of us. I think in a lot of institutions people question the value of the librarians. I mean I think in an old-fashioned way they think of us as the keeper of a collection.

This notion increasingly is becoming obsolete due to the continued advances in library technologies.

On the positive side, librarians do have a technological advantage that spreads the blended space in which they work. Academic libraries offer a substantial connectivity to the university academic collective since they bridge the information gap between the faculty and the student. The actual use of the once-traditional, physical library itself began to shift in the late 1990s (Lougee, 2002). Physical volumes of some journals are being phased out in favor of online subscriptions. The on-campus library is evolving into a smaller study center and less of a repository (Jeevan, 2007; Lougee, 2002). This modification of thought is significant since it made the transition to servicing the campus community in their ubiquitous digital learning much more natural.

Despite this reduction in physical presence, librarians at St. Jerome have several options for outreach and interaction with campus community patrons, such as online information guides (Roberts & Hunter, 2011; Robinson & Kim, 2010) and live and recorded web tutorials (Charnigo, 2009; Dunlap, 2002; Shiao-Feng & Kuo, 2010). However, the popular suggestion to achieve rapid interaction is through virtual communication (Bennett & Simning, 2010; Hawes, 2011), labeled in library-parlance as Virtual Reference.

The premise of virtual reference is simple. The librarian is not tied to a specific reference point, such as a desk or phone, and the interaction is immediate, so the communication is quicker than email. The medium of communication creates the potential for extended hours of service, both on campus and off. Virtual reference includes avenues of written digital communication such as Instant Messaging (IM) (Bower & Mee, 2010; Whitehair, 2010) and video chat, such as via Skype (Booth, 2008).

Virtual Reference grew from libraries attempting to use digital tools in order to provide learning opportunities and communication with patrons who could not directly visit a reference desk. It is a different interaction though from consultations that occur in person.

> Lucy: Even someone who has a lot of experience [with virtual reference] and I think I'm pretty good at that…it can be hard sometimes and sometimes you have to take a step back and realize that you can't show the empathy that you're trying to that you would show in person. You have to be almost more demonstrative and over exaggerate it.

Any form of virtual reference requires patience and training. As Lucy says: "You have to refine your skills to work in that environment." The journey into technology requires a willingness on the part of the librarian to extend beyond the traditional definition and image of a librarian, perhaps requiring a shift in paradigms, both personally and professionally. The ability to extend space virtually enhances the academic librarians' capacity to reach a larger populace.

In an environment where many actual or perceived roadblocks to collaboration exist, technology is a means to bridge many gaps. The usage of virtual reference at St. Jerome continues to increase on an annual basis. For instance, in the calendar year of 2011, there were 1926 questions fielded via IM; in 2012, that number increased to 3016. It is a popular medium through which librarians may interact with the university community, and it represents a viable means to continue to blend professional boundaries in spite of physical and cultural hindrances.

6.1.4 Spaces summary

Technology greatly enhances the third space in which the academic librarians are able to interact and extend their professional boundaries and third space. However, geographic restrictions develop physical and then subsequently cultural silos between personnel at the various libraries of St. Jerome. Their limitations are further complicated by the academic community's misunderstanding of the librarian role as well as the personality and gender traits of the librarians themselves, which is something that will be discussed later in this chapter. These findings indicate that the academic librarians have the ability to blend across different barriers of space, but the existing complications greatly diminish the librarians' effectiveness as blended professionals because the obstacles limit the actual or perceived interactive spaces in which the librarians might work and thrive.

6.2 Knowledges

Whitchurch (2009) asserts that the knowledge or knowledges that a professional retains and distributes creates a blended identity. With tenure-track faculty, this knowledge would be their personal specialty knowledge within their discipline. The liaison librarians at St. Jerome who were interviewed, on the other hand, all provide the ability to find and evaluate materials needed by the academic community. As Maria states: "Our job is to find additional information, or the data, or additional data…whatever they need relevant to whatever experiment that they're doing." That is the basic knowledge that all librarians at St. Jerome may provide by one means or another; it is an expectation of librarians in general. In terms of collaboration and acceptance across boundaries at an academic institution though, secondary abilities and skills earned through disciplinary study also come into play and form a key function of the ultimate success of the blended professional.

6.2.1 Evaluating resources

The knowledges concept of blended professionalism helps explain the unique third space that librarians occupy. Discovering and assessing researchable information is a key function of academic librarians in the context of higher education. The librarians fill that knowledge gap between faculty instruction and student learning. It is a unique academic space occupied by librarians.

Knowledges do vary though, even at the generic level. When asked about the most important knowledge that they might provide, the answers were varied. This is not surprising as knowledge, or perception of knowledge, is subjective and based upon personal experience (Buckland, 1991). However, the most common response regarding significant knowledges dealt with finding and evaluating resources.

> Researcher: What would you consider the most important knowledge or expertise that you provide?
> Melania: Teaching students how to evaluate resources and choosing the right resources to conduct their research.

In the field of library science, the evaluation of information falls into the realm of knowledge management. In general, knowledge management consists of "accessing, evaluating, managing, organizing, filtering, and distributing information in a manner that is useful to end users..." professional judgment-based activities perfected by librarians (DiMattia & Oder, 1997, p. 33). The complexity of the problem addressed will alter the steps in the process and the resources consulted. However, historically this is the basis of the role of librarian: evaluate and categorize materials required by the patronage of that particular library (Rubin, 2004).

Systemic change complicates the distribution of knowledge as well. Modifications in how the library is viewed and used due to the influx of technologies, ubiquitous learning, and philosophical roles impact the blended places of the academic librarians in the academy.

> *The philosophy of knowledge management...is proving to be a catalyst for change – creating an atmosphere in which focus is no longer upon processes taking place in buildings called libraries, but upon knowledge workers as information intermediaries and upon organizing systems to capture that knowledge embedded therein and then transmitting it to those customers who seek answers.*
>
> *Stueart and Moran (2007, p. 45)*

The academic librarians themselves are vehicles of knowledge. They are the individuals that interpret the resources available and "create an interactive knowledge environment" (Whitchurch, 2009, p. 410). As well, this transmission of knowledge may occur in a scheduled or random environment. For example, Gwen relates: "A lot of that is kind of more ad hoc, like in individual conversations with people that I might happen to have about their research. I might mention, like 'Oh we actually have this really great [product]. Have you tried that?'" Synthesis of the problem becomes a seminal part of the academic librarians' interaction with patronage (Bopp & Smith, 2011).

Comfort and understanding related to knowledge management enhances collaborative attitudes (Aharony, 2011). Demonstrating an ability to analyze knowledge effectively, as well as understand and utilize resources, particularly with faculty, sometimes shocks the patronage.

> Lucy: I think that faculty are often surprised by how much librarians do know. But it's getting the opportunity…I think like one of the biggest things is to let faculty see that librarians do know things about student learning and how to align student learning outcomes with research needs and library needs and how to show through assessment measures that something's been accomplished…[but] they don't always let us in that far.

This surprise at the expertise of the academic librarians at St. Jerome extends back to the difference in the production of research discussed in the first section of this chapter. Tenure-track faculty are proficient in the totality of the research process, which, as mentioned, includes the production of disciplinary research. Librarians, however, truly are experts in the evaluation, acquisition, and dissemination of resources and knowledge. This aspect of the findings is key, the universal trait that all librarians retain as blended professionals.

6.2.2 Speaking the language

Every discipline employs its own vocabulary, a language often best understood by those in the discipline. The librarians at St. Jerome are no different, using terms, or jargon, that are specialized and often confusing for nonlibrary personnel and patronage. Adele states that during instruction: "I try not to throw library jargon at them. I don't know if that's a teaching method but I try to use more natural language when talking to them." These terminologies change depending upon the institution. For example, at St. Jerome, the electronic catalog labels a book that has been "checked out" as "charged;" a returned book is "discharged," as opposed to "returned." Still, the campus community not always is privy to such information, and minor language uses such as these potentially isolate the librarians.

More in-depth research terminology has its own code as well. Many librarians employ the use of Boolean Operators for their searches. For instance, if an individual searches for "higher AND education," they will find only materials including both terms. In contrast, if the individual searches for "Higher OR education," they will find more results because the findings will include one or both of the terms. The use of this method often requires explanation. "Oh, okay. You want to use a Boolean search. Oh, you were born in 1995. You don't know what that means." However, it behooves librarians to teach this methodology because it has been shown to enhance research skills in even novice users (Dinet, Favart, & Passerault, 2004). The search engines employed on St. Jerome's library website also operate based upon Boolean phraseology, so students or faculty might accidentally encounter these options and seek librarian guidance for resolution.

Also, while unified service models are being utilized in three of the four libraries at St. Jerome, the largest library, Alexander VI, still utilizes a separate circulation desk and a reference desk. In general, circulation desks are staff by classified, nonlibrarian staff, whereas reference desks are populated by academic librarians. Circulation staff handle the acquisition of the materials (checking out books, ordering materials), whereas librarians at the reference desks help evaluate and locate information for the patron.

The librarians asserted a misunderstanding of the duties of the personnel at the various desks. "I think that everybody thinks that everybody that works in a library is a librarian," to include sometimes even the student workers. As a result, it is not always readily apparent that a student should visit a reference desk in order to find research assistance. Even simple things like this add to confusion to patrons that are newer to the system. Navigating and translating this language allows the librarian to better communicate with the general university population.

In addition, the databases and catalogs also have their own terminologies. For example, in the medical field, there is a vocabulary known as MeSH (Medical Subject Headings). "It is designed to help quickly locate descriptors of possible interest and to show the hierarchy in which descriptors of interest appear" (NIH, 2014). Articles in databases are linked together using subject headings deriving from the language. Demonstrating and communicating the effectiveness of the usage of this language is an important facet of the librarians' abilities.

> Researcher: What's the best way that you can communicate that kind of knowledge?
> Laura: Showing them how to use that language when they're doing searches. So keywords, controlled vocabulary, about things that are relevant. And then contrasting it with how they're doing their current searching. Like if they're using Google Scholar search and then I can take them into [a disciplinary database] and say "We can use this term that's been assigned that might work..."
> Researcher: So distilling their process?
> Laura: Yeah.

The other major cited way to communicate this knowledge is through interactive instruction. During the observed one-shot instruction sessions, when time allowed, the students practiced searching for resources with the librarian present. Often the mistake made by the student was overcomplicating the search. They would use too many words and then return no results. The librarians offered more effective search methods and terms, such as "productive" as opposed to "good." Understanding and applying this knowledge of vocabulary greatly enhances a researcher's ability to find relevant materials in a short amount of time.

While Google and similar search engines have led many to believe that searching for information is a simplistic task, effective research is much more complex. This actuality gives the librarians as blended professionals the ability to interact with a wide range of the university populace. However, in order to gain more intimate acceptance in a disciplinary role, the findings indicate that an additional knowledge in the form of language is often required.

6.2.3 Social language

Speaking the language also extends to social interactions with certain disciplines. The librarians who held a secondary subject master's degrees often cited that degree's ability to open doors.

> Veronica: Oh, knowledge. Well, considering that I do have that [disciplinary] background it seems like I have a little edge in that aspect then because in terms of meeting with my faculty and students since I do have that background I don't have to be shy that I'm not familiar with the programs because I am.
> Researcher: You speak the language?
> Veronica: I speak the language.

Some of this interaction involves verbal communication and terminology. The example previously mentioned during the discussion on one-shot instruction observation is a primary example of effective knowledge of verbal communication. The question fielded by the librarian was so specific that only a knowledge-area specialist would have been able to interpret correctly the question and formulate a precise response.

The other component is the understanding of the social habits of the individuals within specific departments. In-depth interactions provide understanding of the needs of specific academic sectors (Jankowska & Marshall, 2003), which is especially important when effective written or verbal communication is not a forte of members of that discipline (Steiner, 2011).

> *Now this is going to sound really egotistical but I think one of the things that I bring definitely to the department and maybe to the community….is my training in the sciences. We have how many science librarians and how many of them actually have a degree in it? Two. And it's a whole different thought process and I think you know being able to sit in a group of people and say "You don't understand the way the science faculty are really thinking about this or the way they're going to do it."*

It is an acculturation process often learned as graduate students in nonlibrary degree programs (Mitchell & Morton, 1992) and provides a disciplinary identity (Xiaoli et al., 2010).

The surveyed librarians seemingly understand the efficacy of disciplinary language, yet it was not universally mentioned, perhaps because not all of the librarians had multiple master's degrees. Establishing the importance of that knowledge in line with professional success suggests that an additional degree is required, and possibly not all of the librarians were willing to make that commitment. However, consider all of the aforementioned physical and social limitations facing the academic librarians when they perform outreach and seek to gain "admittance" to particular disciplinary departments.

Language, in spite of those obstacles, opens the proverbial door for the librarians. As a result, the particular knowledge of language serves as a key to the effectiveness of the blended professional model. Language and its presence in the librarians' discussions designate its importance for developing collaborative opportunities and extending the boundaries of the perceived third space.

6.2.4 Knowledges summary

The academic librarians at St. Jerome valued their ability to evaluate information and provide methods for their patronage to acquire the resources needed to complete their projects. Speaking the language and having the ability to acculturate oneself into an academic community was a skill specified by the librarians with disciplinary master's degrees. Clearly those librarians who mentioned it perceive language's significance as it almost automatically extends the librarians' third space from the general realm to the disciplinary fields. This is noteworthy in the conversation on blended professionalism because that additional avenue of communication with the university community.

If the library science degree and general librarian role offers the perceived "support" stigma, then the language provides the librarians a means at least to partially overcome that obstacle and gain social and intellectual access to specific factions of the academic community.

6.3 Relationships

Professional relationships "are networks of connections among employees, staff, and external organizations that are primarily relational in nature. They exist to foster and promote good relations among team members" (Olson & Singer, 2004, p. 9). At St. Jerome, these partnerships exist on a variety of vertical and horizontal levels both interior and exterior to the library. They represent the personal third spaces that the academic librarians occupy.

Again, third space is the theoretical sphere built through an individual's ability to interrelate and intertwine with many diverse communities, thus increasing commonalities between varied populations (Whitchurch, 2008, 2009). Real or perceived boundaries have the ability to influence and construct the extending limits of the working third space. In the context of blended professional relationships, this is essential because the third space will influence with whom an individual might develop a professional connection.

As a result, one's blended professional role, specifically at St. Jerome, influences the perspective of the significance of the relationships. For example, academic librarians who manage other librarians have a more holistic view of the institutional relationships and spheres of influence, whereas the liaison librarians tend to focus more on the immediate, departmental networks. The librarians at St. Jerome have connections within a variety of spheres, though again the perceived and constructed limitations of their role inhibit their ability to maximize opportunities.

6.3.1 Managerial perspective

All four of the supervising librarians interviewed conspicuously mentioned the support staff exterior to the library as being significant. This reflects basic recommended library management strategies and reveals their concern for holistic matters regarding their libraries. "Spend time building relationships with partners, key stakeholders, and decision makers…outside your organization" (Olson & Singer, 2004, p. 105). As Maria relates, the point of enhancing and strengthening these relationships is that the alliances with exterior stakeholders allow transitions to occur and progress to be made (Whitchurch, 2009).

> Maria: They're the budget people. They're the facilities people. People that…and again, I don't want to make it sound like I'm game playing but you've got to know what side of the bread your butter is, you know? I'd say I have a good relationship with a lot of the facilities guys just because of some of the adventures that I've fallen into or projects that I've been told to take care of.

Befriending, say, the IT personnel is not politicking or game playing. It is contingency planning. It allows an organization to seamlessly progress when challenges occur. It is also important to gain support from locational influencers such as executives so that they understand what the library intends on achieving. "You will need to gain management buy-in early and often. Involve stakeholders groups in the planning" (Harriman, 2008, pp. 6–7). Therefore, developing relationships with management of exterior and lateral departments becomes important (Kaplan, 1984; Riccobono, Bruccoleri, Harrigan, & Perrone, 2014).

> Catherine: Certainly folks within the University Life and other departments like that…health services…university registrar's office, campus police, the bookstore, info desk…you know, all of those backbone folks, I would say. I don't know as well, say, the folks in my liaisons area. I don't know the facilities guys as well as my access services supervisor, who's also our campus liaison but I know them and they know me.

Without the proper development of these relationships, it becomes difficult to succeed in a constantly changing environment like that at St. Jerome. This is a universal trend, and it is incumbent upon the librarians to build these relationships because the multiplicity of the relationships effectively extends the third space in which the librarians operate.

Two of the supervisors also asserted that one of their primary roles was in the facilitation of the success of their librarians. Maria calls it "servant leadership" and the preservation of a "positive psychic environment." The premise is that her staff was professional, and it was her responsibility to create a positive working atmosphere in which those professionals could succeed.

> Maria: My job was to keep my antennae out to make sure there wasn't too much incoming or other weirdness that would put too much pressure on [them]. I make sure that they've got the platform for what they need to do. So they can jump, spin, run, skate…do what they need to do whatever they need to do within their disciplines or however their disciplines work or how their students work or their faculty or whatever so they can do their job.

The implication of this evidence is twofold. First, it indirectly refers to the factors (described here as "weirdness") that influence and define the boundaries of the librarians' third space. The managerial ideal is that they might mitigate these concerns and allow the librarians to blend further into the university community. Second, if the goal of the organization is to extend the third space boundaries of influence and increase collaboration, the minutia as well as the complex concerns must be addressed so that the individuals charged with the more complex tasks may focus their energy on those instead. It enables the self-sufficiency of the manager's workers (Whitchurch, 2009).

Managers also involve themselves in mentoring, but often, administrative responsibilities limit the amount of time that a manager may devote to such activities. For instance, one manager stated that she very much enjoyed management, but did not have the time to properly develop mentoring relationships with all members of her staff. Five librarians report to this manager. Given this assertion, it seems unlikely that the manager with 11 librarians reporting to her would have better success in this regard.

These conclusions are significant because reality may create issues with professional development because it limits the ability to conceptualize career planning from someone who has achieved a more advanced rank. If librarian third space is seen in the vertical plane in terms of career professionalism, then the lack of mentoring may be a space-restricting complication as well. As a result, a lot of the mentoring falls to colleagues, which were the most cited significant relationships during the interviews.

6.3.2 Colleagues

Mentoring on the lateral level develops skills that enable an individual to succeed at that particular level (Bryant & Terborg, 2008; Parker, Hall, & Kram, 2008). As well, within a geographically diverse community, this type of mentoring extends boundaries and influence because individuals seek guidance from other equally-leveled collaborative partners. There is a "clear link between career success and having a mentor. Many studies provide evidence of this; their findings are fairly consistent in stating that very few individuals advance to the top administrative ranks in an organization without the help of a mentor or several mentors" (Stueart & Moran, 2007, p. 274). However, if the ambition of the librarian is to move up in the chain of command, they might fare better from the advice of individuals already in the position of leadership.

> Laura: The other liaisons have been very supportive and I learn a lot from them just watching what they do. And I would have to say that would be at a lateral level. I don't feel that way [hands mimic moving up].
> Researcher: You're talking about the library administration.
> Laura: Yes. I don't feel like...
> Researcher: Why not?
> Laura: I like the autonomy but I don't like the lack of feedback...the lack of critical constructive evaluation.

In this way, the dependence upon management becomes problematic, especially in an organization such as St. Jerome where upper-level opportunities are not abundant. As will be discussed in the third section of this chapter, a lack of prospects hindered professional development of the librarians. None of the librarians mentioned mentors exterior to their department or St. Jerome as an institution. Only three cited specific mentoring relationships among their immediate colleagues. One wonders if a lack of leadership mentoring relationships helps create this impediment. Organizational structure is also a suspect, and this will be addressed in Section 6.3 of this chapter.

On a basic level though, colleagues become the most important relationship that the librarians might have at St. Jerome because they generally interact with them on a daily basis (Smith, 2014). A positive relationship with colleagues makes the environment bearable.

> Veronica: In terms with colleagues...these are the folks that you work with and every day... so it would be more pleasant if you are on a more friendly or collegial relations with them. Otherwise it will probably be pretty horrendous to go to work every day if your goal is to avoid them at all costs.
> Researcher: So collegiality by necessity.
> Veronica: [laughs]. I guess if you were to break it down that way...well, yeah. We'll go with that.

The librarians do not always interact with members of the academic community outside the library. They may not teach a class or meet with a student on a given day, so as a result, their social interaction is with the people that they see most frequently: their coworkers. As well, given the barriers to collaboration concerning research that the librarians have experienced, the colleagues in the room or department are often the best options for joint projects. Above all, the mission of a particular department is best understood by the individuals experiencing the same environments (Lin & Fraser, 2008).

Researcher: What aspect of those [collegial] relationships makes them significant?
Valeria: I think we get each other. I think we're both here for a similar purpose and we both understand what the barriers are and so I feel like when we work together there is a sense of we're in this together.

The challenges and successes facing the librarians of St. Jerome are somewhat unique to their field. As a result, finding empathy in colleagues makes the daily tasks less daunting. This understanding sometimes extends to professionals in positions exterior to the library as well.

6.3.3 Nonlibrary professionals

The St. Jerome librarians asserted that the professional departmental staff "tend to get what we do a lot more than the faculty," in large part due to their service-oriented roles that created levels of social grading. As a result, "working within formal, hierarchical structures...individuals [are] also developing lateral relationships and networks" (Whitchurch, 2009, p. 409). The staff also "probably get the same brunt" of the approach from the higher-ups. Therefore, developing these lateral relationships is important because "you can build a collaborative relationship with your peers by helping them when they need help- and then asking them to return the favor" (Garfinkle, 2012, p. 4). There is a reflexive understanding, which is important at St. Jerome because of the relative pecking order.

There is a distinct hierarchy in academe, and some faculty treat support staff as subordinates. This is similar to what Laura related about a former corporate role: "I was never on the same level as a physician, or even a nurse, you know. I was a support role and support staff." Librarians have had similar experiences, again in part due to the misunderstanding of the librarians' role. The reality that librarians are in is misconstrued as the "Librarians are here to help the faculty."

The relationships with the staff can be quite fruitful and advantageous though (Garfinkle, 2012). Sofia describes one of her colleagues in a department that she works with:

[There's] another blended professional. She's the PhD adviser for [the disciplinary program] and she and the other professional advising staff in the school have become a real sort of anchor as it were. I learn a lot from them. They sort of help me figure out...they keep me on top of what's going on with their students so opportunities for involvement. So the advising staff are actually...and I'm trying to force that in the other department because it's been so successful in [that department]...the advisers are highly educated people...multiple masters or doctorates...working in that sort of lineal role.

The terminal degree in higher education may not be sufficient to garner worth in that field. The tenure-track faculty focuses on research, and everyone in the surrounding roles becomes supportive. This creates a feeling of camaraderie among the nontenure-track entities on campus that aim primarily to serve the needs of students and faculty. As Jessica states: "We have more in common in that we tend to serve the students and the faculty and honestly they tend to be more receptive than the faculty do."

Still, these internal and external lateral relationships may not be as beneficial as they appear on the surface. When success with outreach is unsuccessful, these relationships tend to become a fallback and may lead to complacency. If the librarians perceive their boundaries of influence only extending to the departmental staff and not the faculty, it artificially creates a boundary to overcome. Outreach for a blended professional should endeavor to extend beyond the perceived limitations of the respective third space and attempt to find audience in both higher and lower levels. It is difficult to engage with, say, the faculty if the professional comfort level is only with the colleagues in the same office.

6.3.4 Faculty

Within higher education, tenure-track faculty occupy a different and elevated level of social space. As a result, developing relationships with faculty can be difficult, in part due to the issues raised in the previous section about research foundations and abilities. As well, it is difficult to portray oneself as a collaborator when the basis of the librarian's work is service. These are both socially constructed and legitimate obstacles to relationship development in the blended professional context. Yet these relationships can be quite successful.

> Gwen: I think faculty support is really important, we definitely…there's some faculty that, you know, kind of couldn't be bothered with us and don't have any interest but on the flip side we have faculty that are really, really big library proponents and always like questioning things and [are] always talking us up and kind of willing to go to bat for us.

Faculty relationships may be beneficial for professional development as well.

> Melania: I have good relationships with my faculty. They're really good and I'm proud of that. And they are important to me…when I've needed recommendations from them they've given them to me and they always acknowledge the contribution that I make.

Elizabeth cited communication as the key developer of relationships with her faculty. However, Elizabeth teaches in a discipline that is more accepting of librarian interaction and assistance, so an enhanced librarian–faculty relationship in that regard seems plausible. The lines are more open for clear objectives and communication. Extension of third space in that atmosphere is prominent and successful.

As a result, the interesting aspect of the librarian–faculty relationship was that the librarians citing those relationships as significant either work in smaller libraries at St. Jerome or taught a significant number of classes. Headway into other fields such as STEM (Science, Technology, Engineering, and Mathematics) and in larger campus environments seemingly was more difficult. A STEM librarian explained the dynamics of her relationship with the faculty in this way:

> *With the scientist aspect it's like they want to fiddle around with it first and then they'll come back to you if they need help. But for the most part, they're like hermits where it's "Let me tinker with it first. I don't need you to tell me what to do."*

Consequently, in addition to the librarians needing to overcome the realities of the representation of their service role, they also need to manage personalities in order to succeed in relationship development with their faculty. This creates an additional border for the extension of the blended professional influence.

6.3.5 Students and classified staff

Significant in the results were two categories of relationships conspicuous by their lack of mention: students and classified staff. When asked about the primary role of the academic librarian, most interviewed librarians replied by describing interactions with students. Yet only one librarian cited students as the most significant relationship.

> Susanna: To me the most important relationship is with the students because you want them to know they come and we'll help. We'll do it. It's always…I think I enjoy working with students more because they talk the field that I learned. It's always nice to have an academic conversation with people and have an academic debate. I think it's really important that I talk with them because I'm with them…my people.

For Susanna, the interaction with students provides an intellectual connectivity with the community. It is what Whitchurch (2009, p. 410) describes as the ability to "enter and understand academic discourse/debate." If the silos of the university are independent Towers of Babel, then here in these relationships, they both speak the same language. However, Susanna and all of her colleagues viewed students as patrons and not potential research partners. This perspective limits what might be the most abundant and productive partnerships available to academic librarians. The librarians in essence are ignoring potentially 34,000 research partnerships!

As well, the term "colleagues" was never meant to refer to classified staff. Many of the classified staff personnel, particularly in the research-oriented departments, have multiple master's degrees or are pursuing doctoral degrees. These staff members have research experience through both education and industry. As well, presumably the staff will benefit from academic productivity, especially if they intend to work in some facet of higher education that requires presentations or publications.

Yet the nonlibrarian staff often is not considered for partnerships on projects, so unfortunately, they are an untapped resource, therefore limiting the internal networks. These discoveries are important in relation to the blended professional model in that they present a mindset that creates an imagined professional border and again limits the third space through which the librarians might thrive by ignoring potential collaborative partnerships. It is a similar manifestation of the socially constructed and somewhat artificial hierarchy that the librarians themselves must navigate at St. Jerome and will be a component of the analysis of the organization in the next section.

6.3.6 Relationships summary

Managers have concerns supplemental to the success of their librarians. If, for example, a snake is found in a chair (this did indeed happen!), then it is beneficial to have a solid working relationship with the facilities crewmembers. Also unsurprisingly, the academic librarians at St. Jerome viewed their colleagues as the most important partnerships. Stakeholders such as faculty, students, and other classified staff were secondary considerations or complete afterthoughts when discussing significant relationships. These findings are significant because they demonstrate the creation of artificial boundaries that encumber the blended professional role. While it initially appears negative, this actuality provides substantial opportunity for outreach and professional development, which leads to the extension of third space and the blended professional role.

6.4 Legitimacies

Legitimacy is something of an abstract perception. Legitimacies can be gained through experience or innate development. For example, some of the qualifications of the librarians addressed practical matters in their ability to perform their duties. One manager stated that her knowledge of management responsibilities enabled her to succeed in her role.

> Catherine: I would have to say all of the management, whether it's time management, resource management...all that understanding of management. Whether it's making sure we meet a deadline. So getting the guideposts in place or if they use the grid or however you take that apart and put the pieces together. But I would say that management component benefits...is broadly based and bleeds into everything.

Other librarians cited personality traits as a legitimizing force in their position.

> Gwen: I think you wouldn't get this from a resume but I think I'm pretty good in terms of, I take a lot of responsibility for projects and I think I carry them through really well, but that isn't something that I think that's just more of innate quality and not something that I've attained.

Yet managerial acumen and personal drive may represent knowledges that may enable legitimacy. In the academy, letters after one's name often determine position and acceptance into various circles of influence and the third spaces that may be occupied. Again though, the findings related to the establishment of legitimacies indicate that the academic librarians at St. Jerome as blended professionals have the capacity to engage across boundaries through the provision of their services and knowledge, but their role is of a lower socially constructed rank than their tenure-track counterparts and therefore provides real hurdles that the librarians must navigate.

6.4.1 Office spaces

In order to understand the legitimacies of the academic librarians as blended professionals at St. Jerome, the physical spaces in which they work required analysis.

In terms of personal space, of all the librarians interviewed, only one had an office space that was accessible to the public within the library itself. Librarian offices at Clement V Library actually are on the second floor of the building, exterior to the library. The rest of the librarians worked in cubicles arranged in offices locked to the public. As well, librarians at Alexander VI frequently meet with students in a public space such as the reference desk because meetings in their cubicles distract coworkers.

The offices or more often cubicles themselves also are not very large. The average cubicle in the Alexander VI Library is 70 sq. ft. A GSA study (2011, p. 30) found that within academic institutions support staff were allotted between 64 and 100 sq. ft of cubicle space; administrative managers were afforded between 100 and 160 sq. ft. The librarian who is assistant head of Alexander VI Library's reference—the equivalent of an administrative manager in the study—has an 80-sq-ft cubicle. According to St. Jerome's own facilities website, administrative/professional faculty (the rank of the academic librarians) are supposed to have a private office of 120 sq. ft. Consequently in terms of space as a legitimizing factor, librarians are negatively influenced.

This observation is significant because the perception of the working space has the potential to undermine librarian legitimacy by placing them organizationally within a nonacademic working space. One of the interviewed librarians specifically cited offices for librarians as a change in a new library.

> Sofia: I would have an office with a door. You know, the first library that I worked at…the Library of Faculty…the faculty had written into their contract "Every faculty member shall have an office with contiguous walls that touch the ceiling without break and a door that locks and is contiguous with all walls. And every one of these shall have a window." They had made it so that you literally couldn't cubicalize the faculty.

The reasoning behind this request relates to both identity and productivity. To the latter, this librarian routinely arrived at the office early in order to focus on research prior to her colleagues' morning arrival and the potential distractions that accompany them. For identity, it undermines authority. Offices are status symbols and cubicles are low in the hierarchy. As Sofia contends, a proper librarian's office "would be professional like a faculty member's office. It's not behind locked doors like a staff person." If one of the primary points of outreach by the librarians is to establish a collaborative academic role within the greater academy, then the librarians may need more traditionally academic space in order to project academic professionalism and extend blended professional boundaries.

If the librarians remain in "cube-farms" for the extended future, then there is opportunity to promote legitimacies within those spaces. In the librarian's space in the Alexander VI Library, there are a lot of blank walls. There are three Employee of the Month awards hanging on the side of the first cubicle. Only two of the recipients still work for the university. There is also a team award on the same wall dating to 2009; only about 60% of the complement of librarians and staff during the time of research were affiliated with the department and therefore able to contribute to that award. The surrounding walls are blank, except for one massive 8 × 4 ft poster from a poster session presentation at an American Library Association conference. It is a major visual representation of research performed by librarians in the room. Nearly all members of this cube-farm have published or presented some materials in the past. If some of these pieces are framed and placed around the room, then those that enter the room, either students, faculty, or library administration, will be able to recognize that productivity is, in fact, occurring within the department.

The most obvious means in which to establish legitimacy in an academic setting is through the exhibition of educational or specialized qualifications (Whitchurch, 2009). In order to examine how the librarians offered their academic or professional credentials, I took field notes documenting relevant materials displayed around their personal spaces. Only two librarians displayed work-related awards. Five displayed materials denoting conference attendance, of which one prominently displayed approximately 25 attendance and presenter nametags. One librarian hung a school pennant. Finally, only one librarian had her degrees framed and displayed on the wall; a second librarian had her degrees in her office, but they were not displayed.

Studies have been done on the psychological reasons behind the arrangement of office spaces; for example, a messy desk denotes creativity whereas a clean desk suggests a conventional thinker (Vohs, Redden, & Rahinel, 2013). This analysis though was more concerned with what the librarians chose to display. Family and vacation photographs were much more prominent that institutional items, perhaps due to a minimal amount of natural light in the cubicle areas (Bringslimark, Hartig, & Grindal Patil, 2011). There have long been discussions on the lack of windows in working spaces and the effects on workers (Finnegan, 1981; Taylor, 1979). During the research, Alexander VI Library was under renovation, and one of the three windows in the liaison librarian's cube-farm had been removed. Due to the ongoing construction, the blinds were almost always drawn, so it was not surprising in that the employees seek to decorate their own personal spaces.

Ultimately, there are opportunities to legitimize the working spaces of the librarians through decorations and celebrations of achievements. It is difficult to project validity in their current professional office environments. If they continue to view the "cube-farms" as a professional slight though, which they appear to believe due to the characterization of the working space during the interviews, then it will take more reformation of the spaces in order for the librarians to view their working spaces as a vehicle of their legitimacy at St. Jerome.

6.4.2 Legitimizing knowledge

Many of the responses from the librarians regarding legitimacies mimicked findings concerning knowledges. In reading these sections, pieces are repetitive, but they demonstrate that knowledge, or better yet the ability to find knowledge, is a legitimizing factor for the librarians. In order to find or acquire knowledge, individuals must navigate the available resources. In this expedition, librarians serve as their guides. That ability retained and demonstrated by the librarians has the potential to validate their overall presence in the community.

Both subject and general knowledges serve as legitimizing forces. Subject knowledge, particularly with the secondary master's, promoted legitimacy first by enabling the librarians to get their position in the field.

> Veronica: I would probably say my disciplinary degree because even applying for this job... when they say "[specific discipline] preferred," I was like "If I can't even get an interview for this position then I don't think that I would have a knack for it."

The ability to "achieve credibility in academic debate/space" (Whitchurch, 2009, p. 410) is gained through specialized understanding of the knowledge field. It extends the conversational and functional space that the librarian might not otherwise encounter.

Not all of the librarians had multiple master's degrees. In these cases, experience provided additional legitimacy. Experience, which theoretically enhances knowledge, may also promote legitimacy and blend the professional role.

> Laura: If I ever get to talk to anybody I can say I've been doing this for 30 years in different ways. But once you hit that you say "and I'm here to serve you. What services can I provide for you?" That's more of a qualification that's they're interested in.

Both service and experience were important factors. Knowledge gained from working in the field legitimized their sense of belonging.

> Jessica: I know libraries and I have a sense of what they don't know. The problem is that they think they know everything and then they don't. Sometimes it's difficult because we're being asked to anticipate what people want and what they may need, which is a funny kind of role. I have libraries, and I have the broad picture. I have the big picture.

At the very least, all of the librarians have the general skills needed to find the basic materials and resources, with a subject specialist providing additional support. As Maria defines herself: "I'd say I'm a generalist. Bottom-line, get them started, let's get going." That mindset comes through, both the education and experience, and extends the blended professional boundaries even when a legitimizing force, such as a secondary master's, is not owned.

6.4.3 Status quo

The only segment of the legitimacies in the blended professional model that the librarians did not specifically connect with is the "challenging of the status quo" (Whitchurch, 2009, p. 410). Valeria connected it to poor marketing.

> Valeria: One of the weaknesses is that we don't do a good job advocating our resources and our services. Describing why a relationship with a library or a librarian is beneficial to a student or faculty member.

Again, misunderstanding of the role of the academic librarians as blended professionals has the potential to place the librarians at St. Jerome in a tenuous third space. Since they are not faculty and have no representation on the faculty senate, they have difficulty addressing the prevailing perceptions around campus. This is an actual barrier to the blended professional abilities of the librarians, and this structuring might have consequences for the longevity of the position.

> Valeria: I think it's probably always been important that libraries promote themselves but I think it's now more so than ever with the advent of the internets...as we call them. I mean, that's how this program with the development office came about. The development officer

> stated "I can't believe we still have a library. Who needs it? Isn't that what Google's for?" And that's what started this whole process. There's just a lot of thinking like that out there.

Therefore, not only do the librarians at St. Jerome need to market themselves, but they require outreach to demonstrate the viability of their institution in the digital age. Contrary to popular belief, Google is not the most effective tool for a researcher (Behrends, 2012). When officer-level members of one's own institution begin to question the value of a library, it becomes exceedingly difficult to promote change within the institution. The librarians interviewed in this study tended to think of themselves in the traditional and conservative role and hesitated to become movers and shakers. Thus, the librarians at St. Jerome are blended professionals, but the limitations of their perceptive positions inhibit their ability to counter prevailing ideologies and perceptions of worth at their institution. This perception may prevent them from thinking and acting "outside of the box" that is their constructed third space. The librarians therefore somewhat unwittingly define their own workable third space by placing or accepting artificial professional boundaries around their role.

In part, social presentation may play a role in the librarians' ability to challenge the status quo. Only one of the four managers wore jeans to the meeting with me. However, 10 of the other 13 librarians wore jeans to the interview, including every librarian working at the Alexander VI Library. This observation was informal. I did not request nor expect the librarians to dress in business casual attire for the interviews. As well, the meetings also took place during the summer session, when dress codes seem to relax.

Still, professional appearance has been shown to affect perception (Keenum, Wallace, & Barger Stevens, 2003) and career promotional prospects (Haigh, 2013). At least one interview took place on every weekday (Monday through Friday), so the relaxed dress cannot be discounted as a "casual Friday" phenomenon. Many librarians spoke of management aspirations though, and three of the four managers interviewed wore business casual attire. Formalizing the dress code might enhance individual and collective legitimacies of the librarians and extend their blended professional boundaries. If they perceive their roles as requiring more professional attire, then perhaps they will interpret their position within the academy in a more legitimized light.

I also examined the professional business cards of the librarians. Nine of the librarians listed their degrees and certifications after their names, including all but one of the librarians at Alexander VI Library. Only one of the remaining eight librarians—all from different libraries—listed their credentials. Part of the siloing between the libraries, specifically cited by Lucy, dealt with the perception that Alexander VI librarians displayed a snobbish attitude toward their counterparts in the other libraries. The hegemonic business cards did not necessarily dispel this contention.

As well, when degrees were listed on the card and the librarian had a secondary master's, the library science degree always was listed second. Some librarians appreciated the pragmatic and professional understanding that the degree provided.

> Ava: I do think the MLS is helpful because I guess I have more of an understanding about how libraries work in the grand scheme of things. It opened my eyes to different modes of learning, different ways of accessing information. So I think in my job that benefits me a lot.

Others were less enthusiastic about the library science degree's ability to promote legitimacy. As Laura states: "I don't think anybody's impressed with an MLS. Pffffh." Indeed, the librarians viewed the subject master's as more important in this regard than the MLS.

> Susanna: I think actually my [disciplinary] degree benefits me the most because I feel like it opens more doors for me than the librarian degree. Because I feel like...if I just had a librarian degree I wouldn't be able to get positions that I care that much about. But because I have the [disciplinary] degree I feel that I have more opportunities to do things that are more interesting to me.

This perception is important because it seems evident that even though the library science degree was the "handshake that got them in the door," the disciplinary expertise held greater esteem and opened other doors and spaces around the academic community.

Therefore, in order for the librarians to effectively challenge the status quo and overarching perceptions of who they are and what they do, it seems that the librarians with formalized disciplinary backgrounds have the best opportunity to flourish. The librarians' established third space limits the likelihood of success in this regard. However, these librarians with multiple degrees have the blended professional traits concerning knowledges that will open doors and provide an audience through which improved legitimacy might be established.

6.4.4 Legitimacies summary

Presuming that the physical offices of the academic librarians at St. Jerome represent their status in the institution, then their legitimacy as blended professionals in the university community may be diminished. The findings demonstrate that while disciplinary backgrounds and degrees open more doors for the librarians, emphasizing these skills inadvertently marginalizes the expertise of the librarian. Yet, while experience or ability to find materials enables the librarian to gain audience with the academic community, their disciplinary knowledge or degree fosters the acceptance.

6.5 Conclusion

In spite of gap-shrinking opportunity provided by technological innovations, geography develops physical and cultural silos throughout the library system, which are perpetuated by the marketing shortcomings of the academic librarians themselves. The librarians are adept at finding and interpreting knowledge, especially in their respective fields, a key and unique function of the librarians in higher education; yet they often underutilize and undervalue their own research, thereby contributing to the misunderstanding of their roles. The librarians, perhaps due to the third space that they occupy or accept, value their colleagues and underappreciate other collaborative avenues, mitigating the true efficacy of their blended role. They are able to "speak the language," but their lack of advanced or doctoral level skills limits their ultimate acceptance and relegates them to a professional third space that is a perceived rung below the faculty at the institution.

Yes, the data collected suggests and demonstrates that the academic librarians at St. Jerome are blended professionals. However, the unique combination of their roles, their perceptions of those roles, places them into a unique third space developed by perceived boundaries that are balanced between the tenure-track faculty and the students. They are fixed in the middle of the hierarchy that is academe at St. Jerome, and this space creates many obstacles to their professional success. These challenges are where the next chapter commences.

References

Aharony, N. (2011). Librarians' attitudes toward knowledge management. *College & Research Libraries*, *72*(2), 111–126.

Bausman, M., Ward, S., & Pell, J. (2014). Beyond satisfaction: understanding and promoting the instructor-librarian relationship. *New Review of Academic Librarianship*, *20*(2), 117–136.

Behrends, S. (2012). Libraries vs. Google in the 21st century. *The Idaho Librarian*. Retrieved from http://theidaholibrarian.wordpress.com/2012/11/12/libraries-vs-google/.

Bennett, E., & Simning, J. (2010). Embedded librarians and reference traffic: a quantitative analysis. *Journal of Library Administration*, *50*(5/6), 443–457.

Booth, C. (2008). Developing Skype-based reference services. *Internet Reference Services Quarterly*, *13*(2/3), 147–165.

Bopp, R. E., & Smith, L. C. (2011). *Reference and information services: An introduction* (4th ed.). Santa Barbara, CA: Libraries Unlimited.

Bower, S. L., & Mee, S. A. (2010). Virtual delivery of electronic resources and services to off-campus users: a multifaceted approach. *Journal of Library Administration*, *50*(5/6), 468–483.

Bringslimark, T., Hartig, T., & Grindal Patil, G. (2011). Adaption to windowlessness: do office workers compensate for a lack of visual access to the outdoors? *Environment & Behavior*, *43*(4), 469–487.

Bryant, S. E., & Terborg, J. R. (2008). Impact of peer mentor training on creating and sharing organizational knowledge. *Journal of Managerial Issues*, *20*(1), 11–29.

Buckland, M. (1991). Information as thing. *Journal of the American Society of Information Science*, *42*(5), 351–360.

Burns, V. (2004). The academic caste system: prestige hierarchies in PhD exchange networks. *American Sociological Review*, *69*(2), 239–264.

Charnigo, L. (2009). Lights! camera! action! producing library instruction video tutorials using Camtasia Studio. *Journal of Library & Information Services in Distance Learning*, *3*(1), 23–30.

Crawford, A. (2012). *New directions for academic liaison librarians*. Cambridge: Woodhead Publishing Limited.

DiMattia, S., & Oder, N. (1997). Knowledge management: hope, hype, or harbinger? *Library Journal*, *122*(15), 33.

Dinet, J., Favart, M., & Passerault, J. (2004). Searching for information in an online public access catalogue (OPAC): the impacts of information search expertise on the use of Boolean operators. *Journal of Computer Assisted Learning*, *20*(5), 338–346.

Dunlap, S. (2002). Watch for the little red light: delivery of bibliographic instruction by unconventional means. *Journal of Library Administration*, *37*, 279–285.

Finnegan, M. (1981). Work attitudes in windowed vs. windowless environments. *Journal of Social Psychology*, *115*(2), 291.

Garfinkle, J. (2012). Getting ahead. *Personal Excellence*, *17*(1), 4.

GSA. (2011). *Workspace utilization and allocation benchmark*. Office of Governmentwide Policy. Retrieved from http://www.gsa.gov/graphics/ogp/Workspace_Utilization_Banchmark_July_2012.pdf.

Haigh, G. (2013). Career mistakes. *Times Educational Supplement*, *11*.

Harriman, J. (2008). *Creating your library's business plan: A how-to-do-it manual with, samples on CD-ROM*. New York: Neal-Schuman Publishers.

Hawes, S. (2011). Playing to win: embedded librarians in online classrooms. *Journal of Library & Information Services in Distance Learning*, *5*(1/2), 56–66.

Jankowska, M., & Marshall, L. (2003). Why social interaction and good communication in academic libraries matters. *Reference Librarian*, *40*(83/84), 131–144.

Jeevan, V. J. (2007). Technology-enhanced library services and the librarian's identity crisis in academic and research libraries of India. *Libri: International Journal of Libraries & Information Services*, *57*(2), 100–109.

Kaplan, R. K. (1984). Trade routes: the manager's network of relationships. *Organizational Dynamics*, *12*(4), 37–52.

Keenum, A. J., Wallace, L., & Barger Stevens, A. R. (2003). Patients' attitudes regarding physical characteristics of family practice physicians. *Southern Medical Journal*, *96*(12), 1190–1194.

Lin, A., & Fraser, C. (2008). The four constructs of collegiality. *International Journal of Evidence Based Coaching & Mentoring*, *6*(1), 57–66.

Lougee, W. P. (2002). *Diffuse libraries: Emergent roles for the research library in the digital age*. Washington, DC: Council on Library and Information Resources.

Marcus, C., Covert-Vail, L., & Mandel, C. A. (2007). *NYU 21st century library project: Designing a research library of the future for New York University*. New York University.

McHenry, L., & Sharkey, P. W. (2014). Of Brahmins and Dalits in the academic caste system. *Academe*, *100*(1), 35–38.

Mitchell, W. B., & Morton, B. (1992). On becoming faculty librarians: acculturation problems and remedies. *College & Research Libraries*, *53*, 379–392.

National Institute of Health (NIH). (2014). *MeSH browser*. Retrieved from http://www.nlm.nih.gov/mesh/mbinfo.html.

Oakleaf, M. (2010). *The value of academic libraries: A comprehensive research review and report*. Chicago: Association of College and Research Libraries.

O'Clair, K. (2012). Sell what they're buying. *College & Research Libraries News*, *73*(4), 200–201.

Olson, C. A., & Singer, P. M. (2004). *Winning with library leadership: Enhancing services through connection, contribution, and collaboration*. Chicago: American Library Association.

Parker, P., Hall, D. T., & Kram, K. E. (2008). Peer coaching: a relational process for accelerating career learning. *Academy of Management Learning & Education*, *7*(4), 487–503.

Riccobono, F., Bruccoleri, M., Harrigan, K. R., & Perrone, G. (2014). Do horizontal relationships matter to production and operations managers? *International Journal of Production Research*, *52*(16), 4731–4746.

Roberts, S., & Hunter, D. (2011). New library, new librarian, new student: using LibGuides to reach the virtual student. *Journal of Library & Information Services in Distance Learning*, *5*(1/2), 67–75.

Robinson, J., & Kim, D. (2010). Creating customizable subject guides at your library to support online, distance and traditional education: comparing three self-developed and one commercial online subject guide. *Journal of Library & Information Services in Distance Learning*, *4*(4), 185–196.

Rubin, R. E. (2004). *Foundations of library and information science* (2nd ed.). New York: Neal-Schuman Publishers, Inc.

Shiao-Feng, S., & Kuo, J. (2010). Design and development of web-based information literacy tutorials. *Journal of Academic Librarianship*, *36*(4), 320–328.

Smith, J. (2014). *10 tips for winning over your colleagues*. 1 Forbes.com.

Steiner, D. G. (2011). The communication habits of engineers: a study of how compositional style and time affect the production of oral and written communication of engineers. *Journal of Technical Writing & Communication*, *41*(1), 33–58.

Stueart, R. D., & Moran, B. B. (2007). *Library and information center management*. Westport, CT: Libraries Unlimited.

Taylor, L. (1979). The natural history of windows: a cautionary tale. *British Medical Journal*, *1*(6167), 870.

Vohs, K. D., Redden, J. P., & Rahinel, R. (2013). Physical order produces healthy choices, generosity, and conventionality, whereas disorder produces creativity. *Psychological Science*, *24*(9), 1860–1867.

Whitchurch, C. (2008). Beyond administration and management: reconstructing the identities of professional staff in UK higher education. *Journal of Higher Education Policy and Management*, *30*(4), 375–386.

Whitchurch, C. (2009). The rise of the blended professional in higher education: a comparison between the United Kingdom, Australia and the United States. *Higher Education*, *58*(3), 407–418.

Whitehair, K. J. (2010). Reaching part-time distance students in diverse environments. *Journal of Library & Information Services in Distance Learning*, *4*(3), 96–105.

Xiaoli, J., Di Napoli, R., Borg, M., Maunder, R., Fry, H., & Walsh, E. (2010). Becoming and being an academic: the perspectives of Chinese staff in two research-intensive UK universities. *Studies in Higher Education*, *35*(2), 155–170.

Yang, Z. (2000). University faculty's perception of a library liaison program: a case study. *Journal of Academic Librarianship*, *26*(2), 124.

Obstacles to professional success 7

Chapter 6, "The academic librarian as blended professional," discussed how perceptions of the academic librarians' role created a unique third space. Working within this constructed third space creates a blended professional identity for the academic librarians at St. Jerome. The data obtained additionally found acknowledged obstacles related to their professional success and development as blended professionals.

This was a chapter that I struggled to write during the research process because I kept projecting my own expectations on the librarians. When you hear complaints about lack of time and money, for instance, it is easy to compare the complaints to your own experiences. During the course of this research, I worked two jobs (one full-time and one part-time), while at the same time, I studied in graduate school. In the libraries, I made far less money than any of the librarians and still had professional academic aspirations and expectations. I was in the same system but lower down on the totem pole, so to speak. So for me, I at first was offended somewhat by these findings. During the revision process, I received a great deal of feedback that illustrated how incorrect my initial mindset had been.

Obviously my original approach is a disservice to the interviewed librarians because it simultaneously dampens their voice when a primary goal of this type of exercise is to provide a venue for them to speak and be heard. As well, I was not walking in the librarians' shoes, either professionally or personally. These were interviews, but they were not comprehensive life stories where the librarians revealed everything about themselves. I am sure that some of them had struggles far greater than I could have imagined from my semiblinded vantage point. Therefore, I encourage you as researchers who might use this model for your own purposes to step back and consider the individuals behind the perceived identities.

Regardless, when compared with the data from the chapter "The academic librarian as blended professional", the additional consideration does not change the results. Instead, the supplementary layer of information amplifies the difficulties that the academic librarians at St. Jerome experience as blended professionals by creating extra difficulties to navigate in their professional roles.

Thematically, three distinct obstacles to the librarians' success in the blended professional model arose during the interviews: time and money (or compensation), gender, and organization. Again, these impediments were at times artificially created through perception, but in other instances, the concerns were very real and tangible. The problem with contrived obstacles is that they may have the same effect as real limitations if the individual perceiving them allows the issue to affect how they function.

Fig. 7.1 represents the categories of obstacles to professional development of the academic librarians at St. Jerome. Chapter "The academic librarian as blended professional" established that the blended professional identity of academic

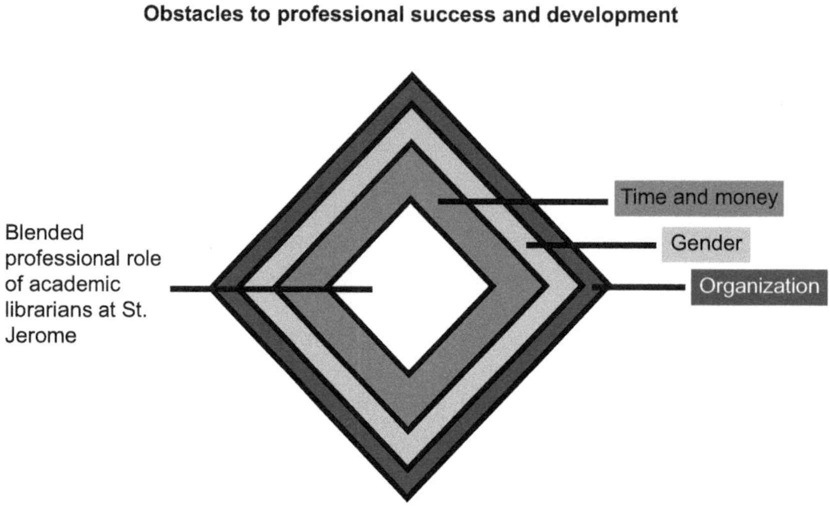

Figure 7.1 This figure symbolizes impediments for librarians as blended professionals to success and development. The working third space of the academic librarians is in the center, surrounded by additional obstacles. The boundaries indicate the severity of the obstacle, with the innermost being perceptually the least serious and the outermost being the most difficult.

librarians and categorized the boundaries of their unique, working third space. Further fencing surrounds this identity, creating supplemental difficulties to the blended role.

The additional obstacles in Fig. 7.1 are categorized by their basis in reality. Analysis of the data suggests that time and money are perceived impediments. The librarians believe that they exist so that perception affects how the librarians view their positions. However, since they are supposed instead of actual concerns, these might be alleviated with dissemination of comparative data.

Gender as an obstacle is not black and white. While some of the librarians viewed aspects of their gender as impacting their ability to do their job effectively, the sentiments were not universal. Gender perception has the ability to hamper the professional development of the individual if they consider their gender an influencing factor, but not all librarians may consider—either deliberately or subconsciously—gender as an obstacle. Yet bias is real. The historical overview in the chapter "Historical roles" documented the challenges facing women in the higher education workplace. Female librarians face this reality every day, whether they acknowledge it or not. Therefore, gender as an obstacle balances between perceived and real.

The structure of an organization is more concrete as an obstacle. The librarians have the ability as blended professionals to maneuver between different social environments interior and exterior to the library, but organizational policies, practices, and procedures truly impede the librarians' effectiveness in their endeavors. The following chapter begins by analyzing the perceived complaints about time and money, transitions to a discussion on gender, and then concludes with an analysis of the organizational complications and impediments that act as a definitive hindrance to the librarian role.

7.1 Time and money

The absence of time to complete their required duties as blended professionals and a lack of funding or compensation to undertake said activities arose frequently during the course of the interviews. Of the concerns raised by the librarians regarding the obstacles to their professional development, time and money seemed to be the most straightforward to address in a reasonable discussion because the limitations they produce in this particular environment are artificial in creation. Time and compensation may be limited for the academic librarians of St. Jerome. However, their situation is not terrible, especially when compared to the tenure-track faculty (or librarians in over settings); still, the librarians think that it is, and this generates an artificial obstacle.

7.1.1 Time

Time was overwhelmingly cited as an obstacle to the professional success. However, the activities of the librarians at St. Jerome must be considered prior to making an assessment on demands on their time. Bridget defines their role as "reference, instruction, collection development, [and] outreach." Since the administration is also emphasizing research, that enterprise becomes another facet of their position.

The fact that the administration is promoting academic professionalism creates a shift in the librarians' initial role at St. Jerome. "The outputs librarians are measuring are not directly associated with specific practices that lead to improved lives for the people we serve. If we cannot make that connection, we have no way of knowing how well we are doing our jobs" (Bonfield, 2014). The librarians at St. Jerome were hired to provide reference services to the university community. Publication was not significant in this task, despite the current interpretation of the Librarians' Handbook by the present administration. The standard duties of the librarians have remained similar (reference desk shifts, individual consultations, instruction, collection development, etc.).

> Valeria: The idea that you could ask a librarian that's responsible for a collection, a service desk, a building that may be open 24 hours a day (which it is at most libraries these days) and to ask them to publish in the same way in which you would ask someone on a 9-month appointment. That doesn't make sense.

The added expectation of research requires supplementary time for such productivity, which was something often cited as an obstacle to professional success because they are still expected to perform the outreach required by a blended professional, but the added job requirements limit that ability.

The librarians at St. Jerome have the opportunity to apply for up to 10 days of research leave per year. However, even when they receive the additional leave, they have difficulty scheduling absences from their desks.

> Lucy: I've got research leave but I can't figure out when to take it because when you get back you have all these things, you know, that...especially when faculty are often building their courses during the summer for fall or spring delivery. Luckily I just got a new staff person, but somebody has to train him. I can't just go on leave for a week when he's new so it's tricky because the research leave is supposed to be the way to solve this but no one covers your responsibilities when you're on research leave.

Clearly, some librarians think that research time is hard to obtain. The traditional time for research is often during the summer. However, the American Library Association's Annual Conference is always scheduled at the end of June, a few weeks after the spring semester ends. This allows the librarians to make travel plans and last minute research adjustments if they are presenting at that conference. Marketing and preparation for outreach also takes up a considerable amount of time in the summer, as librarians attend orientations multiple times per week for most of June, July, and August. There are other ad hoc issues, such as assisting faculty in their development of course reserve materials and preparing online tutorials and webinars for the upcoming semester. In short, summer is already a demanding time for the librarians at St. Jerome.

Even so, it is difficult to quantify the librarians' duties and time management. Again, it *appears* to be less than what is expected by the tenure-track faculty.

> Researcher: In terms of time, do you think the amount of time that's expected for a librarian is similar to what's expected for your [academic discipline's] field?
> Sofia: [laughter].
> Researcher: Okay.
> Sofia: No. [laughter] Not even close.

Consider first instruction. Tenure-track faculty instruction is more time-consuming and substantive than all manner of instruction taught by academic librarians, particularly at St. Jerome. Susanna relates:

> *The difference is that I don't do as much [work as tenure-track]. My sessions are only 30 minutes long and they don't happen very often. I feel like they spend a lot more time and effort figuring out and organizing how they're going to set up the session, how they're going to set up their courses, their syllabi, and things like that. Whereas it takes me maybe a couple hours to figure out a lesson plan for an instruction session.*

The differences exist for varied reasons. First, the resources and generic information covered for the librarian instruction sessions rarely change. The librarian will demonstrate usage of the resources available to the students, specifically library catalog(s), periodical database, electronic journals, research portals, and material acquisition. This formulaic aspect of the instruction means that a librarian will not have to spend an inordinate amount of time preparing for each individual class.

One librarian estimated that she taught 30 classes in a semester, which could include 20 min to 3 hour sessions. This librarian was in the top three librarians at St. Jerome in terms of courses taught. Therefore, her in-class instruction time was significantly higher than some of her peers. For an estimate, let us say that the average class length for this librarian was 1.5 hours. If the librarian spent 1 hour preparing for each of those classes, this would equate to 75 hours a semester spent in the classroom teaching ((30 classes × 1.5 hours class time) + 30 hours preparation time).

In contrast, consider for example an instructor teaching Western Political Theory as a seminar that meets weekly for 3 hours. The material for each course changes as the course topically progresses. One week may be spent reading Machiavelli, whereas the following week, Rousseau may be the focus of discussion. This necessitates continual preparation. In fact, the American Faculty Association (AFA) estimates that an instructor should prepare 2–4 hours per 1 hour of class time taught (American Faculty Association, 2012). As Irene succinctly says: "Yes, I may do instruction but in a whole year I may teach the same class 44 times whereas the instructor is teaching three classes every semester, so the preps are different." Therefore, for a 15 week seminar course, that equates to between 135 and 225 hours a semester devoted to classroom teaching (Classroom Time (1 class × (15 weeks × 3 hours)) + Preparation Time ((1 class × (15 weeks × 3 hours)) × 2 (or 4)). If the faculty member is teaching two or more classes, then that time is doubled or tripled.

Even if one considers the reference consultation time into the total instruction statistics, the librarian time spent teaching still falls short of the tenure-track faculty. The librarians at Alexander VI Library average about 30 consultations per semester. If a generous estimate of 1 hour per consultation and a very generous 1 hour of preparation time is allotted, then the librarians spend 60 additional hours per semester in this instructional capacity. This amounts to 135 hours of librarian instruction time per semester (75 classroom instruction hours + 60 consultation hours). If a tenure-track faculty is teaching three classes in a semester, then they will devote to instruction between 270 and 540 hours based on AFA estimates. Time-wise, library instruction and tenure-track instruction are two different animals.

However, reference and instruction are the only two of those activities to which a reasonable calculation of time may be applied. For those two activities, they are in a fixed location for a specific amount of time. In contrast, librarians might schedule time for collection development or outreach, but the productivity of the time spent (books purchased and appointments scheduled) does not necessarily reflect the time and effort placed into the enterprise.

Research is the most nebulous of the activities. Collecting relevant materials for a literature review constitutes research, and the time spent could vary, depending upon the difficulty of the process of acquiring those materials. Organization, composition, and editing of research articles and writing varies depending upon the individual. Therefore, it is difficult to effectively estimate the amount of time librarians actually spend on their daily research activities aside from counting the number of citations listed in the quarterly *University Librarian's Newsletter*. In 2013, the liaison librarians in the Alexander VI Library collectively published two articles.

Many of the librarians telework, either on a scheduled day or unplanned, based upon the need for them to be physically present on campus. There has been research that suggests that teleworking increases productivity by eliminating in-office distractions (Manley, 2002; Pace, 2004) and aids in the retention of staff (Smith & Van Dyke, 2008). The potential for distraction might be higher than that for the tenure-track, given their office arrangements. A tenure-track faculty member may shut their office door for privacy; the same level of seclusion is difficult in a "cube-farm." Therefore, teleworking does make logistical sense.

Conversely, teleworking might be less successful in developing staff relationships (Fay & Kline, 2011), and attitude toward the job directly influences productivity (Neufeld & Fang, 2005). "The common fear among…the managers is that without the vigilant eye of a supervisor or the snoopy gaze of a coworker, what typical employee is not going to resist the temptation to sleep late, watch television, take naps, snack often, and quit early" (Manley, 2002, p. 124). It was difficult to gauge the productivity of the librarians at St. Jerome who telework, especially from where I worked. While the librarians might send productivity reports to their supervisors, these were not public documents.

I also am not a proponent of teleworking because I have seen and heard of it being abused in a variety of settings. For example, in my current job, there is one (nonlibrarian) staff member who wears a Fitbit fitness tracker that counts the number of steps that she makes in a day. The device is linked to other members at the university who also use the tool so that friends and colleagues might see each other's numbers and collectively motivate themselves. The staff member routinely surpasses step numbers impossible to achieve in a small house while "teleworking." In short, there is no chance that this person actually is working from home. Given that this is a somewhat biased example, a wholesale damnation of the teleworkers seems a bit out of place.

However, specific to my own experience within libraries, I have worked in a number of organizations where librarians teleworked. In one instance, the librarians would telework in order to work on their research articles, yet no articles would ever materialize and be published. It is possible that publishable research was being conducted by the librarians and it simply never made it past the peer review process, but when telework was mentioned, there was a roll of the eyes from those librarians' colleagues that indicated the telework did not constitute substantial effort by those using that work option.

Admittedly though, the illustration of these stories in combination with my own informal observations of the librarians at St. Jerome biases my opinions, particularly concerning usage of time. I am sure that some or all of you might relate. For every instance that I saw a librarian working late or on a weekend, there is another where I walked past a cubicle and noticed mahjong being played on a desktop computer.

In order to obtain an improved, more impartial understanding of how the librarians were utilizing their time, I examined the librarians' schedules for the week of Monday, September 22, 2014, through Friday, September 26, 2014. I then compiled and tabulated the activities. The results are displayed in Table 7.1.

Given the fluctuation in instruction assignments, the week was chosen at random during the fall semester. The statistic that stands out is the final one: miscellaneous/unscheduled. The assumption from the researcher was that the librarians each worked a 40 hour week during the examined time. As seen in Table 7.1, only about 30% of their days were formally scheduled; the rest of the time was open. Perhaps during that 70% of their time, a random student or faculty member visited for a research consultation, but it represents a lot of unplanned time from individuals who stated that they had little time to spare. Conceivably, a more in-depth analysis of the librarians' usage and scheduling of their time, either by the individual librarians or management, might illuminate more open time to engage in activities such as research.

In the end, how one views their role may do more to influence their productivity than any external factor. The perception of the impediment creates an artificial boundary that renders blended professional activity less effective. For example, many librarians view the librarian role as subservient to the faculty place in the campus hierarchy. As Laura states: "Yes, I am definitely a support role to tenured faculty…I really do see it as a support role and not on the same level." There is nothing that legislates this as

Table 7.1 The percentages here represent the amount of a 40-hour workweek spent in the described activity

Activity	Time spent in activity (%)
Reference desk	8.5
IM	1.4
Teaching in library classroom	2.8
Teaching in nonlibrary classroom	1.6
Office hours	3.9
Training staff	0.7
Professional development	3.2
Meetings	7.5
Miscellaneous/unscheduled	70.4

fact. Yet the librarians accept this position because they believe it to be accurate. This mentality creates the belief that the librarians should not perform similar activities, regardless of ability, as faculty because it is not their perceived role in the university. This, in turn, limits the librarians' success as blended professionals because it constructs boundaries on their sphere of influence. A lack of time is ultimately just an excuse that manifests from this accepted perception.

The academic librarians, once they become fully cognizant of the situation, have the choice of whether to let a perceived lack of time undermine their professional successes. On the other hand, success, as Sofia relates, can be an alternative choice.

> Sofia: So the idea that time...do you have time? Bullshit. If you have to do it, you do it and that's it. But for me, the thing that made me so flip was I didn't have to do this. Why do I have to do this? I didn't need a second degree. I could have been a stay at home mom. I choose to do these things. I don't have to publish articles in my field. I don't have to see if I can get my book out. I don't really have to do ALA stuff. I could do something much more micro. I choose to do all of it. I also exercise. Regularly. And have hobbies that aren't exercise and do those. How? Because my day has 48 hours, thank you. I actually live in a space time warp thing.
> Researcher: I understand.
> Sofia: Yeah. So the time thing, I get...and especially because of the pressures on research and instruction faculty. Our job is not even remotely equivalent. Not even remotely equivalent.

Clearly the academic librarians at St. Jerome do not expect to produce at the level of their tenure-track counterparts. If librarians had a better holistic perspective of how their counterparts spend their time, then the librarians' perspective might be altered. Acknowledging this notion will help break down a wall and amplify the blended abilities of the academic librarians within the St. Jerome community.

7.1.2 Money

Financial concerns occasionally entered into the organizational level, such as with insufficient funds to order proper marketing and outreach materials. However, the lack of personal financial backing to do their strongly encouraged professional academic pursuits was an oft-cited complaint of the librarians. "Go publish. Go present. Here's 50% of what you need." It led to some amusing conversation.

> Susanna: Money is the most significant obstacle. Because everything else is pretty easy, especially if you're thinking of professional development terms for a librarian. As long as you can afford it, you're golden. But...
> Researcher: Can you afford to go to as many conferences as you want?
> Susanna: Noooo...no I can't. I get really...I get...this is really sad and pathetic. I convince my parents sometimes to go on vacation in the towns where my conferences will be as a way to save money so that I don't have to pay for housing.

Many librarians extended their conference travel into vacations. As Julia states: "There's nothing wrong with going on a conference and building in a little vacation but it still costs a lot of money to essentially go somewhere where I wouldn't choose to go." Strategically planning conference attendance became a prime tactic. Attending a conference in Las Vegas, NV, during the middle of the summer or Boston, MA, during the dead of winter were not popular choices but instead necessities due to the scheduling of national conferences.

Admittedly though, there are some concerns with the way that money is allotted for travel. Due to preferences from the administration, librarians stated that they generally would receive more money to attend a disciplinary conference instead of a library conference. As well, more money was allotted to present at a conference than to just attend. The distance of travel also influenced compensation. Aside from that, there did not appear to be any standard disbursement of travel monies. Therefore, an academic librarian presenting a paper at a disciplinary conference would stand a greater chance of receiving significantly more financial backing than the librarian merely attending a library-oriented conference across the country.

This manner of money distribution placed the librarians in a bind concerning academic professionalism. Most of the librarians did not have the academic aptitude to present at disciplinary conferences. If the librarians conducted research, then it most likely would be offered at a library conference, thereby garnering lower financial support. In this way, the deck was stacked against librarians being afforded maximum funding for professional development in the form of conference attendance, much to the librarians' chagrin.

The assumption from many of the librarians was that the expectation for publications and presentations from the administration was not matched with monetary compensation.

> Lucy: So that can be really challenging because how can you ask people to present and to further themselves professionally by going to conference and presenting and you're not going to pay them and [what] they make... isn't bad depending on where you live, but isn't like a lot.
> Researcher: It's less than tenure-track faculty?
> Lucy: Yes, definitely. No matter where you live it's less than tenured faculty.

In reality, however, there is not a significant variance. The Bureau of Labor Statistics listed the median compensation for postsecondary instructors in the United States as $68,970 (Bureau of Labor Statistics, 2014). A whistleblower website in the state that St. Jerome operates lists the salaries of all state employees. In 2011, the average salary of the librarians interviewed for this project was $62,057. Therefore, the academic librarians at St. Jerome were only making about 10% less than their tenure-track counterparts.

What about travel stipends? The travel allotment from the university forces librarians to make decisions about which conferences to attend. As Lucy states: "We get travel but the way it's done here we never get the full amount. And if you ask for two things, you get each partially, but very partially so that you almost have to decide which one to take." However, this assumes that the tenure-track faculty receive a significant amount of travel money. At St. Jerome, the maximum award for conference travel for tenure-track faculty is $500, although some individual departments offset the cost with additional financial support. It is similar at their peer institutions. For example, at Florida State University, the maximum is $1500. It should be noted that the librarians at St. Jerome are strongly encouraged to present and publish, but it is not required. Tenure-track does not have the luxury of choice in this regard.

Consider as well the cost of investment. The National Center for Educational Statistics lists the average tuition and required fees at public institutions in the 2009–10 academic year as $8763; at private institutions, the tuition and fees were $20,368 (National Center for Education Statistics, 2011). It takes ~2 years of full-time study to complete the credits required for the library science master's degree. A PhD or equivalent doctorate needed for tenure-track employment takes at least 5 years. Two years at a public institution would run a student $17,526; 5 years in the public system would cost $43,815. If the doctoral student is not being subsidized through a research stipend, then they will have many more loans to pay upon completion of their program, which will also occur 3 or more years after a librarian may have entered the workforce.

Ultimately, compensation should not be perceived as a limitation to a blended professional role or professional development, as there are low-cost means to build legitimacies and other facets of the model. For example, many academic journals require little or no publication fee. The lack of produced research, for any of the variety of previously mentioned reasons, is the true obstacle to professional success in this context, not the lack of compensation.

7.1.3 Time and money summary

Tenure-track faculty might not have a substantially better financial situation than their librarian counterparts. Based upon the estimated time spent during instruction covered earlier, they almost certainly have less time. Many of the perceptions of the librarians appear based upon assumption, particularly that tenure-track faculty are significantly more compensated. It might not be fully appreciated because the librarians are being asked to perform more tenure-track associated duties in addition to their blended professional. However, similar to the issues regarding a lack of time, a better understanding of the totality of the financial situation at the university might demonstrate that money is not as unique a concern to the academic librarians as they might believe. Neither concern realistically should obstruct the academic librarians' roles as blended professionals. Addressing these perceptions either individually or through the counsel of management may alleviate some of the artificially created boundaries impeding the academic librarians' blended professional role and career development.

7.2 Gender

Gender is not a consideration featured in the blended professional model. This might be in part due to the fact that a woman's role in the working world has evolved past the expected jobs of teacher or nurse (Boyd, 2009). No one is suggesting that there is equality in the workplace. Even if I believed that there was equal footing in the profession, which I most assuredly do not, as a reasonable, male researcher, I do not believe that I could make an effective argument that would even be considered as valid.

Yet Whitchurch considered the model in an age when gender did not have as severe of a restriction on professional opportunities. Additionally, the questions fielded by the librarians during the interviews pertained to the blended professional model's characteristics and generic professional roles and challenges. During the course of the interviews, I never asked a question along the lines of "How does being female affect your professional opportunities?"

Still, during the proposal stage of this project and prior to the start of the interviews, the expectation was that gender identity would come up in the course of conversation much more frequently than it did. It is possible that my identity as a male researcher made the topic less comfortable for the female interviewees to talk about. As well, while age of the interviewees was not asked, for the most part, the more veteran librarians voiced their concerns about gender more regularly than their younger counterparts. Yet, during the analysis of the interviews, I did begin to understand that some of the conversations regarding gender manifested in different, less explicit forms, all of which created additional professional hurdles for a blended professional to clear.

The librarians already occupied a unique third space as blended professionals at St. Jerome. Their place within the structure of the university was determined by their respective blended professional abilities, and these relative attributes, in combination with perceived limitations, provided the boundaries of the libraries blended role. The additional consideration of gender placed an extra fence around their sphere of influence.

7.2.1 Age and appearance

Some aspects of an individual's identity may be acknowledged and potentially modified if it is deemed negative or a severe inhibition. For example, the predilection toward introversion previously mentioned might be viewed as a limitation due to the restriction on the ability of the librarian to market their resources. One librarian offered the suggestion of putting small headshots on the library marketing materials sent out to the various departments. This way, the faculty and students of the department will have a means to attach a name and a face, even without the need for the sometimes difficult social interaction.

I made this suggestion to some of the librarians, and it was met with mixed reactions. My immediate assumption was that those librarians who objected to the idea were making the decision due to vanity reasons, which I had witnessed in practice before. For instance, as opposed to university-supplied headshots, some librarians represented themselves as caricatures or other fabricated images on their personal webpages. This is a normal practice, observed all the time in the form of social media avatars. However, another librarian pointed out that they felt uncomfortable having their picture available due to the risk of unwanted, potentially dangerous attention. There was a history of public patronage bothering some of the librarians in some of the libraries at St. Jerome. This is not something that I would have considered as a male, but it is legitimately a concern for the female librarians.

Other aspects are more ingrained within the individual, such as of the gender identity of the person. For some of the interviews, gender was not specifically mentioned as an obstacle to professional success, but it appeared unspoken in other conversations. For example, age and appearance seemed to emerge in conversations contextually associated with gender.

Susanna stated that she was more comfortable interacting within the student crowd as opposed to faculty. "I feel intimidated by faculty, whereas with students…I guess I see myself as a student more often than not. I feel more comfortable working in that kind of environment." Susanna is still a student and seemingly never transitioned from that role to an equal collaborator with faculty members. At the same time though, she is also one of the youngest librarians interviewed. Age also was perceived as a negative in advancement.

> Gwen: As someone who's younger in this profession…I feel like it's not so easy. I had a lot of friends that really wanted to work in academic libraries and couldn't get those jobs and so work in public libraries and that's kind of where they are now. So I feel like the profession is skewed against younger people. I know for a fact [that it is] in this particular organization.

It must be acknowledged that there is a notable dearth of open positions. Three of the four upper management positions at St. Jerome (to which Gwen might advance) have remained filled by the same individual for at least 15 years. The connection with gender and Gwen's perceptions arises from the social dynamic in management mentioned by another colleague.

> Lucy: And it was hard too because some of the librarians that worked with me ended up working for me and that was hard because some of them were males my father's age. And it was very hard to be their supervisor because they had no respect for…you know, "You're young. And you're female. Why should I listen to you?" So I'm sure that it happens in almost every field, but it's almost ironic that it happens in the librarian field because we're female dominated. This should be no surprise to males that become librarians that they will have a female boss at one point.

A portion of that experience derives from age and learning to manage one's elders in the workplace. However, the gender of the subordinate employees might not be considered if the manager was male.

All the same, appearance does affect professional perceptions. Based upon her appearance, one librarian received a unique welcoming into an instruction session.

> Lucy: [In my previous job] there were a lot more males. I was the business librarian and it was hard at first. When I first started, a lot of the business faculty had been there for a long time. I called them the "Gray Beards" because I couldn't tell them apart. They all wore gray beards, I swear. And they were all middle-aged, white men and it was very homogenous. And they did not want to have much to do with me.

I probably shouldn't tell you this, but I went into a class once and the professor was like "Little girl? Little girl? I think you're in the wrong room." Yes, I did look young for my 28 years, but it's mortifying being told that in front of a class when you're coming in to do instruction for his class.

Even physical presence during presentations may put women in a precarious position. Taller women make more money (Sinberg, 2009), as do individuals with lower voices (van Vugt, 2013).

> Adele: Now that I'm thinking about it the majority of places that I've been the chairs have been male.
> Researcher: Why do you think?
> Adele: Because we live in a sexist society? Yeah, I would say it probably relates to the gender bias anyway. And sometimes I'm guilty of it too, you know, when I talk about the authority that goes along with the male voice versus the female voice. Just thinking of the Chronicle of Higher Education article that came out years ago where they were talking about women with deeper voices earn more respect just naturally in the classroom or in the administrative setting.
> Researcher: It could be appearances too. I mean, if both you and I are dressed in...we're standing in front of a room. I'm a lot taller than you. My voice is a lot deeper.
> Adele: It is and I kick myself too, but I'm guilty of it on occasion too. I think there is something engrained either if you want to say it's socialized or learned behavior. There is something to that I think.

Appearance can almost be a double-edged sword for women in the workplace. Studies have shown that if they gain weight, they will make less money (Sinberg, 2009). "Being very attractive can especially make it difficult when it comes to co-workers who might have assumptions as to how you got your job, which means that you have to work even harder to prove yourself" (Madell, 2014). One case cited a Harvard librarian who was passed over for 13 promotions on the grounds that she was too pretty (Nicole, Sheppard, Irish, & Spence, 2006).

Being male, it is difficult for me as the researcher to fully grasp the experiences and perceptions of the interviewed librarians regarding gender, age, and appearance, especially when the findings were connected sometimes through my own interpretations of unspoken intimations. All four who specified those three factors (gender, age, and appearance) are under 40 years of age. Without having a qualified rating system, the women all look their ages. It seemed that the confluence of their age and gender inhibited their perceived values in the workplace. Since they *thought* that it affected their production, so it, in fact, actually did.

Additionally, the phrase "I probably shouldn't tell you this but..." came up in various forms during a lot of conversations. It was as if they felt like they were gossiping, and that was somehow wrong because female gossipers have a negative stigma in the workplace (Farley, Timme, & Hart, 2010). That conceptualization itself is a form of gender bias; in casual conversations, men "converse," whereas women are said to "gossip." Lucy defined the social interactions as potentially malevolent.

> *I think as far as gender goes the department that I work with that are more mixed seem to work better. And that seems like a very un-feminist thing to say, but it seems like if there's more balance between men and women in the library there's better results. My experience has been that reference departments that were exclusively or almost exclusively female were very catty. So there's that...at least in the profession there's that reputation, you know?*

Gossip has been suggested as a customary tool of female aggression in social settings (McAndrew, 2014; Miller-Ott & Kelly, 2013). The librarians at Alexander VI were described as very "clique-y" in a negative connotation by their counterparts at the other libraries. According to the most senior members of the staff there, the department always has had a female majority. It is difficult to say how much gender has an influence on this reputation, although colleagues at other libraries apparently believe that it contributes to the atmosphere there.

7.2.2 Ingrained learning

Characteristics may be ingrained and learned in addition to being perceived both professionally and through formal educational experiences. For example, to many faculty, the role that the librarians have is of a glorified graduate assistant.

> Jessica: As we were being taught by our senior librarians…about how to be a liaison, how to act…we, the librarians, were supposed to be [the faculty's] academic handmaidens. "Anything we can do for you. Anything we can get."

Compound this ideology with the traditional view of women in service (Johnson, 2013; Wilson, 2014) within the workforce, and the librarians are almost automatically placed in a tenuous spot.

> Laura: I know that there's a role that we can serve but I really do see it as a support role and not on the same level.
> Researcher: Okay, so more hierarchical?
> Laura: Yeah. And that's gender related by the way.
> Researcher: Why would you say that?
> Laura: Because, you know, unfortunately the idea of woman being of service and being in a service profession.

This data is significant because it seemingly indicates that gender influence on place in this context reemphasizes the service focus and resulting blended professional sphere of influence described by the librarians at St. Jerome. In this professional case, the limitations created by external factors and interpretations of the librarians' role by the faculty impede their blended professional influence and confine their third space. This ideology again is perceived and not legislated. In fact, the administration is pushing collaboration with faculty, which is antithetical to the handmaiden role, since it promotes partnership and not subordination.

Educational opportunities also are often divided from an early age. As a consequence of sex differentiation, "the girl…does not learn to assert herself, has not studied science, technology and 'heavy' craft [and]…is primarily handicapped in the [labor] market, because she lacks the skills which lead to higher-paying jobs" (Delamont, 1990, p. 4). These behaviors begin in grade school and then persist within higher education (Huhman, 2012). Interactions between the librarians and STEM (Science, Technology, Engineering, and Mathematics) faculty often perpetuated a service or subordinate role.

> Jessica: There's still a lot of weird gender stuff outside the libraries. When I [worked with STEM faculty], you know, I think there was a weird gender thing going on with the male

faculty members. "Oh, you. You do my work for me." I've had strange expectations from library users about what we would do for them. Every so often, it's a little weird.

Due to a lack of numbers, women in the sciences do not often have a position of authority. In 2010, women represented only 28% of the workforce in engineering and the sciences (Neuhauser, 2014). There is a notion of gender equality in education that attempts to provide equal footing for women and men from an early age.

> *Gender equality in education not only implies that both girls and boys have equal access to schooling, but also that the process of education provides all girls and boys with a range of equal opportunities and experiences for expanding their capacities to the fullest potentials in a manner that they are able to contribute to the making of a just, responsible and compassionate society.*
>
> *Jha, Page, and Raynor (2009, p. 1)*

At this point though, statistics do not support the realization of an equal educational system. Social constructs preserve existing constructs in the education field.

Researcher: A lot of them have issues with the self-marketing and that inhibits their ability to reach members of the community. Do you feel that's accurate?
Valeria: I don't feel that's accurate for me but I do feel that it can be accurate. One of the interesting things you talk about is how many women there are. Women by rule are not taught to promote themselves, to "lean in" as we like to talk about it in the current vernacular. The other thing you have to realize is that a lot of the people who go into the field…and again I'm generalizing…is that it's a helping profession and you want to help people and that doesn't mean putting yourself first. Helping, but staying behind.
Researcher: Serving?
Valeria: Serving, you know? I think that's a key difference.

This conclusion is noteworthy because it suggests that the passive or servant behaviors of some of the librarians discussed in the context of their roles and the perceptions of their positions are learned. That makes change very difficult and affects the flexibility required to maximize the blended professional role. At the same time, it is possible that awareness of these issues may provide opportunity to manage them so that they do not inhibit professional growth.

7.2.3 Family

Women in the household raising children while the husband works is not a worldwide gender role. "On the whole people who have studied anthropology tend to incline toward the idea that gender is socially created, because every culture discovered across the world has such different norms for 'masculinity' and 'femininity.' Childrearing is *not* a women's task universally" (Delamont, 1990, p. 8). Yet it does persist in the psyche of women.

For instance, when my wife and I were discussing the prospects of having children, she suggested that she might stay home to raise any kids while I worked. The issue with that scenario is that in her field my wife made substantially more money than me. She still earns more now, even with me holding a doctoral degree, and her career trajectory is probably on a higher arc than my own. If either of us were to be stay-at-home parents, then economically it would make sense for me to put my career aside. Yet due to conventional beliefs, my wife immediately thought that she should make that sacrifice. The term "sacrifice" also is apt because such familial responsibilities would hamper promotional opportunities in the workplace, and particularly in higher education as the literature reviewed in the chapter "Historical roles" suggested. Indeed, some of the librarians interviewed here connected their limitations to gender roles in the household.

Bridget directly related the lack of funding for conferences and salary to the fact that administration expected the female librarian to be the secondary breadwinner in the household.

> Bridget: Professional development funding is very restrictive and this is a common theme among librarians because they are not the main breadwinners. So my professional travel is funded on the fact that my partner makes a good salary and says, "If you want to do this, don't worry about it." Or we go together.
> Researcher: So it's almost like you're saying...the administrative views it as a gender...
> Bridget: No, what I'm saying is that we're primarily a female-dominated profession...we are able to live a comfortable lifestyle...and define that however you wish...but because our partners can support us. And our partners can support our professional development activities. If I didn't have [my partner] I would be making a lot of difficult choices. I would not be going to mid-winter and annual. I would have to turn down committee appointments because I could not meet the committee requirements.

Again, money is a concern for the librarians, but the connection between compensation and gender is something wholly different. Here it constructs a professional limitation based upon the expectation that a (presumably male) spouse would support professional academic endeavors. The logic in Bridget's presumption is not flawless because one wonders then if compensation would rise if the female librarian were single or in a same-sex partnership. The answer is likely no, since complaints about money were uniform in spite of mentioned relationship statuses. At the same time, though, it raises a concern because the perception of the librarian is that she is compensated for what she is, as opposed to what she has done or might do professionally. Bridget, in essence, thinks that she is paid less because she is female with a significant other.

Other librarians specifically cited their familial roles as limitations in the professional aspirations. Catherine mentioned a lack of professional development opportunities at St. Jerome due to a contentious relationship with a male supervisor. She believes that her only hope for advancement will come elsewhere. Accordingly, she has pursued options.

> Catherine: For me, my personal life...I don't want to say kept me here, but has influenced my not going anywhere else. My kids are in absolutely in great schools [here] with opportunities their cousins don't have, whether they're in Florida or Ohio or Southern Virginia. They don't have that. So as a mom and a parent and a spouse as well as other things in my life...you make decisions.
> Researcher: Do you think if you went elsewhere your opportunities would be better, equal, or worse?

Catherine: I interviewed about a year ago. I was offered a library director position. It was not a good fit for my family. It was a fabulous opportunity for my career. Yeah. I know I could. I'm quite sure there are a lot of things out there that I can do but I chose to have a husband. I chose to have two kids. And on balance I would say that take more priority than my career. And I had my career for many years before I had them so I knew what I was headed to with what I was investing in my career. For me, I'll get there. But these folks in my life need me to be where I'm at right now, so that's...yes. I know I could.

Despite a belief in her own abilities, Catherine seemingly defaulted to the familial role. Yet another librarian described balancing multiple jobs (and roles) in order to support her family.

I'm trying to figure out...it's entirely possible that this job that I have right here...if I do this and [a second job], I can float financially. Sleep is for the weak. I can manage. I can see my kids just enough to qualify as a parent. I could be at a sweet spot where I'm balancing two roles. I could stay here. Just saying. It's a possibility. I'm not sure. We'll see...maybe sleep is just for the weak.

Parts of that interview were difficult to conduct because I could sense that the librarian was "burning out" from the dual stresses of professional and family life. Overall, there was no indication that the librarians who mentioned family regretted their decisions, but it was clear that limitations arising from family obligations and their personal roles therein made those particular librarians' ability to negotiate professional opportunities much more challenging. With the increasing expectations of the female librarians in the workforce, it remains difficult for women, despite improvements in work-life balance, to have an equal work-life balance (Slaughter, 2012).

7.2.4 Gender summary

The mention of gender with respect to the blended professional is in itself significant. The model is based upon how one views their role as a professional. The construction of this perception is personal and gender—in this case—appears in some ways to influence the academic librarians' perception of their role at St. Jerome.

Again, from my male perspective, the obstacles that gender may present to a blended professional librarian are difficult to assess. It is clear though that perceptions of gender identity present inherent difficulties for the female librarians to overcome. At the same time, changes in attitudes and beliefs of the individual librarians will only address so much of the problem. At St. Jerome, it is systemic.

A librarian mentioned that she spoke with the male library director about her forthcoming marriage. The director asked questions particularly concerned about the financial stability of the groom, which the librarian took mean that the male library director was questioning whether or not she would leave the library job if the librarian's fiancé found other employment. Similar questioning arose when she became pregnant. A colleague echoed similar frustration.

Susanna: I feel it's always easier for promotion for the male librarians than it is for the female librarians. Mainly just because...it seems like to me there's this feeling like "Oh

God, once she gets married just write them off. They're here in body, but…they're going to be gone soon. Let's not bother with the continuing on with their training or anything like that." That's honestly how it always feels. It feels like you get fewer opportunities to do things.

This is the atmosphere—a uniquely gendered third space—in which the librarians are attempting to advance their careers. It is definitely a challenge, since it creates limitations to the effectiveness of the female librarians in the blended professional role because in addition to the already constructed boundaries of influence, gender also generates challenges. Change will come slowly, as evolution requires that society and perceptions change.

7.3 Organization

In terms of organization, the libraries operate in an academic caste system that previously was mentioned. It is what Bolman and Deal (2003) refer to as a "structural frame." In essence, the organization is configured of "a small number of authority figures at the top and a much larger number of grunts at the bottom" (Bolman & Deal, 2003, p. 41). In smaller settings, there are political interactions with individuals playing people and resources off of each other for personal gain. There is also symbolism with St. Jerome colors around the library and on print and electronic materials circulated within the community.

However, no one is citing the key to their day as demonstrating the St. Jerome spirit and fulfilling the mission of the university. Instead, the librarians tend to perceive the hierarchical levels within the system. With respect to the blended professional model, the regimenting of their organization creates institutionally constructed restrictions that inhibit the librarians' ability to truly blend their role and modify their third space. The genuine limitations of their skills and abilities within the blended professional role, the perceived concerns about time and money, and the additional consideration of gender all are compounded by the structure of the organization and the problems therein.

Even as blended professionals, the librarians are, in effect, boxed in. Faulty communication, lack of professional mobility, overly structured job descriptions, and poor use of talent within the organization all hinder the librarians' professional development. These factors perpetuate the limits on the third space that they might extend by creating impediments to personal growth, outreach, and success.

7.3.1 Communication

Active communication is an important element in the blended professional role because it facilitates contact and collaboration. There was mention of some typical organizational concerns during the interviews, particularly dealing with vertical communication. On a personal level, there was evidence of poor communication with respect to the manager–employee relationship. One manager cited her managerial skill and acumen as her best asset on the job. Yet a librarian on her staff cited that manager as the key obstacle to her own professional development. Clearly something was amiss in that relationship.

Larger organization-wide communication concerns also emerged in the interviews. Bolman and Deal (2003, p. 46) suggest that the structural organizational approach exists to act as "a blueprint for formal expectations and exchanges among internal players and external constituencies." When this system fails, obstacles appear. Recall, for instance, the librarians' uncertainty on the expectations for promotion. In addition, many changes occur in the system without clear written or verbal communication, and this was cited as an obstacle.

> Researcher: So you're kind of being limited by…
> Irene: Administrative decisions that we were given no input in!

The most frequently mentioned during these interviews was the forthcoming change to some of the reference duties of the librarians. Basically, in order to encourage outreach, some of their reference desk duties are being eliminated. Given the discussion about introversion and outreach challenges, it is not surprising that this initiative has proved unpopular.

This is not to say that administration does not have the right or ability to make wholesale changes to the roles and duties of the workers. However, in cases of major change, it benefits the organization as a whole to have the ability to offer feedback or be "bought in" by managerial notice. Otherwise, conflict occurs, and the absence of bargaining promotes extended disputes (Bolman & Deal, 2003).

Helgesen (1995) argued that the hierarchical structure was created by a male-dominated leadership force. In more inclusive systems designed by women, "lines of communication were multiplicitous, open, and diffuse" (Helgesen, 1995, p. 10), often with a center-out instead of a top-down structure. This feedback is significant because it suggests that the librarians in their roles do not feel that they have open lines of communication with their superiors. Even if the communication is acceptable by traditional organizational standards, the librarians at St. Jerome perceive it to be a concern. Reorganizing communicational structures with this thought in mind might alleviate some of these concerns.

7.3.2 Recognition and advancement

It was previously mentioned that some librarians did not appreciate the push to produce professional academic works when the administration was not publishing in kind. That annoyance is compounded when the recognition offered those librarians who do engage in professional work falls short of their expectations. "One cause of disappointment is [the] failure to recognize that excellence requires much more than sermons from top management" (Bolman & Deal, 2003, p. 400). Congratulations on successful work can be very minimal.

> Adele: Maria and I were talking about the poster for ACRL (Association of College & Research Libraries) last year and the director had come in to ask her a question about something else. So Maria was showing him "Oh, Jessica and Adele are doing this poster…blah blah blah." No "That's great!" No "Congratulations!" His comment was "Oh, I hear those [posters] are really expensive."

Researcher: To make?
Adele: To buy. I'm just like "That's your feedback?!" And I just feel like in some ways it's very indicative of the problems here where they don't understand that this helps us…this gets us national attention. I do find that frustrating.

The project is precisely what the administration has been pushing—academic productivity recognized on the national level—yet the major expressed concern was cost to the department. This is not to say that there should be a party or the individual should receive a reward for every significant academic artifact that they produce. However, it is difficult to motivate employees to succeed when there is little to no acknowledgment.

An additional problem was the lack of advancement opportunity within the system. When asked about developing a new library, Susanna said:

> *I probably would promote myself because…the one thing that I really hate about libraries is that it's really hard to move up. It's almost impossible to find ways to promote yourself up a level. So I would just naturally throw myself up there. And I don't know if I'm ready to be a supervisor, but I'm going to promote myself to a higher level.*

Promotion is hard to gain and demonstrates a non-human resources organizational frame (Bolman & Deal, 2003). Successful companies recruit employees with pay and benefits. "To keep them, they protect jobs, promote from within, and give people a piece of the action" (Bolman & Deal, 2003, p. 137). That does not occur in this organization.

At St. Jerome, three of the four director level positions have been filled by the same (male) person for at least 15 years. The female in the fourth position recently replaced a (male) veteran of 14 years. Yet in order to be considered for management positions, librarians must have supervisory experience. Since most of the librarians do not have professional supervisory experience, the rare promotional opportunities are filled from outside the university.

The librarians understand this is the system in which they work, yet this working environment generates an issue with motivation. What is the incentive to push boundaries if there is not an opportunity for reward or advancement? Why push the third space boundaries for collaboration? This is the mindset that curtails the necessary outreach for a blended professional to be successful in their role.

7.3.3 Differentiation and integration

The academic librarians at St. Jerome are blended professionals. Unfortunately, due to organizational restrictions, many of their colleagues reside in more fixed roles. Bolman and Deal (2003, p. 49) specify two key elements of the organizational structure: "how to allocate work (differentiation) and how to coordinate roles and units once responsibilities have been parceled out (integration)." Feedback from the librarians interviewed suggests that St. Jerome has issues with both of these features. Productivity, morale, and the professional environment are impacted by the structural realities of the organizational system at St. Jerome.

First, differentiation is difficult in St. Jerome's system due to the distinctions between classified staff and the professional or administrative faculty. A general characteristic of these two roles is that classified staff tend not to have the MLS, whereas the faculty academically are trained and credentialed as librarians. There are levels of both forms of employee; the more advanced the rank, the more responsibilities allocated to that particular role. In theory, this should be successful because "clear, well-understood roles and relationships and adequate coordination are key to how well an organization performs" (Bolman & Deal, 2003, p. 44). At St. Jerome though, the limits on the duties are very strict because the responsibilities correspond to statewide classifications.

> Jessica: It gets into class differences more or less and...we actually lost...I don't know if you knew [a former classified staff member], but my understanding from hearsay is that...well we all knew that he did spreadsheets. The man was a wizard at spreadsheets. And he wanted to do more with the data but they would not give him a more professional role so he said, "I'm done. I'm done with stats. Someone else can deal with it" because he felt like he was doing more than what was required by the position and he was not being rewarded for it. And I can understand that.

If a worker exceeds the responsibilities outlined in their respective job description, then the state mandates that they should be compensated for the work. That becomes problematic when economic constraints make raises and reclassification of positions impossible. Work, therefore, at St. Jerome is differentiated between the ranks, but the ability to blend roles within the organizational structure is limited by the constraints of specific rankings.

The functionality of the roles, for the most part, is based upon skills and knowledge (Bolman & Deal, 2003). Each library has separate units, such as reference or circulation, that vary in size based upon the needs of that particular location with other factors, such as shift time or geography, playing lesser roles. This becomes awkward at St. Jerome because the integration of the skills of the classified workers sometimes intersect with those of the librarians.

> Jessica: I've been hearing a lot of bits and pieces from conferences and elsewhere where the role of librarians and the role of non-librarians is becoming a lot more fuzzy. I don't think that's necessarily a bad thing but part of me says "I went to library school, darn it!" I wouldn't have gone to library school if I hadn't had to. I only went because that's how you got a job, otherwise I would have never gone to library school. I'm not really sure that I can say that the MLS should be required. I feel like the fact that...I feel that the quote paraprofessional role and the librarian role...I'm not seeing a clear distinction these days.

Think back to the conversation on the quality of library school education. The degree did not so much legitimize the professional as much as it simply opened the door. The skills of the job are pragmatic and experiential, and therefore acquirable by staff performing the same duties as the librarians. "The concept of a non-MLS librarian may appear to demean the profession by suggesting the degree is not essential to being a librarian in the sense that the degree serves as a professional credential indicating mastery of theory and practice of librarianship" (Simpson, 2013, p. 2). The librarians do not appreciate the infringement upon their professional territory, especially when they are simultaneously vying for credibility and legitimacy around campus themselves.

Part of this hierarchical argument may be seen in the titles assigned to the classified staff in the libraries: paraprofessional. The term itself denotes assistance to the licensed professionals, which in this case are the librarians. Librarians can be keen to point out this difference in ability.

> Bridget: And I'm not…this is not an insult to the paraprofessionals at all because I think you know I think you guys are awesome…but I think there's…maybe I'm generalizing and maybe that's too much because I like to think of what I do on the reference desk. The student does not know the question they need to ask. But through my experience and my opportunities, I'm like "Oh, that's where you need to go."

At St. Jerome, paraprofessionals attached to liaison librarian departments were additionally labeled "librarian assistants" or "LAs," further creating a role distinction, which is not necessarily beneficial to the professional environment or productivity.

> Lucy: When it becomes a distinction I think it creates an atmosphere that's not good for anyone and I feel that distinction is definitely made more at Alexander VI then it is maybe at the other libraries. And truthfully a lot of our LAs or whatever we call them nowadays have higher degrees or are pursuing higher degrees or have more academic research than the librarians get, so I mean, yeah. I think the reason we're so hung up on the MLS is there has been pockets where that…idea that an MLS is even necessary is being challenged.

In the quotes presented by Bridget and Lucy you see some of the hegemonic wording that I mentioned in the chapter "Introduction", specifically in this context "paraprofessional" and "LA," or "librarian assistant." This is where my connections to the higher education community at St. Jerome aid in the analysis, as the following perspective was relayed to me by several tenure-track faculty members at the institution during informal conversations.

Whether purposeful or not, this type of terminology structurally confines the classified staff to a rank lower than the librarians. That is fine and natural, since within a structural frame, there are ranks and levels. The problem with this approach, aside from its impact on collaboration and collegiality, is that it simultaneously lowers the standing of the librarians as well, since many of the classified staff have similar functional roles in terms of instruction, reference service, and other duties to those of the academic librarians.

The external academic faculty are very ignorant to the practical and theoretical duties of the academic librarians. In the following chapter, it will be suggested that the library administration might alleviate some of the misconceptions associated with the librarian role by providing better information and high-level outreach to the stakeholders external to the library. In the current state, though, the appearance from the vantage point of the faculty is that the classified staff perform similar duties as the academic librarians. It diminishes the social standing of the academic librarians, since the collective plane of academic capital and contribution is reduced to a position far below that of the tenure-track faculty.

The librarians, of course, also are guarding the legitimacy of their position in opposition to the classified staff for financial reasons. A 2011 study found that 78% of library directors consider budget as a significant reason for hiring non-MLS holding individuals as librarians (Simpson, 2013). The classified staff makes less money than the faculty-level librarians. If the financial situation dictated change, then what would be the sense of hiring an MLS-holding librarian when a nonlibrarian staff member can do the same or very similar job for 75% of the salary?

At the same, the managers realistically cannot ask classified employees to complete the same duties as a librarian or a higher-ranked classified staff member. This creates a motivational and potentially disciplinary concern as well. The state system makes discipline very complicated though.

> Gwen: [In order to fix the system] I might change the fact that we can't terminate people here or then it's such a like arduous process.
> Researcher: 18...18 months to terminate anybody who's classified.
> Gwen: Yeah. I would maybe change that. My husband always says to me that no actual business could function the way your library functions. There's just no way. Businesses couldn't be profitable if they have people that just kind of showed up and then went home. So I would probably change that and I recognize there's benefits the system that we have now, but that's something that I would change.

The constraints of the role description for classified staff make the integration of motivating tasks for the employees. If the employee balks at change, they will have three 6-month-long disciplinary reviews prior to termination. Systemically, the structure of the organization makes management and mobility very challenging.

The totality of these findings is significant because they demonstrate the difficult structural environment in which the librarians attempt to blend professionally. The librarian role transcends a great deal of organizational boundaries. Unluckily though, the classified personnel who might amplify the success of the academic librarians in their blended role through collaboration and high-levels of cooperation are unable to extend out of a restricted positions.

7.3.4 Use of personnel

In the course of the differentiation and integration of the various roles within the library system, the rigidity of the classifications impedes librarian blended professional development and growth. The issue is recognized by several managers and senior librarians, yet they lack the ability to enact true change. "Experienced managers...understand the difference between possessing a tool and knowing how to use it. Only experience and practice bring the skill and wisdom to size up a situation and use tools well" (Bolman & Deal, 2003, p. 13). Too often though, screwdrivers are being used to pound in nails.

> Jessica: We should be grooming people and that's one of the things that we have not done. Actually that is a barrier since there's a tendency to see people in little pegs. You do this job, you do that job, and you do that job, and there hasn't been as much interest in letting people do things that are a bit broader and fuzzier.

A measure of the matter is that St. Jerome must work in the boundaries defined by the state. At the same time though, the system retards the development of ambitious classified staff by limiting their practical experience in their current position. It leads to a high amount of turnover among that level of staff.

> Gwen: I feel like I'm hiring people that are either out of undergrad or out of library school. They want some experience and I expect them to leave, like they're going to get bored. They want to learn new things and I can only offer so many training opportunities or responsibilities and they're going to get bored and then they're going to move on and I expect that.

Some of the managers actually suggested utilizing staff in more substantial roles for the classified staff. As Catherine proposes, "I see the [LA level III] as almost an administrative librarian in their role. Because you want folks to grow…and we don't have that for those folks in those [classified positions]…so I would change that." This type of change would require a systemic overhaul of the function and ideology of the libraries though, and the economic realities of a publically funded institution create an unlikely scenario in which this change might occur.

This system also potentially impedes the productivity of the librarians themselves. Part of the reasoning behind the paraprofessional label was that the classified staff would be in place to aid the librarians on projects. Librarians state that they do not have enough time to complete substantial research. As well, library school may not have equipped them with the abilities to complete significant quantitative or qualitative methodological studies. As Lucy asserts: "You are the stats guy and there is no way I would deny that. If I were going to have a stats question, I would ask you, because you know stats. It doesn't matter if you have an MLS." At the same time though, not all librarians are willing to ask for help from the lower ranks due to perceived statuses. Therefore, this insight gains importance because it denotes both the librarians' weakening of their blended professional role external to the library by restricting the collaborative opportunities internal to the organization itself.

With such feedback, it is clear that some of the academic librarians are aware that these restrictions might impede cooperative opportunities between classified staff and librarians or lateral projects between multiple librarians with classified staff support. In spite of my classified title of "Reference, Research, and Instruction Specialist," the creation and dissemination of research was never part of my actual role. The official research that I conducted was in support of basic librarian projects. It never really amounted to much more than administrative support, aside from very specific committee work.

During my annual reviews as classified staff, I would always advocate for drafting my position's job description to include the production of academic professionalism so that I could cultivate research collaboratively with the academic librarians. Since publishing or conducting actual methodologically sound research was seen as "above my paygrade" or ancillary to my actual role, I informally was discouraged from developing projects on the job. Personally, I always viewed research and productivity as a means to bolster the image of the department. Instead, the organization viewed such work by the ranks of the classified staff as contributing to the gains of the individual and not the collective whole. There often was classified staff who had the capability and desire to contribute to the academic productivity of the librarians. Unfortunately, the organization cultivated an environment where such collaborations were difficult to undertake.

Finally, the appropriate use of personnel is inhibited by the same siloing mentioned previously that affects internal collaborative opportunities.

> Maria: In general, I think we're really bad at recognizing peoples' innate talents and interests and trying to develop those professionally. I've always thought that. You get these people and you see them 3 months out, 6 months out, maybe even a year out and you say "Gosh, well I didn't know they could do that." Well they said they could do that on their resume but I didn't know they *did* this. You know what I mean?
> Researcher: Compartmentalization.
> Maria: Thank you. And I think for all their talk about de-siloing they reinforce it by not recognizing the innate skills of people and maybe putting people with like skills together in a unit. Not just a temporary taskforce...not just a team...but you structure it.

Librarians perform service work on a variety of committees within the library system at St. Jerome. Temporary fixes have not resolved the organizational issues due to the aforementioned communication concerns and structural restrictions. Again, St. Jerome would require major systemic change in order to find realized success for the librarians as blended professionals.

7.3.5 *Organization summary*

It seems somewhat ironic that a project detailing how the academic librarians at St. Jerome are blended professionals suggests that the organization within which they work structurally prevents the success of that very model. Yet their professional growth is stymied by the same organizational system that allows for their roles to branch across sectors of the academic community. Vertical communication is poor, and internal opportunity is exceptionally limited. Also interesting is the experience of rank denial that the librarians experience within faculty circles is then passed on to the classified paraprofessionals. Unless regulations on the roles of the classified staff and librarians improve, the organizational culture seems as if it will be a self-perpetuating cycle of semidysfunction.

7.4 Conclusion

Time and money (or compensation) are big complaints of the academic librarians at St. Jerome. However, it appeared that they based their opinions on misconceptions about their tenure-track counterparts. Increased tenure-track-like research responsibilities are encroaching on their schedules. Still, the amount of time spent on their activities does not approach that of the tenure-track.

Money is also a specious complaint. How many people enter the academy due to financial motivations though? The tenure-track faculty might make slightly more on average than the academic librarians, but the differences are not great. Still, the perception that time and money are impediments to the academic librarians' success as blended professionals. Better understanding of the expectations of the librarians through improve communication from the administration might alleviate some of these misconceptions.

Gender is a far more complicated obstacle than either time or money to address, in part because some of the complaints were implied. It is apparent that perceptions of gender identity offer intrinsic challenges for the female librarians to address. At the same time, alterations in outlooks and beliefs of the individual librarians will only speak to so much of the dilemma. At St. Jerome, it is organizational.

Organization brings the final professional obstacle identified by the librarians. The structural frame of the organization inhibits personal and professional growth and enables a caste system to stymie any opportunity. Promotion is not often available, and the use of personnel often results in counterproductivity. While time and money were the most often cited complaints, the true professional obstacles lay in the gender identity of the academic librarians and the structure of the library organization at St. Jerome. With these obstacles identified, the conversation will turn toward the modifications of the blended professional model with respect toward these discoveries and offer suggestions that might mitigate some of the illuminated concerns.

References

American Faculty Association (AFA). (2012). *Hours for teaching and preparation rule of, thumb: 2–4 hours of pre for 1 hour of class*. American Faculty Association. Retrieved from http://americanfacultyassociation.blogspot.com/2012/02/hours-for-teaching-and-preparation-rule.html.

Bolman, L. G., & Deal, T. D. (2003). *Reframing organizations: Artistry, choice, and, leadership* (3rd ed.). San Francisco: Jossey-Bass.

Bonfield, B. (2014). *How well are you doing your job? You don't know. No one does. In, the library with the leadpipe*. Retrieved from http://www.inthelibrarywiththeleadpipe.org/2014/how-well-are-you-doing-your-job-you-dont-know-no-one-does/.

Boyd, D. (2009). Teaching, nursing, and second wave feminism. *Apophenia*. Retrieved from http://www.zephoria.org/thoughts/archives/2009/10/19/teaching_nursin.html.

Bureau of Labor Statistics. (2014). *Postsecondary teachers*. Retrieved from http://www.bls.gov/ooh/education-training-and-library/print/postsecondary-teachers.htm.

Delamont, S. (1990). *Sex roles and the school* (2nd ed.). London: Routledge.

Farley, S. D., Timme, D. R., & Hart, J. W. (2010). On coffee talk and break-room chatter: perceptions of women who gossip in the workplace. *Journal of Social Psychology, 150*(4), 361–368.

Fay, M. J., & Kline, S. L. (2011). The influence of informal communication on organizational identification and commitment in the context of high-intensity telecommuting. *Southern Communication Journal, 77*(1), 61–76.

Helgesen, S. (1995). *The web of inclusion: A new architecture for building great organizations*. New York: Doubleday.

Huhman, H. R. (2012). STEM fields and the gender gap: where are the women? *Forbes*. Retrieved from http://www.forbes.com/sites/work-in-progress/2012/06/20/stem-fields-and-the-gender-gap-where-are-the-women/.

Jha, J., Page, E., & Raynor, J. (2009). School, gender and stereotypes: despair and hope. In E. Page, & J. Jha (Eds.), *Exploring the bias: Gender and stereotyping in secondary schools* (pp. 1–32). London: Commonwealth Secretariat.

Johnson, M. (2013). Women and work: current situation. *CQ Researcher, 23*(27), 660–662.

Madell, R. (2014). *Your looks and your job: Does appearance affect advancement?* Career-intelligence.com. Retrieved from http://career-intelligence.com/appearance-affect-advancement/.

Manley, W. (2002). Telework, or watching television? *American Libraries, 33*(4).

McAndrew, F. T. (2014). The "sword of a woman": gossip and female aggression. *Aggression & Violent Behavior, 19*(3), 196–199.

Miller-Ott, A. E., & Kelly, L. (2013). Mean girls in college: an analysis of how college, women communicatively construct and account for relational aggression. *Women's Studies in Communication, 36*(3), 330–347.

National Center for Education Statistics. (2011). *Average graduate and first-professional, tuition and required fees in degree-granting institutions, by first-professional field of study and control of institution: 1989–90 through 2010–11.* Retrieved from http://nces.ed.gov/programs/digest/d11/tables/dt11_352.asp.

Neufeld, D. J., & Fang, Y. (2005). Individual, social and situational determinants of telecommuter productivity. *Information & Management, 44*, 1037–1049.

Neuhauser, A. (2014). Minorities, women still underrepresented in STEM fields study finds. *US News & World Report.* Retrieved from http://www.usnews.com/news/stem-solutions/articles/2014/02/06/minorities-women-still-underrepresented-in-stem-fields-study-finds.

Nicole, P. F., Sheppard, C., Irish, M. S., & Spence, B. (2006). Work appearance isn't skin deep. *Working Mother, 29*, 19.

Pace, A. K. (2004). Librarians not in libraries. *Computers in Libraries, 24*(9), 32–35.

Simpson, B. (2013). Hiring non-MLS librarians: trends and training implications. *Library Leadership & Management, 28*(1), 1–15.

Sinberg, L. (2009). Think looks don't matter? Think again. *Forbes.* Retrieved from http://www.forbes.com/2009/12/05/appearance-work-pay-forbes-woman-leadership-body-weight.html.

Slaughter, A. (2012). Why women still can't have it all. *The Atlantic.* Retrieved from http://www.theatlantic.com/magazine/archive/2012/07/why-women-still-cant-have-it-all/309020/.

Smith, D., & Van Dyke, T. B. (2008). A telecommuting interlibrary loan librarian's, experience: the views of both the telecommuter and the on-site supervisor. *Journal of Interlibrary Loan, Document Delivery & Electronic Reserves, 18*(4), 449–455.

van Vugt, M. (2013). Naturally selected: understanding the human animal in the workplace. *Pscyhology Today.* Retrieved from http://www.psychologytoday.com/blog/naturally-selected/201306/the-sound-leader-ceos-deep-voices-do-better.

Wilson, E. (2014). Diversity, culture and the glass ceiling. *Journal of Cultural Diversity, 21*(3), 83–89.

Analysis and possible resolutions 8

The previous chapters provided the key findings from the study. This chapter will compare these discoveries with respect to the existing literature on the librarian's role and the blended professional model. Since the assertion formally has been made that librarians are in fact blended professionals, the conversation then will consider how the academic librarians at St. Jerome might address some of the limitations that persist in their role as blended professional. The chapter will conclude by proposing pragmatic means to enhance the success of the blended professional role of the academic librarians at St. Jerome and how they might address and overcome the real and perceived obstacles to their professional success.

8.1 Place within the literature

Contrasted with the existing literature on the topic of librarians as faculty members, this study finds cohesion with the argument that suggests the duties of the academic librarians do not compare equally with tenure-track counterparts (Coker, van Duinkerken, & Bales, 2010; Hansson & Johannesson, 2013; Schrimsher & Northrup, 2013). While it is clear that librarians do publish (Baruzzi & Calcagno, 2015; Lamothe, 2012) and instruct (Clark & Chinburg, 2010; Cooke & Rosenthal, 2011; O'Malley & Delwiche, 2012; Shaffer, 2011), the level of productivity and complexity of the role found in this study is not on the same level as tenure-track faculty. Academic librarians at other institutions, in fact, might dispute some of these findings because the arguments may not accurately reflect their role at their particular institution (Dunn, 2013) and reiterate the benefits of full-faculty status for librarians (Parker, 2011). That is acceptable and somewhat expected when a case study is performed. These findings firstly consider St. Jerome. The method may be applied to other colleges and universities, and then comparisons and debates may commence.

At the same time, exterior entities' opinions of the academic librarians and their purpose from faculty and nonlibrary administration are sometimes misguided (Hardesty, 1991; Katz, 2003; Rogers, 2012). At St. Jerome though, the academic librarians occupy a tenuous third space predicated by the real and perceived institutional silos and boundaries that inhibit their blended abilities. Defining this third space and the resulting obstacles serves to provide a model where other libraries might examine the specific roles of their librarians and illuminate prevailing challenges. This work provides the basis of a model for the understanding of librarians' perceptions of their duties and position within the context of higher education.

Still, this project does not imply that librarians do not deserve to be considered faculty or have a role within the governance of the university, which is a predominant assertion within higher education literature (Association of College and Research Libraries, 2012; Welch & Mozenter, 2006; Wyss, 2010). The libraries and their academic librarians just fill a unique and different role and space within the educational process. As a result, this study further refines the definition of the librarian role when compared to existing literature.

As stated, the librarians' blended role is much more direct to the curricular student learning process than other noninstructional faculty or student affairs positions. Yes, significant student growth and personal understanding may be found through a student affairs organization, such as a special interest club. However, academic librarians provide the access to and evaluation of researchable material that may directly contribute to student academic success, which is a core mission of any higher education institution. Library literature often focuses on the assessment of library instruction (Oakleaf, 2009; Sobel & Sugimoto, 2012), which is only a portion of the student's academic lifecycle (Passehl-Stoddart & Monge, 2014).

Verdicts here suggest that the librarians have the potential for a more significant impact on student learning through their blended role. When unimpeded, librarians have the capacity for more substantive collaborative projects as opposed to mere instruction of information literacy (Baruzzi & Calcagno, 2015) and tangible academic value (Oakleaf, 2010). In this way, the application of this blended professional model to academic librarians allows for the argument that the librarians at the very least should be included in more significant communication around the St. Jerome campuses in organizations such as Faculty Senate and curriculum committees.

The argument here also disagrees with literature that suggests that libraries "do not seem to directly contribute to gains in information literacy, to what students gain overall from college, or to student satisfaction" (Matthews, 2007, p. 77). Academic librarians have the ability to be integral cogs in the machinery of student learning. Restrictions on their abilities to blend and interact with different segments of the university community though, both internal and external to the library organization itself, require attention. This study, by applying the blended professional model to the library role, adds another layer to the literature that searches for definitions of librarian role and working space, and enhances the arguments that suggest librarians have significant contributions to university students' learning.

This study is very distinctive in that it applies a higher education-focused model to the role of academic librarians. This is something rarely seen in literature because higher education theorists seldom consider librarians as faculty. Library literature infrequently takes this approach also. A great deal of library-oriented literature related to the function of librarians seeks to make a direct comparison to the faculty (Coker et al., 2010; Welch & Mozenter, 2006). This usually fails to make an impact because, as asserted in this study, the librarian role is much different than most faculty, and the faculty do not fully understand the actual role of the librarians.

By utilizing the method demonstrated here, this study advocates that librarians have a shared but different role in the production of educated students and scholars. This does not extend fully to the librarian literature that suggests librarians and faculty are equal in their charges. Instead, this work applies the blended professional model in order to codify the working third space of the academic librarians with respect to the faculty position. Simply put, this method employs the indirect route to validation and may gain more traction because it is not a frontal assault overstating the librarian role.

It was telling that Whitchurch did not consider applying the blended professional model to librarians in her original studies, yet she examined other blended positions such as individuals working within academic advising. This perspective is understandable and expected, having read the existing literature. The librarians' degrees are not respected or (often) at an equivalent level to the rest of the faculty around collegiate campuses, and the function of their role is misunderstood. Whitchurch's model is just another example of librarians and their contributions being overlooked by the higher education community. This study differs in its approach and provides the mold in which to amend that consistent oversight in higher education and librarian literature.

Yet by employing a research model originating in higher education, this study provides the blueprint for inclusion of librarians in the conversation involving faculty and collegiate educators. It merges two fields of academic thought so that librarians might conceptualize themselves as higher education professionals in addition to being library experts. This philosophical nudge empowers the librarian role by demonstrating its significance in the total context of higher education.

8.2 Modifying the blended professional

The blended professional frame was intended to analyze the professional roles and identities of the traditional conception of academic faculty. The librarian's blended professional experience never was considered. Whitchurch's model is also relatively new (published in 2009), so the application of the theory to varying classifications of faculty has yet to occur. As a result, there is no direct comparison in the literature to which the findings of this study might be compared. This study is an entirely new addition to the literature in that regard.

Therefore, the foremost contribution of this dissertation concerning the blended professional model is the study's application of the frame to a new professional in the academic realm, the academic librarian. The employment of the blended professional model on academic librarians demonstrates the malleability and usefulness of the frame when applied to nontenure-track or traditional faculty members of the university collective. As well, Whitchurch (2009, p. 408) described the experience of blended professionals as navigating the "history and tensions between different factions and groups". This held firm for the librarians studied here. The academic librarians must negotiate the expectations of the library administration, interpret the ever-changing needs and requirements of the student populace, and perform outreach to faculty, all while combating the historical role of a librarian as a mere administrator of the university repository. With this in mind, it is clear through this analysis that academic librarians are blended professionals.

Additionally, aspects of the model netted sundry or completely different attributes when applied to librarians. For example, the spaces for librarians are clearly library-centric. Everything originates from the understanding of the library, its resources, and the navigation thereof. In contrast, spaces for other blended professional would extend out from either an academic department or the classroom. This should be expected due to the fact that librarians functionally have different roles than the professionals studied in the original model. All of these factors intertwine and aid in the construction of the librarian as a blended professional.

For the most part, the existing blended professional model generally retains usefulness when analyzing current professional identities within traditional higher education settings. What the model does not fully take into account is the driving force behind an individual's change from a traditional, encased role to that of a blended professional. Whitchurch (2009, p. 418) implies that the institutional environment or management promotes the blended role. For example, "leadership was described variously as 'a facilitator,' 'identifying new initiatives and projects,' 'creating opportunities' and 'releasing potential'". This is certainly one of the catalysts at St. Jerome, as administration is promoting more academic professionalism and librarian outreach. Other factors, such as financial cuts that create the elimination of positions and encourage the development of cross-training skills to account for personnel shortfall also surely are a facilitator of professional change. However, both of these influences ignore the major consideration of technology, especially within the libraries.

My first job in a library as a graduate student involved "sweeping" bound journals once an hour. Library patrons routinely left piles of these periodicals by photocopiers because print copies of these materials were the only way to obtain them. Approximately 10 years later, the majority of print periodicals are in offsite storage because patrons find access to journals online. That student role in the libraries is completely different due to technological advancement.

The academic librarians' roles surely have changed as well, from their understanding on how to obtain the materials to the navigation and interpretation of the resources. Their working third space undoubtedly is more extensive with the availability of online resources and interactive materials. As well, the librarians' ability to interact with a larger populace in a less fixed environment has also shifted. Technology will have a greater impact for some sectors of blended professionals in higher education like librarians than it will for other workers in different departments.

If this model was applied in 2005, the results and perceptions of professional identities of the librarians and other professionals likely would be different than the findings of this study, or one conducted in another 10 years. Although this is a case study analyzing one segment of the university community, the educated guess is that such insight would help professionals other than librarians gain the most practical information when applying the frame. Granted, the goal of a model such as this is not to examine the catalysts of the development of professional roles and identities, but rather the forces shaping the conceptualization of that identity once it is formed.

The blended professional model consequently provides an accurate snapshot of the perceptions of current working conditions, but the usefulness of findings might have a short shelf-life due to factors promoting changing roles. Therefore, being cognizant of the causes of changes regarding blended professional identities will help further identify solutions for the obstacles to professional success and development that impede blended professionals and their organizations because it will offer a total understanding of the role. While adding considerations on causes to the actual model is not recommended, the addition of a question regarding the perceived factors initiating or perpetuating blended professional activities should be added to the qualitative questions, as it will provide supplemental perspectives on the formation of the subjects' professional identities.

Also, while the blended professional model as a whole is exceptionally useful for gaining insight into the professional identity of higher education professionals, there is another distinct suggestion for revision that warrants more attention than technology. Whitchurch's frame does not have an actual consideration of the impact of gender identity on professional identity. This is a case study analyzing the perceptions of 17 female workers in one segment of the university community. As well, not all interviewed librarians even explicitly stated that gender influenced their perception of their job. This reality limits my ability to promote a wholesale change to the process of professional identity investigation.

Still, a modification to the blended professional model allowing for the impact of gender might be in order for future studies that seek to employ it. See Fig. 8.1 for an illustration of gender as an additional component of the blended professional model. Though gender-related obstacles were not a universally-cited concern with the interviewed librarians in this case, additional studies utilizing the blended professional model might consider employing questions that directly ask about perceptions of gender.

Librarianship is statistically two-thirds female, and at St. Jerome, that percentage is even higher. Other blended professional fields in higher education where employees also have professional faculty status, such as career services, have a high percentage of female employees. For example, at St. Jerome, there are 20 full-time employees in the career services department; 17 are female. Consequently, multiple blended professional fields in higher education will have a significant female presence.

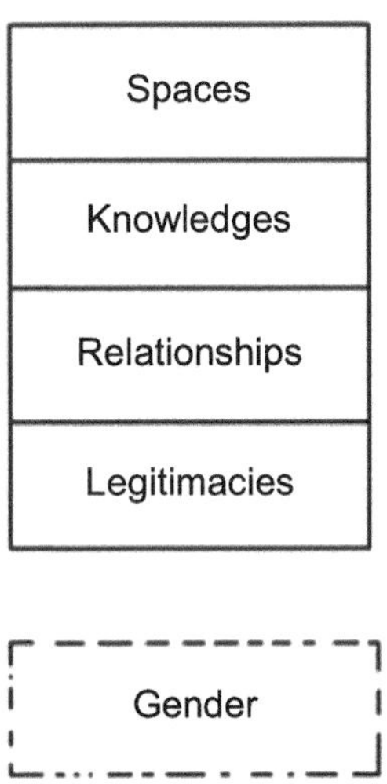

Figure 8.1 This image illustrates the addition of gender as a potential fifth component of the blended professional frame.

In addition, existing literature suggests that women often already possess blended roles (wife, mother, employee, etc.) (Couzy, 2012; English & Callaway, 2013; Rao, 2003; Stefanisko, 1997). Several conversations in this study confirmed this assertion. It has been established that women do not have a fair chance for professional equality in higher education (Clarke, Hyde, & Drennan, 2013; Schuster & Finkelstein, 2006). Literature also states that women as professionals are hampered by inherent and existing gender biases (Bagilhole & White, 2008; Fulmer, 2010; Garn & Brown, 2008). Again, the findings from this work verify that some women indeed are obstructed professionally by gender prejudices.

Therefore, it is reasonable to postulate that, given these biases that exist in the workplace and higher education as a whole, female professionals in fields other than library science might have an altered perspective on their roles within the academy due to experiences with blended roles and confrontations with partiality. Logically, this indicates that examining gender as an influencing factor for the development of professional identity of female blended professionals in higher education is valid. The application of the blended professional model with respect to gender melds these conversations—women in higher education and blended professionalism—and provides for a further understanding of women's role within the academy.

This is especially important within the context of all higher education because the literature has demonstrated that there is a consistent lack of egalitarianism and opportunity for women in the academy (Bowen, 2005; Chisholm-Burns et al., 2012; Fowler et al., 2004; Guillory, 2001; Lanier, Tanner, & Guidry, 2009; Mason, 2011; Schuster & Finkelstein, 2006). Gender has been demonstrated to have an effect on professional identity and career path in female-dominated careers such as social work (Lewis, 2004). These realities very likely have an effect on the spaces and relationships that a blended professional might inhabit and develop by placing real or artificial boundaries around the professional third space. Are the knowledges and legitimacies of working women equally mitigated? With librarians, the limits of their education inhibited the extension of their profile. Do female blended professionals with doctoral degrees still face biases regarding knowledges and legitimacies? The assumption based on existing literature and this study is yes, the biases persist. The application of the blended professional model with additional questions or categories considering gender may better codify the concern and elucidate realistic solutions.

Despite the focus on the female identity in higher education, gender identity issues have the ability to impact other genders. For instance, gender also has the ability to influence the professional identity when the individual works in a field accepted or viewed as belonging to the opposite gender, such as male nurses (Hoeve, Jansen, & Roodbol, 2014). Often, the nursing field is viewed as subordinate to medical doctors (Hoeve et al., 2014), which would be akin to academic librarians conceptualizing their role as in service to the needs of tenure-track faculty. Since librarianship traditionally emerged as a female occupation, explorations on the influence of the stereotype on male librarians have been considered (Gordon, 2004; Holland, 2007). It was noted earlier that library administrators (both at St. Jerome and elsewhere) tend to be male. However, perhaps in this instance, gender has the inverse effect on the equity and opportunity throughout the academy for the male frontline liaison-level librarians.

This potential addition to the blended professional frame would give researchers a viable means by which to examine any measurable impact that stereotype has on male librarian's blended professional identities and working third space.

Even on the smallest scale, explicit questions regarding gender should be asked of interviewees in order to assess the amount of influence this factor has on their professional identity development. If a significant number of respondents in the future studies indicate that gender does play a major part in their professional identity, then formally adding gender as a fifth category in the blended professional frame will become more reasonable.

For librarians, this was a micro-study that provided the model for the analysis of their role in the larger context of higher education. Reflexively, the application of gender to the blended professional model demonstrates its usefulness on the macroscale. This work suggests that gender has, at the very least, a partial impact on the perception of professional identity for one segment of workers in the higher education community. However, by adjusting the blended professional model to reflect the influence of gender, this study establishes another means by which to codify the experience and perception of women in higher education on a much larger level. It is another argument in the conversation on how unequal treatment in the workplace may negatively affect the worker and the organization.

Again, the size of this study does not allow for a conclusive argument suggesting a major overhaul to the blended professional model. This book is one very small enhancement to the literature on the female academic librarian role with respect to professional identity. Yet the anticipation is that an expansion of the frame will benefit the codification of the blended role within all of higher education. This approach for future studies will give a more comprehensive understanding of the blended role because it specifically addresses an issue that continues to be a concern in higher education: the impact of gender on professional role, identity, and development.

8.2.1 Practical recommendations

In terms of pragmatism for the immediate study, the findings presented in the previous chapter indicate that the librarians at St. Jerome are indeed blended professionals. However, restrictions of space and professional challenges prevent the librarians from being fully effective in their capacity as blended professionals on an academic campus. The following is meant to offer potential solutions that will address directly the some of the cited concerns from this case study and hopefully alleviate some of these difficulties for the academic librarians at St. Jerome.

At the same time, through the analysis of the interviews and the librarians' comments and concerns, I became more cognizant of my own standing within the community of librarians interviewed. As a result, I am attempting to provide illumination of issues and potential solutions without projecting my own personal perspectives or work ethic on that of the librarians. This admittedly is a difficult and challenging mission. While this work furthers my empathy regarding the role and professional identities of the librarians at St. Jerome, the experiences of the interviewer and interviewees inherently remain separate and unequal. Simply put, my role at the time of research and those of the academic librarians are different on a social and logistical plane.

This work additionally is an opportunity for an underrepresented or unheard faction of the university community to voice their opinions and beliefs about their role. It is therefore crucial that the suggestions for situational improvement do not trample these views by projecting them as mere musings of a disgruntled sect. The findings presented illustrate valid opinions of these female academic librarians and symbolize a unique insight into one specific yet significant campus group.

Take the deliberation about lack of time, for instance. The implication is that there is more time available to complete tasks and projects that might improve the social and cultural standing of librarians at St. Jerome. However, my own perception of time might be wholly different from the librarian quoted earlier in the book as having difficulty managing the complexities of work, life, and motherhood. The goal then is to detail these concerns and perceptions without undermining their validity through biased interpretation.

At some point, the obstacles becoming impassible realities. Consider the librarian who had a great opportunity to advance her career but chose not to leave her current job due to familial reasons. She geographically is limited in the scope of options, and there are few, if any, opportunities to advance in her current role. In that case, considerations external to the job converge with the realities of the role to create a substantial, if not immovable, obstacle. Situations like this make any proposed resolution suspicious due to the most significant professional obstacle detailed: the library organization and administration at St. Jerome itself.

I do believe that aspects of the organization must change in order to benefit the librarians' experience. On the microscale, librarians might address concerns with colleagues and managers in hopes of improving on the basic obstacles to the librarians' professional success. However, for several reasons previously asserted—organizational structure, poor communication, and inability of the administration to maneuver around itself—I do not believe that wholesale revolution in this environment is a likely outcome.

It is understandable that some librarians might not want to or cannot leave St. Jerome for any variety of personal or professional reasons, yet they still might desire improvement in spite of organizational limitations. At that point when the situation is not likely to change, the only option is that the individual's reaction to the circumstances must be altered. The librarian then might focus on the aspects of the job in which they find the greatest enjoyment. Many librarians cited working with students and faculty and interacting with the community at St. Jerome as gratifying. Focusing on the positive facets of the role might, in some cases, be the only true real or perceptual change that a particular librarian might make at this point in their lives.

Again, the argument here is not to mitigate the concerns raised by the librarians but instead alleviate some of the obstacles standing in their path. While many of the forthcoming suggestions might address some of the concerns, in some cases, comprehensive change is not realistic. In those circumstances though, even small perceptual alterations, however pedestrian that proposal might seem, might improve the overall situation.

8.2.2 Spaces

A few of the recommendations provided here will bridge multiple characteristics of the blended professional. For instance, office space improvements speak to both spaces and legitimacies. If an office is a sign of a legitimate faculty member on the St. Jerome campus, then the academic librarians appear lacking in that regard. Fortunately, there is an ongoing construction project at the Alexander VI Library that will completely redesign the working space of the librarians. Each librarian presently is slated to have their own office. This will mean that all of the liaison librarians at St. Jerome libraries, except those at the Urban II, will have personal working spaces in the form of legitimate offices. The librarians and managers at St. Jerome should be cognizant of the preexisting perception of Alexander VI Library-oriented decision-making biases. The difference in office provisions might further divide Urban II librarians from their colleagues through perceptions of unfair practices.

Increasing an understanding of the technologies used also would enhance the spaces in which librarians might develop. There has been some reluctance to incorporate technologies into the daily routine of librarianship at St. Jerome though. As Lucy states:

> *[Librarians] don't want to admit that they don't know how to do it. So that's the worst thing. If you say "Yeah, I want to help but I don't know" I'd be fine with that. But some people say that they know how to do it but then when you work with them you find that they really don't and they don't want to admit to ignorance.*

Right now, all of the librarians use virtual reference, but not as many use Skype, the Blackboard portal tool Collaborate, One Button Studio video maker, and other forms of interactive technology. There is a learning curve for these technologies, and not all products are useful to every discipline. Discretion should be exercised when deciding which technologies to harness and master.

The speed at which institutions adopt technology often is outpaced by the users' need or desire to utilize that specific equipment. For instance, the Alexander VI Library had a graduate research assistant who knew how to develop Quick Response (QR) codes. By the time he received approval to move forward with a QR code project for the library, the trend had passed and students no longer were scanning these codes in an attempt to gather information. Even so, while there still is significant value in the physical space of a traditional library, in order to maintain a presence with the ubiquitous learners frequenting the campuses of the 21st century, the understanding of a librarians' third space must now extend to the virtual realm as well.

8.2.3 Knowledges

There is no reasonably quick development for some knowledges. Take, for example, the librarians who cited their job experience as the factor that led to their ability to navigate the resources. That type of knowledge simply requires time and effective practice. Other aspects, though, have much more rapid resolution.

The inability to conduct high-level quantitative or qualitative research due to a lack of coursework and training during their graduate education confounded many of the interviewed librarians. A simple solution to that obstacle is to enroll in methodology courses in order to gain the education needed and desired to complete these research projects. Coincidentally, St. Jerome offers 12 free credits of course study per year (with a maximum of 6 credits per semester) to all full-time employees.

This suggestion might be met with scrutiny by the librarians that suggest their time already is at a premium. This is also where it is very difficult for me not to project my own expectations and experiences on the academic librarians. I completed a doctorate while having a full-time job and a part-time job. I also managed several individuals who were working on master's degrees in library science or other disciplines who were in the same situation. Is sitting in class until 10 pm one or more nights a week always enjoyable? No, it is not. However, it serves the purpose of increasing the knowledge of a blended professional at a minimal cost.

There are some current librarians at St. Jerome that take advantage of this benefit. Other librarians enroll in courses at external universities (at their own expense). It might be worth either the librarians themselves or managers consulting these individuals in order to ascertain how they are able to balance the roles of librarian and student. Perhaps librarian schedules might be modified in order to accommodate the professional growth associated with knowledge development.

8.2.4 Relationships

Around campus, expanding relationships into certain sectors is difficult, if not impossible. Some of the faculty simply has no interest in having the librarians in their classes, nor do they wish to work with them on projects. No amount of academic productivity or outreach by the librarians will change their minds. Aside from direct orders from their department dean, there is no chance of developing a relationship with these types of individuals.

One current library administration-backed project is the Balanced Scorecard, which is a management strategy designed to align personnel activities with institutional missions (Balanced Scorecard Institute, 2014). Because it attempts to apply numerical expectations to activities that are difficult to quantify, such as research or outreach, its intrusion is not appreciated. The end result is academic librarians attempting to navigate what is perceived to be unnecessary or unrealistic change, producing frustration and exasperation.

As an administrator, I understand why St. Jerome's library management, as part of the Balanced Scorecard, is pushing the academic librarians to increase (numerically) partnerships throughout the university. It is an attempt to implement a strategic planning system that aligns the institution's missions with the activities of the employees. However, it puts the librarians in a bind because so many of the components of these types of initiatives are inappropriate for the environment in which they are to be executed.

Here, being realistic makes sense. First, get rid of any statistical pressure to "make friends" in different departments around the university. The library is not a sales department. Productivity should not be measured through factors that require persuasion of individuals into equal partnerships. Second, keep the door open if these resistant faculty ever wish to ask for assistance, but do not spend the effort on a lost cause. Work with the faculty who are receptive, and strengthen those relationships. If the librarians focus on the productive partnerships, then it will save a lot of time and energy over the long haul.

The relationships internal to the library also have to extend beyond the boundaries of the individual libraries and campuses. Schedule visits once a month to libraries on the separate campuses in order to maintain or develop rapport and keep colleagues abreast of current projects. Travel between campuses can be difficult with the traffic congestion, but once a month. 12 visits per year, is not too much to endure if the activity is meaningful. As well, these may be informal meetings over coffee or lunch. Formality is not a necessity for relationship development, and in some ways, casual gatherings might serve as a welcome relief from the daily librarian grind.

The librarians also must broaden their pool of prospective research partners. Specifically, they must begin to regard both students and classified staff as potential collaborators. As liaisons, they have access to many graduate students working on theses or dissertations. Also, many of the classified staff workers within the organization, often in the same department, have advanced degrees and experience in high-level research and publication. Start projects with these folks. Both students and staff members benefit from collaboration with the librarians because they enhance their research skills and resumes so that they might advance in their own fields. The librarians also profit because they are performing service and outreach, thereby increasing their blended role and producing academically as well.

One of the better ways to develop a research pipeline is to connect with one or more individuals on prospective projects. It reduces the total workload per research venture, thus allowing for the researcher simultaneously to complete multiple studies. This ideology simply provides the partnerships.

8.2.5 Legitimacies

Similar to the discussion with knowledges, coursework provides the opportunity to expand legitimacies of the academic librarians at St. Jerome. Taking the suggestion a step further, completing a certificate or degree program may increase legitimacy by providing the librarian with the all-important hegemonic device of higher education: the letters after one's name. The additional knowledge of program language further extends boundaries and opportunities for the academic librarian.

Again, this recommendation might find protest due to the time required for collegiate study. Nevertheless, if the librarian seeks to use only the 12 free credits per year, their student status will remain part-time. While taxing with a full-time job, family, and social life, this represents a reasonable opportunity for motivated individuals.

This proposition may be trickier, though, than merely enrolling in research methodology courses due to the potential for inadvertently creating a student–faculty relationship instead of a librarian–faculty association. Building collaborative relationships becomes problematic when the librarian registers for a course taught by a member of the department for which they liaise. This is especially so if the librarian performs poorly as a student!

At the same time, a good performance in the class might provide for the development of future collaborations by establishing a working relationship. The librarian truly concerned by this might strategically avoid certain faculty throughout their studies or simply seek to define the roles with the faculty member prior to the start of the class or program. In the end, enrolling in a degree or certificate program is a cost-effective means to add layers to the blended professional role.

8.2.6 Final thoughts on blended professionalism

The above suggestions represent what the librarians as individuals might do in order to be successful in their blended positions. The librarians cannot succeed alone in their endeavors though. In total terms of increasing the blended professional role and third space of the academic librarians at St. Jerome, the administration also must aggressively promote these professionals' skills. Maria provided the following analogy.

> *That's where I think the sales job needs to come from the director. Sales job...I think I've used this analogy before. The director is the sales guy out there with the plow. He's plowing the field, sowing some seeds, you know. Gosh guys, over here is going to be the wheat, over here is some corn, over here are the soy beans, we're going to let this sit fallow...bah bah! Your librarians come in behind. Okay, we're the wheat guys. We're the corn guys. We're the soy bean guys and let's get this crop going here. But I think your leader...your top dog...is your lead liaison, if you will. He's the top salesman. And that's the person who's in these meetings with deans and directors here.*

As Maria asserts, that library director position has the ear of the executive levels of the university and can bridge some of the silo gaps that encumber librarian outreach, especially with highly resistant faculty. In general, my overall understanding was that the librarians did not feel that director of the libraries or his direct subordinates did well enough to work at promoting the research accomplishments of St. Jerome's librarians.

If the director is analogous to the "sales guy," then currently the librarians are his assistants making cold calls on his behalf because he does not have enough active leads. The academic librarians have specialties that would promote promising collaboration. They just need some additional support from the top that endorses the variety of the blended professional abilities that they might offer.

8.3 Additional pragmatic implications

As suggested, some of the obstacles perceived by the academic librarians at St. Jerome appear artificial in creation. Yet the perception of the hurdles as truly existing may affect the views that the librarians have of their own roles. For instance, nearly every librarian interviewed mentioned time and money as chief concerns. However, the chapter "Obstacles to professional success" suggested that the perception of these factors as obstacles was misguided. Other factors, such as gender or organizational structure, were less tangible, yet provided very real hurdles to professional success. The following is meant to suggest resolutions that might alleviate some of the consternation for the librarians at St. Jerome.

8.3.1 Time

Time is a frustrating topic to discuss when librarian activities are actually tabulated and measured within the larger context of higher education. Previous discussions (and feedback from the librarians themselves) in this work suggested that other activities of the librarians did not encompass as much depth or breadth as other professionals on campus. The bottom line is that the academic librarians at St. Jerome have more time than their faculty counterparts in most of their activities. What they perceive as constricted time is actually not that bad! However, the fact that the librarians perceive their time to be overly saturated with activities creates a tangible obstacle to professional success and suggests that additional perspectives and analysis from colleagues or managers are needed.

For matters of time, librarians might do a desk audit of their schedules and keep track of their hourly activities for a week, a month, or longer. This will demonstrate how their hours are being used, and when discussed with a manager or colleague, viable scheduling plans might develop. In the short run, this method might open the librarians to micromanagement by allowing an increased inspection of their respective activities. However, the overall understanding of productivity and time management benefits the librarians in the end by providing means for increased efficiency. If time constraints really do heavily affect the productivity of librarians, then spread some of their responsibilities to the classified staff in order to lighten the load (and provide the classified staff with new or expanded professional development opportunities). In this way, the librarians might maximize their ability to stretch their operational third space in a more efficient manner.

8.3.2 Money

Librarians presume that having the responsibility, or at the very least strong encouragement, of the production of tenure-track-level research remains unfair due to the discrepancy in comparative salaries and compensation between the two factions. The chapter "Obstacles to professional success" suggested that the gaps in pay are far less than the librarians believed. Yes, there are STEM (Science, Technology, Engineering, and Mathematics) faculty and full professors walking around St. Jerome's campus who annually make well into the six figures. However, there also are plenty of PhD-holding assistant professors making $53,000 as well (that's a meager salary for the general locale of St. Jerome).

Truthfully though, a lack of a high salary or compensation should not prevent research productivity. The concept of pay-for-productivity is a mentality best suited to a sales environment, not a research department in a higher education library. At the very least, the librarians who produce scholarship are adding valuable lines to their curriculum vitae. Holistically though, academic professionalism benefits the individual(s) because it increases understanding of the research process, which is seminal to an academic librarian's role.

Also, thousands of journals do not charge for publication, and there are a variety of cost-effective conferences to attend. In fact, with many of the free qualitative and quantitative research programs provided by the library, conducting research and producing scholarship can cost nothing at all. If substantial funding is required, then apply for grant funding. This is not meant to be groundbreaking advice; it is an encouragement to be realistic and work with the limited funding to the best of one's ability.

The benefits received by the librarians meet the standards of the field. Few people enter higher education to become rich. It seems foolish then to fault low compensation as a hindrance to success in that chosen field.

Again, when I conducted this research, I was classified staff and not a librarian. Hierarchically, I was a subordinate. In my current role at another university, I work outside of the libraries, and I still am not a librarian. As a result, if I myself asserted my findings concerning librarian compensation during a staff meeting, it is likely not to be well received. However, if librarian peers or managers illustrate this reality, then contextually some of the concern might be assuaged through reasonable discussion.

8.3.3 Gender

It was stated that I, in fact, was surprised by the rather reserved representation of gender in the comments by the librarians. It must be noted though that perhaps the librarians have become accustomed to the situation in which they work, or they have become complacent with the role and space. Unless prompted, they might not even perceive a gender difference because this is their daily existence. In addition, I am male. Some of the librarians might have been more forthcoming speaking with a female interviewer. Hopefully, this project at least provided the interviewed librarians with an opportunity to reflect upon their jobs with respect to gender and contemplate how it might affect their blended professional role.

In terms of change though, there have been numerous studies suggesting ways to create positive change toward gender equality in the workplace. In order to provide equal pay and opportunity for working women, there have been suggestions to add benefits such as onsite daycare (Alsever, 2013), the proposal of legal initiatives demanding equal pay from as high up as the White House (White House, 2014), and the establishment of higher quality mentoring programs in order to promote female managers (Ibarra, Carter, & Silva, 2010). These are great suggestions, but St. Jerome already has a daycare facility, actively encourages managers to consider equal compensation and promotion in spite of gender, and has several faculty and staff mentoring programs in action. Yet in spite of these and like initiatives, concerns persist.

The goal here then is not to suggest overarching modifications. Realistically, if I actually had drastic solutions to these concerns, I would be assessing corporations professionally, and I would be far, far richer. Instead, the hope is that the recommendations will serve this immediate case and potentially expand through further research and assessment.

On a university level, perhaps an increased positive understanding of the academic librarian role at St. Jerome throughout the university community would provide the continued opportunity for the librarians to assess their professional challenges. Again, the misunderstanding by the faculty may directly relate to the conflicted role that the librarians have of themselves. They view themselves as service providers, yet the administration emphasizes collaboration. Collaboration suggests equal or at least similar standing in role. Service retains the connotation of "servant." These are wholly different ideologies that are difficult to reconcile, resulting in a lack of shared ventures and a reduction in blended space.

Given the feedback that many of the female librarians felt like "academic handmaidens" or "minions" of the faculty, administration should adhere to one identity and stick to it. If the administration desires collaboration, then promote the academic achievements of the librarians instead of emphasizing service. If service is to become the main provision, then the administration should be cognizant of how this identity effects the perception of the role for female librarians and be prepared to address any potential fallout.

In the hierarchy of higher education, academic production is valued over service. Therefore I would recommend the focus on academic professionalism in order to bolster collaborative opportunities. How might this be accomplished? Promote the positive academic contributions of the female employees.

However, the librarians at St. Jerome seem apprehensive at personal self-promotion, in part due to personality. For example, introversion was suggested as possibly preventing outreach. Lucy confessed: "I think a lot of librarians by default are more introverts. Yeah, let's just face it. By librarian standards I am not an introvert but by regular human standards I am." This inward-facing mentality was apparent when many librarians cited individual consultations as opposed to classroom instruction as the most pleasant contributions to a good day in the library. Julia echoes many similar statements when she says: "I think that the most important thing that I do is working with students individually." Studies have shown that 65–75% of the general population is extroverted, whereas approximately 63% of librarians are introverted (Milford & Wisotzke, 2011). Compound this with the "service-first" mentality that many of the librarians hold due to gender expectations. It is possible, therefore, that librarians excel at one-on-one interactions and consultations but fail to thrive in outreach endeavors (Milford & Wisotzke, 2011).

Therefore, in lieu of personal outreach, the female librarians might benefit from administration-led outreach. Individual librarians might make contacts with some of the faculty in a department. However, the administration has a better opportunity to gain the ear of deans and department heads due to the relative equality of the professional levels. As opposed to opening a few doors, this approach may open all of them. This is especially important in fields where a female presence is lacking, such as STEM.

Another basic recommendation is for the increase in the diversity of the librarians. Ethnic identification was not asked of the librarians during the interview. However, within the American Research Libraries in 2011–12, 85.8% of the librarians identified as Caucasian; only 14.2% held minority status (Chang, 2013). Anecdotally, this trend continues at St. Jerome, and this is something that may affect the productivity in the libraries. As Lucy states:

> *I think one of maybe the big problems with stagnation with some of the libraries that I've worked with or in that were bad was that the demographic was all the same. Very similar in ages, background, ethnicity whatever. I think that's one of the problems with attracting the diversity and having a vibrant field is that there's been a lot of concentration of people who think the same and we need more perspectives. We need more diversity, period.*

It seems kind of odd that one would suggest decreasing the percentage of white women in a position in order to advance their role within an organization. However, a different professional and personal experience brought to an organization by a diverse group of individuals provides the opportunity for a dynamic workplace. Diversity provides the chance to view problems from a variety of perspectives not necessarily available to a homogenous group. In order to further the collective roles of the female academic librarians at St. Jerome, it would be useful to have individuals with specialties and voices who might interact and blend professionally with a greater population of the university community.

St. Jerome has generic faculty and staff mentoring programs in place. However, a formalized library-based mentoring initiative might help increase support and promote cross-departmental collaboration. The interviews suggested that any mentoring, either vertical or lateral in nature, originated and stayed within contained departments. Some librarians even expressed disappointment with the inability to work together with librarians on different campuses. This compartmentalization might hinder professional growth and development by limiting the viewpoints and alternatives presented regarding professional options.

There are female leaders within the libraries, and many took different paths to their current roles. How did they get into their position? What was their career path? If a director in, say, the Urban II Library met with an Alexander VI librarian, it would offer additional professional perspective not available necessarily within the department. Due to the geographic and cultural silos that presently exist, this sort of partnership might require the intervention of administration in order to ensure that the program commences and maintains activity though.

This paper certainly is not going to solve the longstanding issue of gender inequality within higher education. Like it or not, biases exist that make it very difficult to encourage positive change, especially in systems as regimented as a state institution of higher education, where evolution occurs at a glacial pace. However, awareness of the issue and internal and external conversation by the female academic librarians at St. Jerome is a start, and hopefully in some small way, this project may increase their blended professional roles through cognizance.

8.3.4 Organization

Finally, one of the benefits of a case study is that the recommended pragmatic changes occur on a microscale. It is much easier to address operational concerns on a university level than to attempt to produce system-wide changes. Communication seemingly is the easiest to address. These suggestions serve St. Jerome; while they may apply at different universities as well, prior blended professional research and institutional assessment must transpire prior to consideration.

The first matter to consider is the organization itself. To start, in a hierarchical system, positive change occurs from the top (Bolman & Deal, 2003). Administrators have the opportunity to lead by example. For instance, if the desire is to promote librarian academic professionalism and productivity, then the administration might publish or present as a means of inspiration. The librarians at St. Jerome do not feel that this occurs, however. As Bridget said: "There's also very much a level of 'you all do this [academic productivity]...' But I don't see the administration doing any of it. And that sort of hypocritical situation is sort of frustrating." This is a relatively simple resolution for the administration. If they are not publishing, then seek to publish. If they presently are successful in these pursuits, then effectively communicate so that subordinates may know and appreciate the efforts.

Continuing with communication, many of the librarians noted that the personal or electronic contact from the director level of administration particularly was poor. For instance, at the Alexander VI Library, the reference desk is being eliminated. The general understanding is that the initiative will increase customer service and provide librarians with more time to perform outreach. Still, the librarians do not understand the "how" and "why" this change is taking place. This particular issue might be resolved with an open forum, yet it has festered since prior to the interviews for this project. This does not suggest that nonmanagerial employees should know all of the reasoning behind executive decisions. However, in order to "gain the buy-in," proper and timely explanations regarding significant role changes or other pertinent concerns should reach the appropriate constituent parties. The effective communication will benefit the organizational morale and productivity by removing the specter of uncertainty in their daily activities.

Another major hurdle for change concerns professional advancement. As mentioned, the librarians do not have many upward options within the St. Jerome system. While presumably the four individuals at the VP level eventually will retire, this cannot be counted on as a means for future librarian advancement due to the lack of a timetable. As a result, administration must consider other internal leadership opportunities for the academic librarians. Currently, there are 2-year appointments for organizational needs, such as Graduate Research Assistant Coordinator, Virtual Reference Coordinator, Assistive Technology Coordinator, and Alexander VI Reference Department Assistant Head. These are effective offerings that allow the academic librarians to bolster their resumes for both internal and external opportunities when they arise.

Still, these positions codify and formalize basic activities that already existed within the library system. Wholly new opportunities for the librarians should be considered. For instance, the administration encourages academic professionalism. Why not create a research-oriented position as well? This position might coordinate grant writing, presentation proposals, article submissions, and so on. Such a position and role simultaneously would cater to the needs of administration and librarians.

Also contemplate classified staff. The "paraprofessional" title of classified staff that works in the libraries creates the illusion that the present job is a stepping stone. For example, the expectation during the course of research for this project that I, and all the other classified staff that earn graduate degrees while working within the library system, will graduate and find employment elsewhere. Immediately following the interviews, nearly all the librarians asked, "What are you going to do next?" implying that I would leave as soon as an opportunity presented itself. In my case, I did take an external professional position soon after I completed the doctorate. Ideally though, I would have stayed in that position or a slightly more advanced role for the time being due to matters in my personal life. What if another staff member needs to stay due to personal or professional reasons? What happens if the staff member actually *wants* to stay?

Organizationally, that is a mindset that needs to change. From a human resources perspective, it makes little sense to train employees on a professional level and then let those skills walk out the door. The resources invested in creating a marketable and productive employee will benefit the future employer, not the St. Jerome libraries. As well, it produces stagnation in the advancement of the employee. Along with my then-colleagues approaching the end of their studies, after I reached ABD status, I no longer received on-the-job professional development, since it is viewed as "wasted energy" spending time improving someone who inevitably will depart. It is a detrimental system for both the individual and the organization.

Obviously, the need for St. Jerome to work within the guidelines designed by the state inhibits some of the opportunities for individual's growth and advancement within the organization. In fact, one of the librarians with the most seniority estimated that since the mid-1990s, only four classified employees were promoted to the professional faculty level. That amount of opportunity paints a bleak picture for classified staff currently within the system.

Yet there is opportunity to redesign the classified roles so that the employee might expand their responsibilities on the job. Recall the classified staff member mentioned by Jessica who excelled at analyzing spreadsheets but grew frustrated with formal restrictions and a lack of recognition. Management may modify the employee work profiles of classified staff at any point during the calendar year. Why not rework job descriptions and reward these employees for their productivity and enterprise? Elevation from classified staff to administrative faculty may not be possible with state and budget restrictions, but the demonstration of flexibility promotes the idea of opportunity and answers the concern about employee differentiation and integration.

It is at this point that the hierarchy that exists in the St. Jerome organization will mitigate the efforts to change. Not all proponents of change have a viable means to express their opinions. Ultimately, following the completion of the research, I offered the findings and suggestions to my line manager and other midlevel personnel. As classified staff, I was not a member of Librarians' Council, which is the group that has the most control over policy within the libraries at St. Jerome. As a result, aside from publishing the findings, I really had no voice or audience to speak on a larger level, which is similar to what the librarians themselves experience, being absent from St. Jerome's Faculty Senate. If the academic librarians truly would like change, then they will have to address the issue themselves through petitioning of the administration. Whether that happens or whether it will be successful remains to be seen.

8.4 Conclusion

The academic librarians of St. Jerome face a number of challenges in their role as blended professionals. However, there are means by which they might overcome some of the difficulties, and the implementation of this model will allow researchers, librarians, and administrators to identify some of the chief concerns. As well, by utilizing a research model originating in higher education, this study provides the outline for the inclusion of librarians in the conversation involving faculty and collegiate educators. This study promotes the idea that librarians have a shared but different role in the production of educated students and scholars.

There are aspects of the blended professional model that do not completely address the development of professional identity for all members of the higher education community. Due to the influence of technology, the model provides only an ephemeral snapshot for academic librarians' perceptions. Additionally, gender likely plays a greater part in the development of professional identity to certain segments of the higher education population, depending upon the actual professional role. This was a case study, and the findings cannot be deemed wholly conclusive for the entirety of higher education. However, my inclination from both the research and professional experience is to believe that gender has a significant place in the formation of the blended professional's identity. It is just up to future research to prove this consideration and formally add gender as a fifth frame to the model. The avenues of potential prospective inquiries guide the discussion to the final chapter.

References

Alsever, J. (2013). Which tech company offers the best child care? *Fortune*. Retrieved from http://fortune.com/2013/10/14/which-tech-company-offers-the-best-child-care/.

American Faculty Association (AFA). (2012). *Hours for teaching and preparation rule of thumb: 2–4 hours of pre for 1 hour of class*. American Faculty Association. Retrieved from http://americanfacultyassociation.blogspot.com/2012/02/hours-for-teaching-and-preparation-rule.html.

Association of College and Research Libraries (ACRL). (2012). Guidelines for academic librarians without faculty status. *College & Research Libraries News*, *73*(3), 161–162.

Bagilhole, B., & White, K. (2008). Towards a gendered skills analysis of senior management positions in UK and Australian universities. *Tertiary Education & Management*, *14*(1), 1–12.

Balanced Scorecard Institute. (2014). Balanced Scorecard Basics. Retrieved from http://balancedscorecard.org/Resources/About-the-Balanced-Scorecard.

Baruzzi, A., & Calcagno, T. (2015). Academic librarians and graduate students: an exploratory study. *Portal: Libraries and the Academy*, *15*(3), 393–408.

Bolman, L. G., & Deal, T. D. (2003). *Reframing organizations: Artistry, choice, and, leadership* (3rd ed.). San Francisco: Jossey-Bass.

Bowen, R. W. (2005). Gender inequity. *Academe*, *91*(2), 128.

Chang, H. (2013). *Ethnic and racial diversity in academic and research libraries: Past, present and future*. Association of College and Research Libraries. Retrieved from http://www.ala.org/acrl/sites/ala.org.acrl/files/content/conferences/confsandpreconfs/2013/papers/Chang_Ethnic.pdf.

Chisholm-Burns, M. A., Spivey, C. A., Billheimer, D., Schlesselman, L. S., Flowers, S. K., Hammer, D., … Vaillancourt, A. M. (2012). Multi-institutional study of women and underrepresented minority faculty members in academic pharmacy. *American Journal of Pharmaceutical Education*, *76*(1), 1–13.

Clark, S., & Chinburg, S. (2010). Research performance in undergraduates receiving face to face versus online library instruction: A citation analysis. *Journal of Library Administration*, *50*(5/6), 530–542.

Clarke, M., Hyde, A., & Drennan, J. (2013). Professional identity in higher education. In *The academic profession in Europe: New tasks and new challenges* (pp. 7–21). Netherlands: Springer.

Coker, C., van Duinkerken, W., & Bales, S. (2010). Seeking full citizenship: a defense of tenure faculty status for librarians. *College & Research Libraries*, *71*(5), 406–420.

Cooke, R., & Rosenthal, D. (2011). Students use more books after library instruction: an analysis of undergraduate paper citations. *College & Research Libraries*, *72*(4), 332–343.

Couzy, M. (2012). *Conflicting roles: Balancing family and professional life- a challenge, for working women*. Master's thesis. Sweden: Linnaeus University.

Dunn, S. (2013). Do librarians need tenure? Depends on which ones you ask. *The Chronicle of Higher Education*. Retrieved from https://chroniclevitae.com/news/139-do-librarians-need-tenure-depends-on-which-ones-you-ask.

English, L., & Callaway, K. (2013). Business woman, earner, mom: a new and growing role. *Working Mother*. Retrieved from http://www.workingmother.com/research-institute/business-woman-primary-earner-mom-new-and-growing-role.

Fowler, N., Arens, K., Gilbert, L. A., Payne, S. M., Reichl, L. E., & Staiger, J. (2004). Graphic stories: representing the status of female faculty. *Feminist Studies*, *30*(3), 689–701.

Fulmer, C. L. (2010). Unpacking evidence of gender bias. *Journal of Women in Educational Leadership*, *8*(2), 81–97.

Garn, G., & Brown, C. (2008). Women and the superintendency: perceptions of gender bias. *Journal of Women in Educational Leadership*, *6*(1), 49–71.

Gordon, R. S. (2004). The men among us. *Library Journal*, *129*(11), 49.

Guillory, E. A. (2001). The black professoriate: explaining the salary gap for African-American female professors. *Race, Ethnicity & Education*, *4*(3), 225–244.

Hansson, J., & Johannesson, K. (2013). Librarians' views of academic library support for scholarly publishing: an every-day perspective. *Journal of Academic Librarianship*, *39*(3), 232–240.

Hardesty, L. (1991). The bottomless pit revisited. *College & Research Libraries*, *52*, 219–230.

Hoeve, Y. T., Jansen, G., & Roodbol, P. (2014). The nursing profession: public image, self-concept, and professional identity. A discussion paper. *Journal of Advanced Nursing*, *70*, 295–309.

Holland, A. (2007). Gender bias in libraries? *Library Journal*, *132*(1), 64.

Ibarra, H., Carter, N. M., & Silva, C. (2010). Why men still get more promotions than women. *Harvard Business Review*. Retrieved from http://hbr.org/2010/09/why-men-still-get-more-promotions-than-women/ar/1.

Katz, L. S. (2003). *The image and role of the librarian*. New York: Routledge.

Lamothe, A. R. (2012). The importance of encouraging librarians to publish in peer-reviewed publications. *Journal of Scholarly Publishing*, *43*(2), 156–167.

Lanier, P. A., Tanner, J. R., & Guidry, B. N. (2009). A comparison of gender and gender-related issues in the business disciplines. *Public Personnel Management*, *38*(3), 51–70.

Lewis, I. (2004). Gender and professional identity: a qualitative study of social workers practising as counsellors and psychotherapists. *Australian Social Work*, *57*(4), 394–407.

Mason, M. A. (2011). The pyramid problem. *The Chronicle of Higher Education*. Retrieved from http://chronicle.com/article/The-Pyramid-Problem/126614/.

Matthews, J. R. (2007). *Library assessment in higher education*. Westport, Connecticut: Libraries Unlimited.

Milford, R., & Wisotzke, T. (2011). Introverts and customer service in the library: an unexpected fit. *OLA Quarterly*, *17*(3), 22–26.

Oakleaf, M. (2009). The information literacy instruction assessment cycle: a guide for increasing student learning and improving librarian instructional skills. *Journal of Documentation*, *65*(4), 539–560.

Oakleaf, M. (2010). *The value of academic libraries: A comprehensive research review and report*. Chicago: Association of College and Research Libraries.

O'Malley, D., & Delwiche, F. (2012). Aligning library instruction with the needs of basic sciences graduate students: a case study. *Journal of the Medical Library Association*, *100*(4), 284–290.

Parker, C. A. (2011). How law schools benefit when librarians publish, teach, and hold faculty status. *Legal Reference Services Quarterly*, *30*(3), 237–253.

Passehl-Stoddart, E., & Monge, R. (2014). From freshman to graduate: making the case for student-centric institutional repositories. *Journal of Librarianship & Scholarly Communication*, *2*(3), 1–11.

Rao, K. (2003). Coping and subjective wellbeing in women with multiple roles. *International Journal of Social Psychiatry*, *49*(3), 175–184.

Rogers, J. (2012). Killing fear part 1: the problem. *Attempting Elegance*. Retrieved from http://www.attemptingelegance.com/?p=1640.

Schrimsher, R. H., & Northrup, L. A. (2013). Helpful hints for every librarian's nightmare: publishing an article. *College & Undergraduate Libraries*, *20*(1), 87–94.

Schuster, J. H., & Finkelstein, M. J. (2006). *The American faculty: Restructuring of academic work and careers*. Baltimore: The Johns Hopkins University Press.

Shaffer, B. A. (2011). Graduate student library research skills: is online instruction effective? *Journal of Library & Information Services in Distance Learning*, *5*(1/2), 35–55.

Sobel, K., & Sugimoto, C. R. (2012). Assessment of learning during library instruction: practices, prevalence, and preparation. *Journal of Academic Librarianship*, *38*(4), 191–204.

Stefanisko, M. C. (1997). Understanding how women make meaning of their multiple roles: a cognitive-developmental analysis. (Order No. 9809402, University of Massachusetts Amherst). *ProQuest Dissertations and Theses*, 168. Retrieved from http://search.proquest.com/docview/304350930?accountid=14541.

The White House. (2014). *Expanding opportunity for all: Ensuring equal pay for women, and promoting the women's economic agenda*. Retrieved from http://www.whitehouse.gov/the-press-office/2014/04/08/fact-sheet-expanding-opportunity-all-ensuring-equal-pay-women-and-promot.

Welch, J. M., & Mozenter, F. L. (2006). Loosening the ties that bind: academic librarians and tenure. *College & Research Libraries*, *67*(2), 164–176.

Whitchurch, C. (2009). The rise of the blended professional in higher education: a comparison between the United Kingdom, Australia and the United States. *Higher Education*, *58*(3), 407–418.

Wyss, P. (2010). Library school faculty member perceptions regarding faculty status for academic librarians. *College & Research Libraries*, *71*(4), 375–388.

Concluding thoughts

9

As I mentioned at the beginning of this book, I do not foresee a future where I pursue a library science degree, so the likelihood of me transitioning back to work in a library again is slim. Additionally, a substantial amount of my research interests now extend outside the realm of academic libraries. Consequently, the implementation of this frame by me in a future study on libraries in all probability will not materialize. While one does not have to work within libraries for this type of analysis to be successful, it holds significant practical applications that would benefit a librarian, manager, or administrator who had the ability to enact more immediate responses to any respective findings.

I also feel that some of the message here will be diminished by the fact that I am not a librarian. It admittedly is easy to write off these findings as the interpretations of a nonlibrarian outsider. If a message created and sent by formal and credentialed academic librarians would be more apt to find receptive individuals, then I would hope that other librarians would conduct this study in order to better analyze and appreciate their organization and the perceptions of the personnel.

Therefore, the majority of the forthcoming work will be produced by you, the readers, and researchers with a more permanent stake in the future of academic libraries. While I can and will proselytize the qualities of academic libraries and their librarians to fellow administrators external to the libraries, further modification must be enacted from within, and the application of this version of the blended professional model is a feasible and worthwhile advancement. With all that of said, here are several avenues of potential future research.

9.1 Future research

The first logical step would be to analyze other academic librarians, both at St. Jerome and other universities, with the blended professional model in mind. If the postulated assertion is that academic librarians are blended professionals, then does this trend extend to librarians working at universities that provide tenure to their librarians? Concerns were raised in the previous chapter about librarians' research preparation in graduate school, the level of the terminal degree, and the amount and quality of research productivity. Since the librarians did not all attend the same institution for their library science master's degrees, and education standards put forth by the American Library Association regulate curriculum in the accredited schools, it is reasonable to assume that librarians in other institutions have similar experiences. It would, therefore, not be surprising if librarians at those colleges and universities, even those with tenure for librarians, experience comparable obstacles to professional success and occupy the same tenuous third space as the librarians at St. Jerome. However, the degree to which the differing statuses affect the blended role of the academic librarian at those institutions must be explored before a definitive proclamation may be made.

Geography might play a role in the development of professional identity. Constructions of social roles in different areas might restrict the blended professional role, even within supposedly advanced communities such as higher education. For example, would a female librarian in the Southeast be afforded the same flexibility as a female librarian in Northeast? What about differences in country? Perceptions of all faculty vary dependent upon nationality. For instance, the role of teacher (and subsequent connotations of faculty) might be more respected or held in higher esteem in, say, Finland, than in the United States. This study obviously considered the United States, but the projected professional identity of academic librarians might by higher if they were to be included in the function of "teacher" in those other countries. The hope is that geography would not have a tremendous impact on the identity, but research is required to determine the presence of challenges in this regard.

A study examining the nature of the institution and its impact on librarian identity would also warrant consideration. Just as there are categorized levels within the context of an individual university such as St. Jerome, there certainly are tiers of institutional rank within the entire university system. Consider implementing this frame on librarians at a lower-tier school or college. If a librarian working at that lower-tier institution had a low perception of their professional identity, then did that college's reputation have an effect on that viewpoint? However, if the librarian worked at a prestigious school like Princeton University or Harvard University, then perhaps that librarian would be more willing to accept their professional identity because there would not be much room for advancement in the library field within higher education. The relative placing of their institution within the total context of higher education might have a distinct effect on an academic librarian's professional identity, and it would be worth investigating.

Since this study also focused on female academic librarians, additionally expanding the demography will provide extra knowledge on the blended role. Is the perception of male librarian counterpart similar to that of the females at St. Jerome? The obvious next step would be to question the male liaison librarians at St. Jerome and gauge their opinions on their roles and the perceptions of their positions within this particular university. The opportunities for promotion are as limited for the males as the females at the university, as there are only so many positions available, regardless of gender. Given the males in the upper-level administration positions though, the few men that work in the liaison positions might not have as harsh of an opinion of the administration. It is not possible to make a conclusion on this subject though without additional research on the influence of gender.

It would also be interesting for someone to study both genders and analyze the obstacles through a comparison in order to determine whether or not the inhibitors persist for the men in academic libraries. As well, if male librarians have experienced significant obstacles to professional development, then what did they do in order to overcome these challenges? Were they gender specific? Could they translate to all individuals?

Whitchurch did include the student affairs professionals in her consideration of the blended professionals, but it was more in the mixed role of the faculty member. For example, in Whitchurch's assessment, the faculty person working as the program's graduate student adviser would be a blended professional due to the mixed roles of the individual. The next step would be to extend the model to the other professional faculty, not in an instructional role whatsoever, such as the career counselors in a career services department.

There are many avenues to expand the conversation on academic blended professionals, both internal and external to the libraries. The hope is that this initial model provides a template to expand on for future research in these separate areas. This research will provide a better understanding of the roles and professional identities of valuable members of the academic community and help identify (and ease) some of the obstacles to their professional development.

9.2 Conclusion

Librarians at St. Jerome are not on the same level as the tenure-track faculty, either in actual function or perception of their role. The librarians have far different emphases with respect to the core activities of research, instruction, and service. However, the librarians functionally operate as blended professionals. Unfortunately, these blended aspects of the librarians' role places structural limitations on their influence; the perceptual and manifest constructed limitations further increase these issues by confining the blended professional effectiveness and functioning third space, which produces both artificial and actual obstacles to professional development.

Geography, the hierarchical system of higher education itself, and socially constructed departmental structures limit the spaces that the librarians might interact within. While librarians gain a significant amount of pragmatic research experience through their profession, library school and disciplinary studies do not always provide sufficient knowledge needed to gain acceptance into research-oriented circles around the institution. Relationships are restrictive in their scope and breadth. Due to their standing within the hierarchy on campus, the librarians find common ground with service-minded staff external to the libraries and within their own immediate social and professional groups, but often the librarians fail to consider how to collaborate more efficiently with faculty, students, and other staff. Degrees and accomplishments often determine legitimacies in higher education, but the librarians do not market themselves in a manner that emphasizes their academic professionalism or credentialing. The librarians have the ability to interact with a wide range of individuals and departments in the academic community, but these restrictions place boundaries around their essential third space and mitigate the blended efficacy.

Some obstacles to professional development result from the librarians' perception of their role. A lack of time and money do not appear to have significant actual weight. Sensitivity to the role that gender plays in the role and the structure of the organization and its functioning ability though create tangible impacts on the perception of the job and the resulting performance therein. While these concerns have no quick means of resolution, awareness of their presence in the minds and actions of the librarians at St. Jerome provides the initial stride toward constructive change.

The academic librarians at St. Jerome have a unique role and ability to contribute to the overall success of the mission of the university. The application of the blended professional model to their role is meant to aid in the understanding of that role and how the librarians themselves interpret their place within the system. In gaining this understanding, the hope is that the findings presented here will illuminate the difficulties facing these libraries and provide context and communication so that they might increase their abilities and successes in their role as blended professionals. Through the provision of these findings and the frame utilized, the added objective is that this method might be applied elsewhere and a greater understanding of librarians within the entire context of higher education might be sought and found.

Appendix A

Dimension of professional activity[a]	Method of inquiry
Spaces • Multiple perspectives on an institution • Works in third space • Adapts to changes in professional boundaries • Not restricted by formal structures	• Qualitative interview • Document analysis (schedule: location of shift, location of instruction session)
Knowledges • Assimilates professional and academic knowledge • Investigates organizational activity • Develops synergistic knowledge settings	• Qualitative interview • Document analysis (Research Portals, Infoguides) • Observation of instruction
Relationships • Functions in academic conversation • Establish alliances with important individuals • Assist or establish independence of own unit • Develop networks	• Qualitative interview • Document analysis (schedule: office hours, embedded hours, etc.) • Observation of instruction
Legitimacies • Academic credentials • Attain suitable standing in academic environment (publish, etc.) • Handle internal and external roles within academic spaces	• Qualitative interview • Document analysis (business cards, cubicles for diplomas, awards, etc.)

[a]Whitchurch, C. (2009). The rise of the blended professional in higher education: A comparison between the United Kingdom, Australia and the United States. *Higher Education, 58*(3), 407–418.

Appendix B

Dear Librarians:

I am currently working on a doctoral degree in the Higher Education Program at St. Jerome University. Under the supervision and direction of Dr. X, and with the support of dissertation committee members Dr. Y and Dr. Z, I am carrying out research for my dissertation entitled: *The Academic Librarian as Blended Professional: Reassessing the Perception of the Position.*

This study emerged based upon my professional experiences at both the Urban II Library and Alexander VI Library here at St. Jerome University. As I am sure many of you can attest, I have witnessed many misconceptions from faculty, students, and staff alike about the libraries and their personnel's role at the university. From the perspective of higher education theorists, the role and identity of academic librarians is often misunderstood. This study will attempt to clarify some of these misconceptions by portraying academic librarians from a viewpoint that utilizes higher education based-theory.

I will argue that the traditional mold of tenure-track faculty does not fit the roles of academic librarians, who are better defined in higher education terms as blended professionals. Blended professionals are individuals who bridge gaps in both institutional and external silos in order to perform their professional and academic duties. By utilizing the blended professional model, the study will better establish the specifics of the position in the context of the professional duties of academic librarians.

Additionally, this study will be gender specific in studying the identity of female academic librarians, simultaneously analyzing the often challenging and complex roles and identities of women and academic librarians within the position of faculty. The study endeavors to determine how the multiplicity of roles impacts the professional identity of academic librarians and how this, in turn, might impact professional development.

Therefore, at its core, this case study seeks to determine what the blended professional identity of female faculty librarians at St. Jerome University is and how this blended professional identity shapes the female academic librarians' professional growth. Your personal insight and experience will be instrumental in exploring these issues.

With the approval of the St. Jerome University Institutional Research Board, I ask you to become a participant in the study. Participation is voluntary, and you are under no obligation to contribute. Interviews should take approximately 30–60 min. Names and identities of participating librarians will be kept confidential.

I hope to schedule and conduct the interviews during the 2014 summer session. If you are willing to participate, reply to this email, and I will accommodate any request based upon your scheduling preferences. My planning to travel to the distributed campus libraries is also expected and not an issue.

If you have questions about this project and would like clarification from someone other than the researcher, email or call my dissertation advisor, Dr. X, Associate Professor of Higher Education (phone: xxx-xxx-xxxx; email: xxxxxxx@xxx.xxx).

Thank you for your time.

Sincerely,
Michael Perini

Appendix C

Can you describe a good day for you in the library?

In what ways is your role as academic librarian comparable to tenure-track faculty?

What would you consider your primary role(s) as an academic librarian?

Would you describe your service affiliations and roles?

In what ways are you included or isolated in specific communities around the university? How do you feel in describing them?

Tell me about your most important work at St. Jerome. Where is it? What is it? What does it add to you as a professional?

What do you consider the most important knowledge or expertise that you can provide to the academic community? How do you provide it? How best do you communicate it?

What is (are) your most significant relationships in the academic community (students, faculty, supervisor, etc.)

What type of instruction do you do? What is your preferred method?

What types of research do you do? (Can you list some of your publication and presentation experience?) What do you enjoy the most about that process?

Which of your professional qualifications and/or abilities benefits you the most? Around campus? With associations?

What are obstacles to your professional success?

Imagine creating a new library. How would it differ from your current library? What would you keep the same? What role would you want in this library?

What else do you want me to know that I have not asked you?

Thank you.

Epilogue

I struggled with how to end this book because the principal purpose of this work is to provide the academic librarians that I interviewed with a voice. Through the course of the text, I interjected some of my personal views and opinions because it benefited the context, but I really attempted to keep such interpolations to a minimum. The vast majority of the quotes and stories were those of the academic librarians. Therefore, I do not plan to deviate from that pattern in these closing remarks. While I am concluding with some additional information about my experience after the research ended, the heart of this book and its message was and remains about the academic librarians.

Aftermath

Throughout the interview process, the librarians routinely asked me "What's next?" in anticipation that I would leave the libraries soon after completing the degree. The funny thing was that I was not committed wholly to moving on at that point. One impetus for staying involved pay; I made a very good salary. In fact, I knew that the difference between my salary at that rank of classified staff and that of a starting librarian in a professional faculty position was negligible.

I also liked the institution and the surrounding locale. The university was progressive and relatively pleasant, and I enjoyed working with my immediate colleagues in my department. Moreover, I had been in the region for close to 10 years, had acquired a mortgage, and had built ties and friendships. I was not keen with the notion of having to uproot and start anew elsewhere.

Finally, my wife and I also were expecting a daughter a few months after the completion of the research. I thought that professional stability would help in that immediate future. This was especially so, given all of the horror stories that I had heard about sleep deprivation with newborns.

As things worked out though, a dean/director position at another university opened up elsewhere. I was fortunate to be offered this opportunity just as I was finishing the paperwork for the submission of the doctorate. The scheduling of the transition was not the greatest because the aforementioned lack of sleep was accurate, but I chose to move forward, and my time in the libraries came to an end.

In part due to my approaching departure, I never had the opportunity to present the results of this study to anyone other than my immediate line managers, and even then, the information passed was informal. It is unfortunate because I truly believe that the librarians who participated in this study would benefit from hearing about how they perceived themselves within this particular environment. By approaching their roles through the prism of a blended professional, I think that those academic librarians might find greater success and satisfaction in their positions because the librarians' identity and third space might be better understood.

At the same time, in order for these discoveries to find optimal success, they would need to gain acceptance from administration, and I am unsure if these findings would be appreciated by that sector of the organization in particular. Given prior interactions with administrators, I believe that a good majority of them would view the source of the information and write it off as the misguided interpretations of a nonlibrarian. This is why I mostly have curtailed the personal anecdotes. These findings are the voices of the academic librarians. The words of the librarians have a better chance of promoting transformation than those of Michael Perini.

Yes, consideration of these results requires self-reflection by individuals in the administration regarding their policies, decisions, and procedures. It is difficult to look in the mirror. However, it is necessary to do so in order to create positive change for both the organization and the individuals therein.

Ever Forward

The work at my new university is challenging. It is easy to get lost in the minutia of administration and forget about the integral parts of the higher education process. It required far less effort to refocus back when I was surrounded by stacks of books and journals because to me, they represented the physical manifestation of learning and of one's educational ambitions. The books created the foundation for students to build a better life. In this way, to me libraries and their books signify hope and spirit. Academic librarians help navigate this chaotic maze. I do miss working with my colleagues, and I do miss the libraries. For me, the library was, and is, the heart of academe.

Who knows? Maybe I someday will end up pursuing a library science degree and wind up back in libraries at some point. Until then, I will advocate for libraries from the higher education administration side and I will continue to support libraries and their librarians as entities of collaboration.

Index

'*Note*: Page numbers followed by "f" indicate figures and "t" indicate tables.'

Kolibri 360 GmbH
Ferdinand-Jühlke-Straße 7
99095 Erfurt, Deutschland
produktsicherheit@kolibri360.de